# UPON THIS ROCK

# THE BAPTIST UNDERSTANDING OF THE CHURCH

UPON THIS ROCK

JASON G. **DUESING,** THOMAS **WHITE,** AND MALCOLM B. **YARNELL III**

B&H ACADEMIC
Nashville, Tennessee

Upon This Rock:

The Baptist Understanding of the Church

ISBN: 978-0-8054-4999-0

Published by B&H Publishing Group
Nashville, Tennessee

Dewey Decimal Classification: 230.6
Subject Heading: CHURCH \ BAPTISTS—DOCTRINES \
CHRISTIAN THEOLOGY

Printed in the United States of America

1 2 3 4 5 6 7 8 9 10 11 12 • 17 16 15 14 13 12 11 10
BP

# Contents

# Acknowledgments

This volume would not be possible were it not for the efforts of the Center for Theological Research and the Riley Center at Southwestern Baptist Theological Seminary. Both of these centers put time and resources into the fourth consecutive Baptist Distinctives Conference held at Southwestern's Fort Worth campus during September 2008.

The Riley Center is a 55,000-square-foot conference center with 55 guestrooms. It attempts to bring positive change to the local churches through hosting theologically organized events addressing culturally significant topics. More information on the Riley Center, including information for scheduling conferences, may be found at http://www.swbts.edu/center.

The Center for Theological Research is currently engaged in a monumental task that will benefit all Baptists. The Web site http://www.BaptistTheology.org makes available to the broader public white papers addressing current theological issues, as well as rare or out-of-print Baptist works online. By providing ready access to these important Baptists resources, the center seeks to preserve Baptist heritage and help educate a new generation concerning the biblical ways of our Baptist forefathers.

The editors wish to express their deep appreciation to the administration of Southwestern Baptist Theological Seminary, especially President Paige Patterson, for supporting the Baptist Distinctives Conference and this publication.

# Dedication

We would have every individual stand on Bible ground, and to take his position there, in the unbiased exercise of his own judgment and conscience. There we strive to take our position; and there, and there only, we invite our brethren of all denominations to meet us. We yield everything which is not required by the word of God; but in what this word requires, we have no compromise to make.

—John Leadley Dagg (1794–1884)

# The *Baptist Faith and Message*, 2000

## ARTICLE VI. THE CHURCH

A New Testament church of the Lord Jesus Christ is an autonomous local congregation of baptized believers, associated by covenant in the faith and fellowship of the gospel; observing the two ordinances of Christ, governed by His laws, exercising the gifts, rights, and privileges invested in them by His Word, and seeking to extend the gospel to the ends of the earth. Each congregation operates under the Lordship of Christ through democratic processes. In such a congregation each member is responsible and accountable to Christ as Lord. Its scriptural officers are pastors and deacons. While both men and women are gifted for service in the church, the office of pastor is limited to men as qualified by Scripture.

The New Testament speaks also of the church as the Body of Christ which includes all of the redeemed of all the ages, believers from every tribe, and tongue, and people, and nation.

Matthew 16:15–19; 18:15–20; Acts 2:41–42,47; 5:11–14; 6:3–6; 13:1–3; 14:23,27; 15:1–30; 16:5; 20:28; Romans 1:7; 1 Corinthians 1:2; 3:16; 5:4–5; 7:17; 9:13–14; 12; Ephesians 1:22–23; 2:19–22; 3:8–11,21; 5:22–32; Philippians 1:1; Colossians 1:18; 1 Timothy 2:9–14; 3:1–15; 4:14; Hebrews 11:39–40; 1 Peter 5:1–4; Revelation 2–3; 21:2–3.

# Author Introductions

**David Allen** (Ph.D., University of Texas at Arlington) is the dean of the School of Theology and professor of expository preaching at Southwestern Baptist Theological Seminary. He has published numerous works, including two forthcoming projects: *Hebrews* in the New American Commentary series, and *The Lukan Authorship of Hebrews* (both Nashville: B&H Publishing Group).

**Bart Barber** (Ph.D., Southwestern Baptist Theological Seminary) is pastor of First Baptist Church in Farmersville, Texas. He has a degree from Baylor University and two degrees from Southwestern Seminary including a Ph.D. in church history. The title of his dissertation was "The Bogard Schism: An Arkansas Baptist Agragarian Revolt."

**Emir F. Caner** (Ph.D., University of Texas at Arlington) is president of Truett-McConnell College. He is coauthor of *The Truth About Islam and Jihad* (Eugene: Harvest House, 2009), *The Truth About Islam and Women* (Eugene: Harvest House, 2009), *The Sacred Desk: Presidential Addresses of the Southern Baptist Convention Presidents* (Nashville: B&H, 2004), *Unveiling Islam: An Insider's Look at Muslim Life and Beliefs* (Grand Rapids: Kregel, 2002), and *More than a Prophet: An Insider's Response to Muslim Beliefs About Jesus and Christianity* (Grand Rapids: Kregel, 2003).

**Jason G. Duesing** (Ph.D., Southwestern Baptist Theological Seminary) is chief of staff in the Office of the President as well as assistant professor of historical theology at Southwestern Baptist Theological Seminary. He has coedited *Restoring Integrity in Baptist Churches* (Grand Rapids: Kregel, 2008) and *First*

*Freedom: The Baptist Perspective on Religious Liberty* (Nashville: B&H Academic, 2007).

**James Leo Garrett Jr.** (Th.D., Southwestern Baptist Theological Seminary; Ph.D., Harvard University) has authored, co-authored, edited, and coedited more than 130 published works, including a thesis, two dissertations, scholarly articles, and books. His most recent publication is *Baptist Theology: A Four-Century Study* (Macon: Mercer University Press, 2009). He taught at Southwestern Baptist Theological Seminary and Baylor University.

**Byron McWilliams** (D.Min., New Orleans Baptist Theological Seminary) is pastor of First Baptist Church in Odessa, Texas. He answered God's call to the ministry out of an established career and has been a pastor since 1997. In 2007, he completed his D.Min. with a project on "Equipping a Select Group of Married Couples of First Baptist Church, Odessa, Texas, in Premarital Counseling Skills."

**Paige Patterson** (Ph.D., New Orleans Baptist Theological Seminary) is president of Southwestern Baptist Theological Seminary. His publications include *The Church in the 21st Century* (Magnolia Hill Papers, 2001), *Christ or the Bible* (Magnolia Hill Papers, 2001), *Heaven*, coauthored with W. A. Criswell (Carol Stream, IL: Tyndale House Publishers, 1991), *The Troubled Triumphant Church: An Exposition of First Corinthians* (Nashville: Thomas Nelson, 1983), and *A Pilgrim Priesthood: An Exposition of First Peter* (Nashville: Thomas Nelson, 1982).

**Joy White** (Ph.D. Candidate, Southeastern Baptist Theological Seminary) is a wife, a mother, and a homemaker who is also writing a dissertation on Titus 2 as the final requirement for a Ph.D. in systematic theology. She has an M.Div. from Southeastern Seminary and wrote the commentary on Acts for the *Women's Evangelical Commentary* (Nashville: B&H Publishing Group, 2006).

**Thomas White** (Ph.D., Southeastern Baptist Theological Seminary) is vice president for student services and communications and associate professor of systematic theology at Southwestern Baptist Theological Seminary. He is the coauthor of *Franchising McChurch: Feeding Our Obsession with Easy Christianity* (Colorado Springs: David C. Cook, 2009).

**Malcolm B. Yarnell III** (D.Phil., Oxford University) is editor for the *Southwestern Journal of Theology*, director of the Center for Theological Research, director of the Oxford Study Program, and associate professor of systematic theology at Southwestern Baptist Theological Seminary. He is the author of *The Formation of Christian Doctrine* (Nashville: B&H Academic, 2007).

# Introduction

## The Duty of Baptists to Teach
## Their Distinctive Views?

*Jason G. Duesing*

I n early 2009, *The New York Times* reported an effort among
many Roman Catholic dioceses to restore some of their "fading
traditions" among what they described as a "self-satisfied world."[1]
Their concern centered on a significant decrease in Catholics practicing confession. The article explains that "[t]o remain in good
standing, Catholics are required to confess their sins at least once
a year. But in a survey last year by a research group at Georgetown
University, three-quarters of Catholics said they went to confession less often or not at all."[2] As a result, the dioceses encouraged
the overlooked tradition of the indulgence to correct the trend.

Although made famous during the Reformation era due to
Martin Luther's public denouncing of the practice, the indulgence,
or the specific offering of the church to spare an individual from
time spent in Purgatory, never disappeared from the life of the Roman Catholic Church. *The New York Times* article explains that

---

[1] P. Vitello, "For Catholics, A Door to Absolution Is Reopened," *The New
York Times* (February 9, 2009), http://www.nytimes.com/2009/02/10/nyregion
/10indulgence.html?pagewanted=2&_r=1&sq=Roman%20Catholic%20resur
gence&st=cse&spc=1, accessed September 24, 2009.
[2] Ibid.

[t]he return of indulgences began with Pope John Paul II, who authorized bishops to offer them in 2000 as part of the celebration of the church's third millennium. But the offers have increased markedly under his successor, Pope Benedict, who has made plenary indulgences part of church anniversary celebrations nine times in the last three years.[3]

Although following the same doctrinal understanding for the indulgence as in Martin Luther's day, the contemporary dioceses are no longer selling them. Instead, the Church hopes that the recovery of the tradition will serve as an incentive for Catholics to return to confession and the practicing of their faith. The article explains, "But for Catholic leaders, most prominently the pope, the focus in recent years has been less on what Catholics have in common with other religious groups than on what sets them apart—including the half-forgotten mystery of the indulgence."[4] Indeed, the article conveys a growing appreciation for a return to Catholic distinctives. "'In our diocese, folks are just glad for any opportunity to do something Catholic,' said Mary Woodward, director of evangelization for the Diocese of Jackson, Miss., where only 3 percent of the population is Catholic."[5]

Most Protestants and Baptists would quickly object to this Catholic revival of tradition as something, like Luther labored to proclaim, that is contrary to Scripture and distorts the saving work of Christ. However, for confessional Protestants and Baptists alike, the recent activities of the Roman Catholics should serve as a mirror of sorts to test our intentions and challenge our reasoning. Just what exactly is the basis for our denominational distinctives? The Bible alone or the Bible plus tradition? Do we see Baptist distinctives as merely a collection of "faded traditions" that we

---

[3] Ibid.
[4] Ibid.
[5] Ibid.

need to repackage to provide incentives for those drifting from denominational ties? Or are they truly doctrinal necessities rooted in the Bible alone? Are our Baptist distinctives only the memories of days gone by when every Baptist church followed the same weekly format, sang the same songs, and practiced the same traditions? Or are they theologically rich cornerstones of faith that easily transcend time, culture, and preference?

Such questions should be asked at the start of any book claiming to focus on the "Baptist" understanding of a particular doctrine. Since the word *Baptist* cannot be found in the New Testament to describe the early gatherings of believers into local churches, the onus to provide a rationale as to why any believer should give consideration to adopting such a name is always on those who are determined to set forth a Baptist perspective. If a New Testament believer in Jesus Christ really only needs the Bible for living the Christian life or forming a local church, then why focus on a particular tradition? And why Baptist?

## THE DUTY OF BAPTISTS TO TEACH
## THEIR DISTINCTIVE VIEWS

In an effort to provide the reader with some perspective of the intentions of both the editors and authors, I have endeavored to answer that question at the beginning of this volume with the aid of nineteenth-century Baptist pastor and professor, John A. Broadus. Broadus (1827–95) served as one of the founding professors and later as president of the Southern Baptist Convention's first seminary.[6] In 1881, he was invited to address the American Baptist Publication Society at their meeting in Indianapolis, Indiana. His sermon, entitled "The Duty of Baptists to Teach Their Distinctive Views," stands as a forgotten, but surprisingly prescient, approach

---

[6] See A. T. Robertson, *Life and Letters of John Albert Broadus* (Philadelphia: American Baptist Publication Society, 1901; repr., Harrisonburg: Gano Books, 1987); D. S. Dockery and R. D. Duke, eds., *John A Broadus: A Living Legacy* (Nashville: B&H, 2008).

to the questions many ask with regard to the necessity and future of denominational, namely Baptist, identity.[7]

## Internal and External Commands: Both Essential

Broadus begins with a text taken from Matt 28:20, "Teaching them to observe all things whatsoever I have commanded you."[8] Referencing Jesus' commission, Broadus identifies that the commands of Christ, given to the disciples, consisted of both "the internal and the external elements of Christian piety."[9] The internal elements, Broadus explains, are more crucial to the Christian faith as they relate to individuals and their relationship to their Creator. However, Broadus clarifies that any primacy given to the internal elements does not mean that the external elements have little value or lack importance. Broadus reasons that if Christ and His apostles gave commands relating to external elements such as the "constitution and government" of churches, then it "cannot be healthy if they are disregarded."[10]

In fact, both internal and external elements are intrinsic in the prerequisite command of Matt 28:19. First, Jesus exhorts the disciples to "go therefore and make disciples of all nations." This mandate speaks of the ultimately internal act of Holy Spirit regeneration that produces a fruit-bearing disciple. As Broadus states, the internal aspect of these commands does take priority. When one of the criminals crucified alongside Jesus asked in faith, "Jesus, remember me when you come into your kingdom," Jesus replied, "Truly, I say to you, today you will be with me in Paradise" (Luke 23:42–43). In this exchange Jesus' affirmation came in response

---

[7] J. A. Broadus, *The Duty of Baptists to Teach Their Distinctive Views* (Philadelphia: American Baptist Publication Society, 1881). Citations follow M. Grace's transcription published in 2006 by the Center for Theological Research, Southwestern Baptist Theological Seminary, Fort Worth, Texas, See http://www.baptisttheology.org/documents/DutyBaptisttoTeachtheirViewsBroadus.pdf.

[8] All texts quoted in the introduction are taken from the English Standard Version of the Bible.

[9] Broadus, *The Duty of Baptists*, 1.

[10] Ibid.

to the outward expression of the internal work in the heart of the criminal. Due to the nature of the circumstances, discussion of Jesus' external commands related to baptism or church order were not as important as the criminal's life after death. This is not to say such commands have no importance but rather, simply, that they are less important than the internal commands which address the question, "What shall I do to inherit eternal life?" (Luke 10:25).

When Paul writes his magisterial chapter on the resurrection in 1 Corinthians 15, he reminds believers that what he delivered to them "first" was the gospel, namely that "Christ died for our sins in accordance with the Scriptures, that he was buried, that he was raised on the third day in accordance with the Scriptures" (1 Cor 15:3–4). Paul clearly wrote to them about many other vital items of an external nature for the local church, but the first instructions he relayed to the Corinthians were of an internal and more important nature.

The priority of the internal teachings of Christianity appear in Paul's letter to the Galatians as well. His expressed concern for believers who were deserting the faith did not revolve around their quibbling over the external teachings related to local church order. Rather, Paul intervenes as a result of the believers entertaining a "different gospel," that is a different teaching of an internal nature than the one Jesus provided (Galatians 1). For those altering the internal message, Paul renders them "accursed" (Gk. *anathema*), a term he does not employ, for example, when speaking of divisions within the church at Corinth over external matters related to church leaders and baptism (1 Cor 1:10–17). The internal commands of the New Testament that speak of the reconciliation of lost and rebellious men and women to a holy and wise God through only faith expressed in the work of God's Son bearing the punishment on behalf of humanity are clearly the first commands the churches should carry forth in obedience to Matt 28:20.

Second, in Matt 28:19, Jesus instructs the disciples to baptize the new disciples in the name of the Father and of the Son and of the Holy Spirit. Here the command to baptize marks an external component in the commission. The external commands are not as important, as they do not directly convey the power to make one "wise for salvation" (2 Tim 3:15; cf. Rom 1:16). However, the external commands are vital for healthy Christian living, preserving the internal message for future generations, and therefore should not be discarded.

When Peter "lifted up his voice" and addressed the mocking and perplexed crowd who did not know how to make sense of the arrival of the Holy Spirit in Acts 2, he proclaimed, "God has made him both Lord and Christ, this Jesus whom you crucified" (Acts 2:36). In response to Peter's wielding multiple Old Testament texts as a sharp, two-edged sword, the crowd was "cut to the heart" (Gk. *katenygēsan tēn kardian*) and asked, "What shall we do?" (Acts 2:37). Peter responded in 2:38 first with the primary internal command, "repent," signaling the need for both confession of sin and faith expressed in belief. Peter's entrance into his proclamation ministry follows the example of Jesus Himself, who began His public ministry saying, "The time is fulfilled, and the kingdom of God is at hand; repent and believe in the gospel" (Mark 1:15).

Peter continues, however, and quickly articulates the external command for the hearers to "be baptized" (Acts 2:38), thus practicing the entire commission of Jesus, with both internal and externals in view. As with Matt 28:19–20, the order prescribed by Peter, first internal then external, shows the importance of one over the other, but it does not negate the essential function of both types of commands. To have eternal life, the soon-to-be disciple must repent and believe (internal). To function as an obedient disciple, professing his faith in the context of a local church community, the new disciple must be baptized (external).

The order and connection between the two commands appears also in the encounter Philip, the deacon, has with the Ethiopian court official in Acts 8. After following the instructions of an angel of the Lord to go to "the road that goes down from Jerusalem to Gaza," Philip discovers the Ethiopian reading Isaiah 53 aloud and asks, "Do you understand what you are reading?" From the top of his chariot, the Ethiopian responds, "How can I, unless someone guides me?" and invites Philip to sit with him. As they travel together, Philip proceeds to explain from the Scripture that Jesus is the sheep that "was led to the slaughter" in Isaiah 53, and the account in Acts relates that Philip, "beginning with this Scripture," told the Ethiopian of the internal message regarding eternal life through faith in Jesus Christ. However, Philip appears also to have communicated some of the external commands as well, for when the Ethiopian's chariot came near a body of water, he said, "See, here is water! What prevents me from being baptized?" How would the Ethiopian have known of his need for baptism after he confessed his faith in Jesus if Philip had not already taught him of this external command? The baptism of the Ethiopian reinforces the notion that the external commands given in the New Testament, while not primary, are nonetheless important and should be incorporated properly into any presentation of the "good news about Jesus."

Throughout the New Testament the local church functions as a repository not only to receive and transmit the internal message of the gospel to the current generation but also to preserve that message for future generations. As a result, the external commands given for the purposes of ordering and governing the church are essential for this task, even though they are not as important as the internal message. When Paul writes to Timothy to instruct him in "how one ought to behave in the household of God," Paul describes the local church as the "pillar and buttress of the truth" (1 Tim 3:15). The idea of the local church functioning as a pillar (Gk. *stulos*) and a buttress (Gk. *hedraiōma*) creates a picture of an intentionally designed (i.e., ordered) structure that, through its strength, has been prepared both to uphold (i.e., present or proclaim) an object as well as protect (i.e., preserve) an object. Jesus' promise in Matt 16:18 that "the gates of hell will not prevail against" the church, reinforces the idea that the local church has been given as an indestructible fortress of strength held together by Jesus Christ himself (Col 1:17).

As a result, Jesus and His apostles have given commands of an external nature that must be taught and implemented. But for what end? The object given to the local church to uphold and protect is the "truth." The "truth" is the message of eternal life—the substance of the internal commands of Christ (1 Tim 2:4; 2 Tim 2:25). The New Testament teaches that this "truth" was, and is, to be handed over or delivered from one generation to the next through the local church. Luke speaks of this at the beginning of his Gospel when writing to assure Theophilus of the certainty of the things he had been taught. Luke states that he has written an "orderly account" of the things that "those who from the beginning were eyewitnesses and ministers of the word" had "delivered" (Gk. *paredosan*) to Luke and the other apostles (Luke 1:1–4). Likewise, in 2 Tim 1:14 (cf. 1 Tim 6:20) Paul instructs Timothy and the Ephesian Church to guard "the good deposit" (Gk. *tēn kalēn parathēkēn*), a reference to the entire message of the gospel he had taught and given to them. In a broad sense the purpose of all of Paul's letters is to deliver the "truth" not only to his immediate recipients but also to all who will read his letters and implement the commands in local churches (Col 4:16).

Jude reinforces the notion that the "truth" is the object the local church exists to proclaim and protect. In Jude 3, he explains that "the faith," or the gospel message of eternal life, "was delivered" (Gk. *paradotheisē*) to the saints. That is to say, the internal command of salvation through Jesus Christ has been handed down to Christians who live out the Christian life in local churches. Jude states that this delivering was done "once for all" (Gk. *hapax*), referencing the complete and final nature of the message rather than communicating that the message had no further need of transmission.

Therefore, the local church, the "pillar and buttress of truth" exists to "guard the good deposit" and "deliver" it to future generations. The New Testament commands that speak of the "truth" are primary. However, the external commands that speak clearly to the order, practice, and health of the local church, while secondary, should not receive treatment as unessential. Instead, the local church also has a duty to carry forth and teach these commands in obedience to Matt 28:20.

Broadus rightfully notes, however, that the trend throughout the history of Christianity has been not to neglect the external commands but rather to "exaggerate or pervert" what he sees as a "very simple pattern" in the New Testament for church organization, government, and ceremony.[11] One example Broadus provides concerns the way the early church continued to "Judaize" Christianity. Broadus states:

> When men began to exaggerate the importance of externals, they would soon begin to change their character. Coming to believe that baptism brings regeneration and is indispensable to salvation, they would of course wish to baptize practicable for the sick and the dying. Beginning to fancy that the bread and the wine really became the glorified body and blood of the ascended Saviour, they not unnaturally took to withholding the cup from the laity, lest their awkward handling should spill some drops of the sacred fluid, which would have been profanation. And, in addition to these tendencies should have a stronger government.[12]

Throughout the early centuries of church history, all too often Christians succumbed to the pressure from outside groups to add more and more to the mandates given in the New Testament. In Broadus's understanding, Baptists have had a long history of expressing opposition to this kind of distorted view of Christ's external commands given to the local church based on "the principle of recognizing no religious authority but the Scriptures themselves,

---

[11] Broadus, *The Duty of Baptists,* 1.
[12] Ibid.

and of strictly observing all that the Saviour has commanded."[13] As a result, Broadus reasons that even though "Baptists differ widely from large portions of the Christian world" on these matters, if they feel that "their own views are more scriptural, more in accordance with the Saviour's commands," then they are required to teach those views in accordance with Matt 28:20.[14] If Baptists believe that their views are not any more Baptist than they are biblical, Broadus contends that Baptists have a duty to teach their distinctive views.[15]

## Reasons Why Baptists Ought to Teach Their Distinctive Views

In the main portion of his sermon, Broadus provides his audience with four specific reasons why Baptists should teach their distinct views as an expansion of his thesis. These four reasons offer a helpful and healthy perspective for tasks set forth in *Upon This Rock* as well as any work that aims to provide an impetus for the practice of Baptist distinctives.

*1. It is a duty we owe to ourselves.* Broadus's first reason argues that because adhering to Baptist distinctives requires Baptists to "stand apart" from other Christians in "separate organizations," Baptists should ensure that the cause for the separation has "real importance."[16] If Baptists determine that the "points of difference" they have with other Christians are of "substantial value and practical importance as a part of what Christ commanded," then Baptists owe it to themselves to teach their views as a matter of consistency.[17] More than that, however, Broadus explains

---

[13] Ibid., 2.

[14] Ibid.

[15] Ibid. In the next section of Broadus's sermon, 2–3, he articulates his understanding of the "leading distinctive views of Baptist churches" as (1) holding to the authority of the Bible alone, (2) the belief that Christian churches are comprised only of believers, (3) practicing only two ordinances, baptism and the Lord's Supper, in nonsacramental fashion, and (4) holding to local church independence, from one another and the state. For a brief clarification of these views see James Patterson's chapter in Dockery and Duke, *John A. Broadus,* 250–51.

[16] Broadus, *The Duty of Baptists,* 4.

[17] Ibid.

that teaching Baptist distinctives also serves as "the only way of correcting excesses among ourselves."[18] Broadus speaks of some "Baptist brethren" who, in their zeal for their denomination, were often "violent" and "bitter" in their defense of Baptist distinctives. Later in the sermon, Broadus describes these preachers as those who were "constantly going out of their way to find such topics through a bred-and-born love of controversy or a mistaken judgment as to its necessity and benefits."[19]

This excessiveness among a few embarrassed many and caused other Baptists to retreat, "scarcely ever making the slightest allusion to characteristic Baptist principles," and who, "afraid of appearing sensational in their own eyes, or in those of some fastidious leaders . . . shrink from saying the bold and striking things they might say, and ought to say."[20] Broadus finds no fault with the content of the violent preachers' message but rather with the harm they cause by their sensationalism in that they drive so many other preachers to the opposite extreme.[21] The only corrective Broadus sees for what he terms "denominational ultraism" is "a healthy denominationalism."[22]

Broadus's observations have merit, in that, for those who understand their distinct Baptist positions as only the outworking of biblical study, to shrink or minimize what they hold as true, is inconsistent practice. If the external commands in the Bible for ordering local churches are counter to the vast majority of the practice in contemporary Christendom, and if Baptists feel as though their views align with the teachings of the Bible, then Baptists owe it to themselves to teach their views. However, such teaching should follow the directive of Paul in Ephesians 4:15 and go forth "in love" for the purpose of building up the body of

---

[18] Ibid.

[19] Ibid., 9.

[20] Ibid., 4.

[21] Ibid.

[22] Ibid.

Christ, not for winning an argument or tearing down other misguided believers.

However, the errors in spirit among Baptists in Broadus's day have continued to exist among Baptists. Too often, zealous members of the Baptist faithful verge into sensational defenses of Baptist views, thereby ostracizing many who agree in principle and practice, just not in spirit and tenor. The result is a cleaving among Baptist brethren whereby the extremists continue to marginalize themselves as they run like the cattle of Pamplona through the narrow aisles of Tiffany & Co.'s fragile wares. Often precisely correct in their views, their methods, however, only overshadow their message and do damage to their cause. The world gains a distorted view of the Baptist perspective, and many otherwise capable Baptists shrink from attempting to offer a corrective.

The shrinking, though, is just as egregious of an error. These embarrassed Baptists often use their rhetorical abilities to caricaturize the extremists, remarking to one another of how baseless and harmful are the sensationalists. However, rarely do these Baptists respond with a defense of Baptist distinctives cloaked in humility and Christian kindness, much less a defense at all. Instead, many are pulled toward the position of minimizing the distinctives as unnecessary or nonessential to the practice of the local church. Broadus described such Baptists in his day as those who "go out of their way to avoid all disputed questions, and want nothing to do with controversy of any kind."[23] Also, his charge to these kinds of Baptists continues to speak as a needed corrective when he advises them to "study the history and recorded writings of a man named Paul. He did not shrink from controversy. Yea, and his Master and ours is polemical on every page of his recorded discourses, always striking at some error or evil practice of the people around him."[24]

---

[23] Ibid., 9.
[24] Ibid.

Broadus's cure is still correct. The way to correct the practice of both extremes, sensationalism on the one hand and timidity on the other, is for some clear-thinking, courageous Baptist preachers to get out in front of both groups and lead the parade. Broadus's plea for the teaching of a healthy Baptist denominationalism will still find favor in the hearts and minds of many believers not only because it is true but also because of how it is communicated. Baptists owe it to themselves to teach their own distinctives. Near the end of his sermon, Broadus provides a response that leading Virginia Baptist Jeremiah Jeter gave regarding how he approaches teaching Baptist distinctives in the right manner. Jeter said:

> I never go out of my way to avoid such topics, and never go out of my way to find them. When natural-ly suggested by my subject or the circumstances, I speak of them, and I try to speak without timid fear of giving offence, and without fierce vehemence, as if taking hostility for granted, but just treating these matters, so far as I can, in the same tone with which I speak of other things.[25]

What is needed are Baptist leaders who will, like Broadus and Jeter, and even like Paul, model their views in such a way so as to say, "What you have learned and received and heard and seen in me—practice these things, and the God of peace will be with you" (Phil 4:9).

2. *It is a duty we owe our fellow Christians.* Broadus con-tends that the teaching of Baptist distinctives is a duty Baptists owe to Christians residing in Roman Catholic or Protestant tradi-tions. Operating from the premise that "there are but two sorts of Christianity—church Christianity and Bible Christianity," Broa-dus argues that both Catholics and Protestants alike are all "hold-ing some 'developed' form of Christianity" in that they have all

---

[25] Ibid.

"added something, in faith or governances or ordinances, to the primitive simplicity" of what he calls Bible Christianity.[26] With specific regard to Roman Catholics, Broadus believes the Baptist position, because of its roots in the New Testament, has an advantage over other Protestants for leading Roman Catholics to embrace evangelical truth.[27] He states,

> If well-meaning Roman Catholics become dissatisfied with resting everything on the authority of the church and begin to look toward the Bible as authority, they are not likely, if thoughtful and earnest, to stop at any halfway-house, but to go forward to the position of those who really build on the Bible alone.[28]

With regard to Protestants, Broadus states one large source of the differences between Baptists and Protestants is "a widespread and very great ignorance as to Baptists" and their views.[29] Broadus explains that Baptists owe it to other Christians to teach their views so that they "may at least restrain them from wronging us through ignorance."[30]

Lest one think that Broadus has elitist motives, he clarifies, stating,

> If there were any who did not care to know, who were unwilling to be deprived of a peculiar accusation against us, with them our efforts would be vain. But most of those we encounter are truly good people, however prejudiced, and do not wish to be unjust; and if they will not take the trouble to seek information about our real views, they will not be unwilling to receive it when fitly presented. Christian charity may thus be promoted by correcting ignorance. And

---

[26] Ibid., 4.
[27] Ibid.
[28] Ibid.
[29] Ibid., 5.
[30] Ibid.

besides, we may hope that some at least will be led to investigate the matters about which we differ. Oh that our honored brethren would investigate![31]

Indeed, Broadus affirms that there are many "noble Christians" within Roman Catholic and Protestant churches.[32] Later in the sermon he advocates that teaching Baptist distinctives to other Christians will only serve to "render them better Christians."[33] Broadus explains:

> I fully agree with an eminent Presbyterian minister who recently said, "We make people better Christians by making them better Presbyterians, better Methodists, Baptists, Episcopalians." There are some very excellent people in our time who think it a merit to be entirely undenominational, and who proclaim that they "love one church as well as another." But, where not deluded, such persons are few and quite exceptional; in general, the truest, most devoted, and most useful Christians are strong in their denominational convictions and attachments. I repeat, then, that by proper instruction in our distinctive views we shall really make our young people better Christians.[34]

If that is the case, then is it not arrogant for Broadus to "wish them to adopt other opinions?"[35] Broadus explains, "It is not necessarily an arrogant and presumptuous thing in us if we strive to bring honored fellow-Christians to views which we honestly believe to be more scriptural, and therefore more wholesome."[36] Just as Apollos received instruction from Aquila and Priscilla, Broadus believes

---

[31] Ibid.
[32] Ibid.
[33] Ibid., 7.
[34] Ibid.
[35] Ibid., 5.
[36] Ibid.

there is a place for Baptists to teach those of other denominations who might be willing to learn.[37] He concludes, "He who tries to win people from other denominations to his own distinctive views *may* be a sectarian bigot; but he may also be a humble and loving Christian."[38]

What served as true for Broadus in 1881 has an even greater opportunity for service in the twenty-first century. In a day when, worldwide, there are as many groups who identify themselves as Baptist as there are countries in the world, the articulation of Baptist distinctives will only help other Christian traditions to understand what a particular group of Baptists believe. As Broadus suggests, if twenty-first-century Baptists believe their views reflect scriptural truth, then there exists a place for Baptists to reach out to Catholics and Protestants, albeit with humility and graciousness. Broadus later advises:

> We must learn how to distinguish between abandonment of principles and mere practical concessions in order to conciliate. . . . One of the great practical problems of the Christian life, especially in our times, is to stand squarely for truth and squarely against error, and yet to maintain hearty charity toward Christians who differ with us. This assuredly can be done. The very truest and sweetest Christian charity is actually shown by some of those who stand most firmly by their distinctive opinions.[39]

However, this might prove difficult for Baptists who have spent energy working to minimize any semblance of their Baptist identity. By this I do not necessarily have in mind the trend to remove the word *Baptist* from a church's name, although it could include that if the church did so out of embarrassment of showing

---

[37] Ibid.
[38] Ibid.
[39] Ibid., 10.

public ties to their denomination. Also, I affirm that the possibility exists for a local church to practice biblical distinctives that Baptists would identify as their own but never embrace the Baptist historical tradition either in name or in cooperative denominational effort. The possibility exists precisely because Baptists seek to derive their distinctives only from the Bible.

These groups are not who Broadus has in mind, and neither do I. My concern rests with those churches who are functionally Baptist, either in name and/or in denominational affiliation. If these churches will embrace their identity as Baptist because they are convinced they find those teachings rooted in the Bible, then churches of all kinds, both present and future, have the potential to draw closer to biblical truth. In an age of financial insecurity, real persecution, and hostile opposition to the gospel, the only churches that will survive are, ironically, the ones who are most fit according to the external commands provided in the Bible.

*3. It is a duty we owe to the unbelieving world.* Broadus posits that Baptists owe the unbelieving world the duty of teaching their distinctive views as his third reason. Explaining that his motive, along with all Christians, is for "unbelievers to accept Christianity," Broadus argues, "They are more likely to accept it when presented in its primitive simplicity."[40] The Baptist reliance on the Bible alone for the composition of their distinctives allays any skeptic's questioning of any corruption that took place in the history of Christianity. Broadus states:

> We can say to the skeptical inquirer, "Come and bring all the really ascertained light that has been derived from studying the material world, the history of man, or the highest philosophy, and we will gladly use it in helping to interpret this which we believe to be God's word;" and we can change our views of its meaning if

---

[40] Ibid., 5.

> real light from any other sources requires us to do so.
> There is, surely, in this freedom no small advantage
> for attracting the truly rational inquirer.[41]

By this Broadus asserts that Baptists have no need to fear any examination of the truth of the Bible. If Baptists believe the Bible is true and authoritative, then this recognition fosters "an instinctive feeling that they must stand or fall with the real truth and the real authority of the Bible."[42] Broadus argues that trust in the Bible produces a feeling of freedom that is "most healthy and hopeful," and this hope is made available to unbelievers, in part, through Baptists teaching their distinctive views.[43]

Broadus's thoughts here are helpful and provide a compelling reason for why Baptists should labor to ensure their distinctives are constructed from only the Bible. When Baptists have grown enamored with their own extrabiblical traditions or even errors, the unbelieving world takes note. One need think only of the Baptist defense and continued practice of slavery in the southern United States only a century ago to realize that distorted views of biblical teaching in one area affect one's ability to proclaim effectively the central message of the Bible to the world that needs to hear the message.

The same holds true for the petty squabbles of local Baptist churches over truly nonessential items that are not part and parcel to biblical Baptist distinctives. Churches caught up in major controversy over such items as reserved seating for church patriarchs, meeting location or service time differences, have led many astray. The lost world needs Baptists who "do all things without grumbling or questioning" that they "may be blameless

---

[41] Ibid., 6.

[42] Ibid.

[43] Ibid. Broadus also affirms the role of statements of faith in this section. He explains, "Confessions of faith we have, some older and some more recent, which we respect and find useful; but save through some exceptional and voluntary agreement we are not bound by them."

and innocent, children of God without blemish in the midst of a crooked and twisted generation," among whom they "shine as lights in the world" (Phil 2:14–15). If Baptists truly are building their distinctives on the foundation of the truth of the Bible, then they do have a duty to teach those to an unbelieving world.

*4.   It is a duty we owe to Christ.* Broadus describes his final reason as "one full of solemn sweetness."[44] When Jesus gave the commission to his disciples recorded in Matthew 28, he did so "under the most solemn circumstances. . . . He met the eleven disciples by appointment on a mountain in Galilee . . . and uttered the express injunction."[45] Broadus concludes that Baptists have a duty to teach their distinctive views as "a matter of simple loyalty" to Christ.[46] He explains,

> The things of which we have been speaking are not, we freely grant, the most important of religious truths and duties, but they are a part of the all things which Jesus commanded; what shall hinder us, what could excuse us, from observing them ourselves and teaching them to others?[47]

For Broadus, teaching and obeying Jesus' commands of an external nature are akin to a Roman soldier who takes an oath of complete allegiance to the empire. He does not then proceed to obey selectively only the commands of his superior officer that he prefers. Rather, he obeys all the commands.[48] Broadus then reminds his audience that he had yet to quote the final portion of Jesus' commission. The end of Matt 28:20 reads, "And behold, I am with you always, to the end of the age." As a parting word, Broadus asks, "Shall we neglect to teach as he required, and then claim the promise of his presence and help and blessing?"[49]

---

[44] Ibid.

[45] Ibid.

[46] Ibid.

[47] Ibid.

[48] Ibid.

[49] Ibid. Broadus concludes his sermon, 6–11, by offering six "means and methods"

Broadus's appeal to one's loyalty to Christ and His commands, whether primary and internal or secondary and external, strikes a chord not often heard in the present day. Yet the simplicity of his argument serves as its greatest strength. If the New Testament speaks clearly to any aspect of local church governance, operation, structure, health, or practice, then followers of Christ, of whatever denominational persuasion, have to come to terms with whether they will obey His commands. Of first importance are the commands to "be reconciled to God" (2 Cor 5:20). However, the secondary commands, such as, "And let us consider how to stir up one another to love and good works, not neglecting to meet together, as is the habit of some, but encouraging one another, and all the more as you see the Day drawing near" (Heb 10:24–25), are also important. If Baptists agree with Broadus that their distinctives are true, then they owe it to Christ to teach them. Indeed, in agreement with Broadus, this volume, subtitled *The Baptist Understanding of the Church*, functions more as an honest attempt of the authors and editors to teach a "biblical understanding of the church" than anything else.

## UPON THIS ROCK: THE BAPTIST UNDERSTANDING OF THE CHURCH

A September 2008 conference at Southwestern Baptist Theological Seminary in Fort Worth, Texas, served as the initial setting for the presentation of the majority of the content in this volume. The conference speakers addressed topics following the discourse set forth in the article on "The Church" in the Southern Baptist Convention's *Baptist Faith and Message* 2000, which reads:

---

for the performance of teaching Baptist distinctives. They include: (1) Teaching others through instruction of our own people. (2) Teaching by everything that builds up our churches. (3) Teaching by understanding those whom we propose to reach. (4) Studying the wise treatment of controverted topics. (5) Cooperating with others as far as we can. (6) Cultivating unity among ourselves.

## ARTICLE VI. THE CHURCH

A New Testament church of the Lord Jesus Christ is an autonomous local congregation of baptized believers, associated by covenant in the faith and fellowship of the gospel; observing the two ordinances of Christ, governed by His laws, exercising the gifts, rights, and privileges invested in them by His Word, and seeking to extend the gospel to the ends of the earth. Each congregation operates under the Lordship of Christ through democratic processes. In such a congregation each member is responsible and accountable to Christ as Lord. Its scriptural officers are pastors and deacons. While both men and women are gifted for service in the church, the office of pastor is limited to men as qualified by Scripture.

The New Testament speaks also of the church as the Body of Christ which includes all of the redeemed of all the ages, believers from every tribe, and tongue, and people, and nation.

Matthew 16:15–19; 18:15–20; Acts 2:41–42,47; 5:11–14; 6:3–6; 13:1–3; 14:23,27; 15:1–30; 16:5; 20:28; Romans 1:7; 1 Corinthians 1:2; 3:16; 5:4–5; 7:17; 9:13–14; 12; Ephesians 1:22–23; 2:19–22; 3:8–11,21; 5:22–32; Philippians 1:1; Colossians 1:18; 1 Timothy 2:9–14; 3:1–15; 4:14; Hebrews 11:39–40; 1 Peter 5:1–4; Revelation 2–3; 21:2–3.

Therefore, as with the presentations given at the conference, the chapters in *Upon This Rock* each examine a section of the article on "The Church." All of the presentations have been revised and edited for publication. What follows is a brief introduction to each chapter and the specific topic addressed.

*A New Testament church of the Lord Jesus Christ . . .*

Chapter 1 functions intentionally as the bedrock upon which the other chapters are built. Malcolm B. Yarnell III labors to provide a comprehensive exposition of the focal text, Matt 16:13–20, with specific regard to understanding the meaning of Jesus' statement, "And upon this rock, I will build my church."

*. . . is an autonomous local congregation of baptized believers,*

In chapter 2, David Allen presents a historical survey of the Baptist understanding of local church autonomy through their confessions of faith. Allen then examines the concept biblically and comments on the relationship between autonomy and the twin Baptist doctrine of religious liberty.

*. . . associated by covenant in the faith and fellowship of the gospel;*

In chapter 3, Emir Caner discusses the necessary correlation between church covenants and confessions of faith. Using historical and contemporary examples, Caner offers three lessons for local churches and their use of covenants. He concludes with an explanation of the role baptism and discipleship provide in a church's covenant relationship.

*. . . observing the two ordinances of Christ,*

In chapter 4, Paige Patterson seeks to reexamine the purpose of the local church's two ordinances, baptism and the Lord's Supper. He argues that they are more than "mere symbols" but are not sacramental. Rather, the two are to work together to enforce the biblical concept of sanctification in the lives of believers and the local church.

*. . . governed by His laws, exercising the gifts, rights, and privileges invested in them by His Word, and seeking to extend the gospel to the ends of the earth. Each congregation operates under the Lordship of Christ through democratic processes. In such a congregation each member is responsible and accountable to Christ as Lord.*

In chapter 5, James Leo Garrett Jr. draws upon his scholarship and expertise and presents a case for the practice of congregational polity as the biblical norm for local churches. Chapter 6 follows with Bart Barber addressing the timely topic of whether there is value or biblical support for local churches cooperating together in denominations.

*. . . Its scriptural officers are pastors and deacons.*

In chapter 7, Byron McWilliams adds a candid reflection and articulation of the relationship of the officers in local churches. His tested experience as a pastor provides a welcomed personal perspective to the volume.

*. . . While both men and women are gifted for service in the church, the office of pastor is limited to men as qualified by Scripture.*

In chapter 8, Thomas White along with his wife, Joy White, seek to answer the questions of whether women can serve as pastors or deacons in the local church. A biblical and theological analysis, this chapter speaks with clarity to a controversial and often misunderstood topic in twenty-first-century Christianity.

*. . . The New Testament speaks also of the church as the Body of Christ which includes all of the redeemed of all the ages, believers from every tribe, and tongue, and people, and nation.*

In chapter 9, Thomas White ventures forth into another area where contemporary Baptists often fear to tread. Bringing clarity and understanding to the terms "local" and "universal," White provides the reader with a ready resource for local church life and practice.

# "Upon This Rock I Will Build My Church" A Theological Exposition of Matthew 16:13–20

*Malcolm B. Yarnell III*

The eight verses in Matthew that describe the confession of Simon regarding Jesus as the Son of God have generated much controversy in Christian history. The subsequent discussions around what has been called the "storm center of New Testament exegesis"[1] have put more attention upon the person and office of Simon than upon the Messiah that Simon confessed. This is unfortunate, for Simon put the emphasis upon his teacher, Jesus, rather than upon himself, a disciple of the teacher, in his own life and writings. The same emphasis, moreover, is evident in the Gospel of Matthew. The hope in this essay is to unravel the controversy in an effort to reemphasize the Christ-centeredness that Simon confessed and Matthew recorded. Let us first recollect the text.

> Coming into the area of Caesarea Philippi, Jesus queried
> His disciples, saying, "Who are men saying that I, the Son
> of man, am?"

---

[1] O. F. Seitz, "Upon This Rock: A Critical Re-examination of Matt 16:17–19," *JBL* 69 (1950): 32.

And they said, "Some John the Baptist, others Elijah, yet others Jeremiah or one of the prophets."

He said to them, "But who do you say that I am?"

And answering, Simon Peter said, "You are the Christ, the Son of the living God."

And answering, Jesus said to him, "Blessed are you, Simon, son of Jonah, because flesh and blood did not reveal this to you, but My Father who is in heaven. And I also say to you that you are *Petros*, and upon this *petra* I will build My church, and the gates of Hades will not be victorious over it. I will give to you the keys of the kingdom of heaven, and what you bind upon the earth will have been bound in heaven, and what you loose upon the earth will have been loosed in heaven."

Then He warned His disciples that they should tell no one that He was Jesus the Christ (Matt 16:13–20; author's translation).

In order to arrive at a proper theological interpretation of this passage, we shall follow a grammatical-historical approach and interact with the major interpretations offered in the history of Christian churches. In agreement with Gerhard Ebeling and Brevard S. Childs, this approach to biblical theology laments the unfortunate divorce of biblical exegesis from the theological interpretation of the church and laments the atomization of the canon.[2] While rejecting the modernist hubris involved in such a willful lack of historical awareness regarding prior Christian interpretations of the whole canon, this approach also rejects any hint that the Christian tradition is the final arbiter of proper theological exegesis. Systematically, after analyzing the linguistic nature of the passage, we shall turn to the historical and canonical context in

---

[2] G. Ebeling, *Word and Faith,* trans. J. W. Leitch (Philadelphia: Fortress, 1963), 79–97; B. S. Childs, *Biblical Theology: A Proposal* (Minneapolis: Fortress, 2002), 1–12.

which it was written, then the historical context in which it has been interpreted. Only then may we attempt to offer some preliminary theological conclusions.

## 1. LINGUISTIC CONSIDERATIONS

### Literary Structure

The literary structure of this passage exhibits a striking "unity" and "symmetry."[3] Indeed, for some modern interpreters, the symmetry is so profound that it is difficult for them to believe that the passage is anything but an interpolation the Matthean redactor has put into the mouth of Jesus Christ. For others, this and the coordinate passage in Matt 18:15–18 resulted from "the strained encounter between Hellenistic and Jewish Christian traditions."[4] Although we find the literary structure of Matthew reflects a highly nuanced redaction, we deny the insupportable presupposition that because the result is theologically complex the words do not fully reflect the teachings of Jesus and the confession of Peter. Moreover, we affirm the canonical presupposition that the author and his text were inspired by the Holy Spirit and, therefore, the original Matthean manuscript remains free of historical error, even as the extant manuscript tradition is infallible (2 Tim 3:16; 2 Pet 1:21).

With these presuppositions made plain, we now turn to the linguistic structure of the passage in question. There are four sections in the subject pericope, with the opening line of the first section and the entire fourth section providing the transitions required for placing the pericope within the historical progress of the Gospel of Matthew. The first three sections of the pericope follow a

---

[3] B. P. Robinson, "Peter and His Successors: Tradition and Redaction in Matthew 16.17–19," *JSNT* (1984): 86.

[4] G. Bornkamm, "The Authority to 'Bind' and 'Loose' in the Church in Matthew's Gospel: The Problem of Sources in Matthew's Gospel," in *The Interpretation of Matthew*, 2nd ed., ed. G. Stanton (Edinburgh: T&T Clark, 1995), 111. Cf. Robinson, "Peter and His Successors," 98.

### Structural Outline of Matthew 16:13–20

*Elthōn de ho Iēsous eis ta merē Kaisareias tēs Philip-pou ērōta tous mathētas autou legōn·*
- *tina legousin hoi anthrōpoi einai ton huion tou anthrōpou;*
  *hoi de eipan*
- *hoi men Iōannēn ton baptistēn,*
- *alloi de Ēlian,*
- *heteroi de Ieremian ē hena tōn prophētōn.*

*legei autois*
- *humeis de tina me legete einai;*
  *apokritheis de Simōn Petros eipen·*
- *su ei ho Christos ho huios tou theou tou zōntos.*

*apokritheis de ho Iēsous eipen autō·*
- *makarios ei, Simōn Bariōna,*
  - *hoti sarx kai haima ouk apekalupsen soi*
  - *all' ho patēr mou ho en [tois] ouranois.*
- *kagō de soi legō hoti su ei Petros*
  - *kai epi tautē tē petra oikodomēsō mou tēn ekklēsian*
  - *kai pulai hadou ou katischusousin autēs.*
- *dōsō soi tas kleidas tēs basileias tōn ouranōn,*
  - *kai ho ean dēsēs epi tēs gēs estai dedemenon en tois ouranois,*
  - *kai ho ean lusēs epi tēs gēs estai lelumenon en tois ouranois.*

*tote epetimēsen tois mathētais hina mēdeni eipōsin hoti autos estin ho Christos.*

conversational format; specifically, Matthew relates a rhetorical discourse of question and answer between a Jewish Teacher, Jesus, and some students, the disciples of Jesus. We have taken the liberty of identifying the structure of the words of the Rabbi and His students in a bullet format. In this way it becomes noticeable that the first and second sections each contain a query and a response, while the first and third sections each contain a triplex delineation.

The threefold delineation of the first and third sections gives special prominence to the second section, which does not contain such a complex delineation. The unique nature of the second section's answer, with its relative simplicity and placement in the structural center of the discourse, thereby grammatically highlights the Christological confession of Simon. That the third section does not contain a query, but nevertheless contains a long response, indicates the authority of the speaker. In other words, the literary structure gives prominence to the Teacher, on the one hand, and to the confession of the student regarding the Teacher, on the other hand.

## Son of Man and Son of God, and Son of Jonah

Also within the purview of linguistic considerations may be considered the frequent wordplays that are employed throughout the pericope and in its relationship with the preceding and following pericopes. Within the pericope the wordplays focus on the mutual naming between Jesus and Simon. To Simon's *su ei*, Jesus responds also with a *su ei*. The wordplays begin with their unique parental generation. Jesus is, on the one hand, self-described as "the Son of Man," a title that could have been taken as an appellation of nothing more than his own humanity,[5] especially when coupled with Jesus' query regarding what other "men" are saying. But Jesus is, on the other hand, confessed by Simon as "the Son

---

[5] B. Gerhardsson, "The Christology of Matthew," in *Who Do You Say That I Am? Essays on Christology*, ed. M. A. Powell and D. B. Bauer (Louisville: Westminster John Knox, 1999), 20.

of the living God," a title that sets off Jesus as so much more than any other human. Indeed, Simon's ascription of divine generation to Jesus is endorsed by the latter as a revelation by "my Father who is in heaven." Jesus, who is the son of man, is concurrently the Son of God. This God is, moreover, no mere deity; rather, He is the only God who lives; He is "the living God."

In comparison with such an exalted ascription, the third time that "son" is mentioned, in the identification of Simon as the "son of Jonah," the listener is reminded not only of Simon's father, John, but also of a rebellious prophet. The fallen humanity of Simon—his limited "flesh and blood"—is thereby placed in sober comparison with the exalted humanity and unique deity of Jesus. The title of "Christ" is also here ascribed to Jesus, and comprises part of the reason for the enthusiastic response by Jesus. But "Christ" was believed to be also a "Son of David," a title already being ascribed to him in Matthew (Matt 9:27; 12:23). Interestingly, "Son of God" had also already been ascribed to Jesus but with increasing degrees of certitude (4:1–11; 14:33).

The critical point seems to be the concurrent accumulation of these titles in a personal confession voiced by a human directly to Jesus. The personal nature of the confession is key to understanding its meaning, as is the accumulation of titles ascribed to the one being addressed. Indicative of the importance of the amassing of these titles is Jesus' similar equation of "Christ" and "Son of God" with "Son of Man." This personal accumulation is the turning point in his trial before the Sanhedrin. The high priest condemns Jesus as an utter blasphemer for having agreed, "under the oath of the living God," that "you are the Christ, the Son of God" (Matt 26:63–65). The contrast between the blessing of God upon Simon (16:17) and the judgment of God upon the Sanhedrin (Acts 4:11; a judgment poignantly pronounced by Peter) is determined by whether one personally accepts or personally rejects Jesus as the messianic Son of God.

## *Petros* and *Petra*

Another wordplay concerns the well-known issue of Christ's renaming of Simon. Simon, son of his father John on earth, is now to be known as Peter because he correctly repeated a revelation from the Father in heaven. This revelation, by the way, was not given to Peter alone but also to the others who heard the Father's voice at the baptism of Jesus (Matt 3:17). Simon is given a new name because Simon has confessed as his own that which had been confessed to him. Simon is renamed because he no longer spoke about a revelation as a distant matter; rather, Simon now received that revelation as his own and confessed it personally as a profound reality. Simon's Christian name is now Peter, literally *Petros*. According to Oscar Cullmann, *petros* in common Greek use "tends to denote the isolated rock."[6] This is where properly interpreting the wordplay surrounding Simon's renaming becomes important, for it is not upon *Petros* but upon the *petra* that Christ will build His church.

There are three important notes to be made with regard to the words *petros* and *petra* in the Greek. First, the masculine form, which becomes Simon's new name, is "used more for isolated rocks or small stones, including flints and pebbles." Second, the feminine form, upon which the church will be built, is "predominately used in secular Greek for a large and solid 'rock,' [such as an] individual cliff or a stony and rocky mountain chain." But, third, "they are often used interchangeably."[7] In other words, morphology may seem to provide a ready solution to the problem, but ultimately, lexicology leaves the question open as to whether one may use the imagery of Peter as a small rock in comparison to the mountain upon which the church is built. Moreover, unlike the *petros*, what the *petra* is to be identified as is not directly stated.

---

[6] O. Cullmann, "Πέτρος," in *TDNT*, vol. 6, ed. G. Friedrich, trans. G. W. Bromiley (Grand Rapids: Eerdmans, 1968), 101.
[7] Ibid., 95.

As we shall see, lexicology has left Romanists and Reformers with no end to their argument in sight.

At this point many interpreters have appealed to the Aramaic, the language of the original statements of which the Greek is a likely translation. However, this effort ultimately relies upon an argument from silence. Moreover, for the one who presupposes the divine inspiration of the Greek text, an appeal to an Aramaic source—largely about which only educated conjectures may be made—is simply not germane. Since the Holy Spirit inspires the biblical author and the resultant text, the extant biblical text—whether written in Greek or Hebrew, or rarely Aramaic—must be deemed sufficient for the task of theological exegesis. If an evangelical or free-church reader ignores the wordplay in the inspired Greek text in favor of a conjectural Aramaic text he implicitly denies one of his own fundamental theological principles, the inspiration of the New Testament. In other words, a vague appeal to the Aramaic, though interesting, does not settle the question.

Without the lexicon and without the Aramaic, the conservative Christian interpreter is left with the Greek text itself, and the Greek text, which is entirely sufficient as inspired, uses not one word, but two. One may not ignore the distinction in noun genders simply because the lexicon does not provide a firm definition regarding their distinct meanings. The fact remains that there are two similar words in use here; and although they are similar words, they are not the same word. Consider this somewhat literal translation: "I say to you that you are *Petros*, and upon this *petra* I will build My church." If Jesus was going to identify Simon himself, now renamed Peter, as that upon which the church will be built, He could simply have used *Petros* in both places. The fact is that the Lord did not do so, and this verbal change is significant, in spite of the inconclusiveness the lexicon generates.

But how significant is the wordplay? Could Jesus and Matthew and the Holy Spirit have chosen to use the masculine and feminine terms simply for the sake of providing a verbal pun?

Now God is not past delivering a good joke—one thinks here of that incredibly funny story of Balaam and his donkey or of Jesus describing the camel squeezing through a needle.

Yes, Jesus could have made a pun, but let us consider the serious nature of the human sinner's eternal *Sitz im Leben* for a moment. Though Jesus was not averse to humor, the serious nature of His vocation was foremost; moreover, wisdom teaches that there are different times for laughing and weeping (Eccl 3:4). It is highly doubtful that Christ, His apostle, and the Spirit would have thrown a meaningless pun into such a carefully structured passage in which wordplay has already indicated profound theological nuances.

Consider the serious issues being discussed in this and the following pericope: God, man, heaven, hell, spiritual war, death, resurrection, Satan. Perhaps the issue is not the wordplay as a simple verbal pun but the wordplay as indicative of a deeper truth. If so, then the use of the feminine *petra* rather than the masculine *Petros* may not be a reference to Peter himself, but to something related to Peter in some way, something related to the reason for his new name. Indeed, if God wanted to refer to Peter, he could have used *Petros* again or the second-person pronoun.

## Sign, Word, Doctrine

One of David Allen's favorite sayings is, "Friends, we deal in words." By this the dean of Southwestern Seminary means that the words of Scripture and the words we preach are extremely important. I agree with him in this. Because they are brought together by the Spirit to form the Word of God, words in Scripture are serious and are to be seriously considered, distinguished, correlated, and formulated into the doctrine that the Christian believes, lives, and teaches. Words formed into thoughts and taken as ultimate truth become our doctrines, and doctrines can give life or take life. Jesus tried to press this truth home when He taught the disciples about their need to search for the depth of meaning in what He spoke. Earlier in this same chapter Jesus gave the disciples two lessons on the significance of words.

First, He told the disciples that the problem with the Pharisees and the Sadducees was that they sought a "sign," but this wicked generation would only be given one sign, the sign of Jonah (Matt 16:1–4). Now, if they had thought about it, they would have remembered that shortly before this, Jesus had explained the sign: like Jonah, the Son of Man would be in the depths for three days and three nights. The sign of Jonah indicated Jesus' impending death and resurrection, and it demanded that sinners should hear Him and repent. Because the religious leadership of Judaism would not repent and believe, they would face a greater judgment than even the wicked Assyrians to whom Jonah preached (12:38–42). Bringing to their minds this previous lesson, Jesus now teaches His disciples another lesson, a lesson regarding the discernment of doctrine.

In the second lesson Jesus warned His disciples about "the leaven of the Pharisees and Sadducees" (16:5–12). However, rather than rising to the occasion and engaging in appropriate theological exegesis, the disciples displayed their earthly narrow-mindedness. The disciples had "little faith" because they did not yet "understand" the meaning of Christ's ministry and words. The words for thought and perception occur numerous times in the second lesson of chapter 16. Jesus was calling His disciples to think according to the gospel, to think as theologians, not to remain rank materialists. The disciple of Jesus should not be characterized by his appetite for sensual gratification but by his desire for divine doctrine. Listen to the thinking words, the focus upon faithful doctrine, in that conversation: "'Oh, you of little faith, why do you reason among yourselves because you brought no bread? Do you not understand, or remember . . . ? How is it that you do not understand . . . ?' Then they understood that He did not warn them about the leaven of bread, but about the doctrine of the Pharisees and Sadducees."

The proper hermeneutical method of a disciple is to look for the theological meaning behind the signs that Jesus worked and the words that Jesus taught. And those visible signs and those verbal signs signified something deeper. In like manner, when we come to a discussion of the words *petros* and *petra*, the contemporary disciple will not get hung up on the *sign* of Peter but will turn to the *doctrine* of Peter.

We are dealing here with words, words that have meaning. Do we not understand whom Christ has been asking them to identify? Do we not remember what Peter has said? The focus of the entire gospel up until now has been upon the Teacher and His doctrine, but with two words, *petros* and *petra*, is the focus now going to shift radically away from the Teacher and His teaching to Peter himself? Perhaps we may surmise that Jesus did not focus on Peter but upon the doctrine of Peter. And do we not understand that the doctrine of Peter that Jesus praised is the epistemological reality of who Jesus is?

Is the *petra* about Peter? Yes, but he is only the sign of something more. Is the *petra*, then, about the doctrine of Peter, the confession of Peter? Yes, but the doctrine of Peter is composed of words, words that function as verbal signs pointing to a deeper reality. As Augustine reminds us, the sign must be distinguished from the thing signified.[8] Is the *petra*, then, Jesus, "the Christ, the Son of the Living God"?

Perhaps the disciples understood that Jesus did not talk to them about a mere man, Peter, but about the doctrine of Peter, the confession of Peter, that is, about Jesus. The passage is concerned with Jesus: Jesus, the son of man, the Messiah, the Son of the living God, the owner of the keys to heaven and hell, the builder of the church, the one who binds and looses on earth because He binds and looses in heaven. Jesus, the one going to the cross, the one to be taken off the cross and laid in the grave—He is the

---

[8] "No one uses words except as signs of something else; and hence may be understood what I call signs: those things, to wit, which are used to indicate something else." Augustine, *On Christian Doctrine*, 1.3.

one who will stride right through the gates of hell, the one who will take the keys from the hands of death and Hades and walk back into life. He is the one who will commission His disciples and ascend into glory. He is the one who will be present with His gathered church while remaining with His Father in glory, whence He will come to judge the living and the dead. Yes, the *petra* has something to do with Peter, but the *petra* is not *Petros*. *Petra* is the confession of *Petros*; *petra* points to Jesus Christ.

### Other Linguistic Considerations

We too often treat scriptural pericopes as independent units of thought. Rarely are they such. Every passage in Scripture must be read in the context of its immediate surrounding texts, in the context of its book, in the context of its genre, in the context of its testament, and in the context of the canon. Matthew 16:13–20 should not be read independently of Matt 16:1–4 or Matt 16:5–12, as we have seen, for those earlier passages highlight the doctrinal context in which Peter's confession is made.

Moreover, Matt 16:13–20 should not be read independently of Matt 16:21–23. The back-to-back pericopes form a verbal diptych teaching the two parts of the Christian creed. If our subject pericope concerns the person of Jesus, or who He is, then the following pericope concerns the work of Jesus, or what He does. In Matt 16:16, Peter confesses correctly who Jesus is; in Matt 16:21, Jesus confesses what He will do. Matthew recognized that a proper Christology concerns not only the person of Christ but also the work of Christ. Peter, however, failed to receive properly the revelation of Christ's work. The Christian is called to remember Peter's fallibility and to avoid it.

Throughout the book of Matthew, Peter and the disciples are shown at their highs and at their lows. The disciples as an anonymous community and Peter as a personal individuality are the examples of what the Christian should be and should not be. Peter and the disciples serve as both positive examples and negative examples.

What is amazing with Peter, the representative disciple and spokesman for the other disciples, is that he charges from one extreme to the other. Compare Matt 16:16–19 with Matt 16:21–23. In one moment Christ is lauding him for confessing what the Father has revealed; in the next moment Christ is rebuking him for denying what the Son has revealed. In one moment Peter is an orthodox Christian, confessing Christ's person; in the next moment Peter is the consummate heretic, denying Christ's work. In one moment Christ is full of praise, comparing Peter with the rock upon which the church is built; in the next moment Christ is full of reprimand, comparing Peter with a stumbling block to the ruler of the church. In one moment Christ has renamed Simon as *Petros*; in the next moment Christ has renamed Simon as *Satana*, the occupant of the pit. In one moment Simon Peter is a powerful force that must be followed; in the next moment Peter is a powerless failure that must be resisted.[9]

## 2. HISTORICAL CONSIDERATIONS: THE BIBLICAL ERA

### The Old Testament Background

Four specific Old Testament passages create the ideological backdrop for Jesus' statements in Matt 16:17–19. These passages may be found in Psalm 118 and Isaiah 8, 22, and 28. What is striking with regard to these passages is that they concern the military governance of the people of God in the midst of war. These passages describe the conflict between two great communities, the people of God and foreign oppressors. The military situation

---

[9] This pattern of success and failure in discipleship continues throughout the book of Matthew, for both Peter and the disciples as a whole. See R. T. France, *Matthew: Evangelist and Teacher* (Grand Rapids: Zondervan, 1989), 245–46; M. J. Wilkins, *Discipleship in the Ancient World and Matthew's Gospel*, 2nd ed. (Grand Rapids: Baker, 1995), 181–85, 264; J. D. Kingsbury, "The Figure of Peter in Matthew's Gospel as a Theological Problem," *JBL* 98 (1979): 72.

probably came to the mind of Christ and the apostles in light of the geographical area in which they stopped to converse. Here at the foot of Mount Hermon—near the modern Golan Heights that have kept Syria and Israel in a state of war—the assaults from the northern powers of Assyria and Babylon first came.

The language evokes the terror of a surge of water from the Euphrates River (Isa 8:6–8), for wave upon wave of soldiers, following established military doctrine,[10] repeatedly swept through the land, bringing total destruction (Ps 118:11–12a). From their vantage point beside Caesarea Philippi, the disciples remembered that this was where Israel had seen "the overflowing scourge as it passes through" (Isa 28:18), overwhelming the people of God time and again. In a panic the Jerusalem and Samarian governments made covenants with the foreign powers—covenants doubtlessly sealed with acts of idolatry with the foreigners' gods—only to be overwhelmed by these foreign powers, prompting the prophet to describe any such agreement as a "covenant with Sheol" or a "covenant with death" (Isa 28:15,18).[11]

The prophets warned Judah that their only hope was in covenant with the living God. Even as the gates of Sheol opened to issue forth their endless hordes of idolatrous warriors so God and His Messiah could become the rock upon which the people of God might rest secure in His fortress. The "rock" or "stone" is the central metaphor of these passages in Isaiah and the Psalms, and the metaphors of "sanctuary," "gates," and "keys" are dependent on that central metaphor. Psalm 118 declared that the "gates of righteousness" would open to allow the believer into the safe presence of the Lord (Ps 118:19–20). For the psalmist, "salvation" within these gates was dependent on an unassailable outcrop of rock previously deemed unfit by the architects of the nation:

---

[10] J. N. Oswalt, *The Book of Isaiah, Chapters 1–39*, New International Commentary on the Old Testament (Grand Rapids: Eerdmans, 1996), 519.

[11] J. Blenkinsopp, "Judah's Covenant with Death: Isaiah XXVIII 14–22," *VT* 50 (2000): 472–83.

"The stone which the builders rejected has become the chief cornerstone" (118:21–22 NKJV).

Jesus Christ, as Matthew reports, applied Ps 118:22 to Himself, too. He asked His listeners whether they had ever read Ps 118:22 and then let them know they were subject to judgment for rejecting the rock (Matt 21:42–44). The critical decision of life depends on one's relation to the rock. As Martin Luther, a man who battled so much *Angst*, recognized, this stone upon which the believer's safety depends is the Christ. It should cause little wonder, then, that the sixteenth-century author of the well-known hymn "A Mighty Fortress Is Our God" claimed this particular psalm "more than any other as his own."[12] For when the attacks are relentless and death itself is haunting us, even with the approval of the Lord, who allows His own to be chastened with death, the believer may cry in faith with the psalmist, "I shall not die, but live" (Ps 118:17).

Like the psalmist, Isaiah also centered upon the imagery of the "rock" or "stone," a metaphor that explicitly evoked the solidity of the divine character. The difficulty for the people of Israel concerned whether they would allow this rock to shelter them or to shatter them. In Isaiah one's response to the divine rock is critical:

> To those who sanctify him, who give him a place of importance in their lives, who seek to allow his character to be duplicated in them, he becomes a sanctuary, a place of refuge and peace. But to those who will not give him such a place in their lives, he becomes a stone to trip over. He does not change; only our attitude determines how we experience him.[13]

Isaiah 8:14 emphasizes the negative aspect of the immutable nature of God: "He will be as a sanctuary, but a stone of stumbling

---

[12] R. M. Hals, "Psalm 118," *Int* 37 (1983): 282.

[13] Oswalt, *Isaiah, Chapters 1–39*, 234.

and a rock of offense to both the houses of Israel, as a trap and a snare to the inhabitants of Jerusalem" (NKJV). Isaiah 28:16 emphasizes the positive aspect of the immutable nature of God and His Messiah: "Behold, I lay in Zion a stone for a foundation, a tried stone, a precious cornerstone, a sure foundation; whoever believes will not act hastily" (NKJV). The last phrase in Isaiah 28, "which may have been understood to be the inscription on the cornerstone,"[14] is particularly interesting, for it links salvation to faith in the rock itself. Isaiah also pictured the keys to the gates of Israel being given to a steward, an instrument of God who would open and close the safe city of God to the people of God (Isa 22:22).

## A Christological Hermeneutic

Jesus Christ and His disciples took their Bible, the Old Testament, very seriously. In the Gospel of Matthew in particular, Jesus affirmed the inviolability of the Old Testament (Matt 5:17–20) and interpreted His own life and ministry in light of their Scriptures (26:56). Then again, it is just as appropriate to say that the New Testament interprets the Old Testament in light of the life and ministry of Jesus Christ (Luke 24:25–27). A Christian may never forget that the New Testament is a Christological text and must remember that the New Testament authoritatively treats the Old Testament in a similar manner. As they rang like music in the minds of the apostles, the metaphors of the Old Testament reinforced the message of Jesus Christ that they recorded in the New Testament, and their interpretations of the Old Testament and of Jesus Christ reinforced the interpretations of the other apostles.

This Christological description of the canon, of course, includes Matthew. According to Birger Gerhardsson, "The Gospel of Matthew is from beginning to end a christological book."[15] Later Gerhardsson repeats this affirmation: "Matthew paints a

---

[14] Ibid., 519.
[15] Gerhardsson, "The Christology of Matthew," 15.

composite and yet coherent picture of Jesus with the aid of diversified material. His Gospel is from beginning to end a christological book."[16] R.T. France agrees with this perspective and furthers it by noting that when it comes to the church, Christology has the priority. Some have referred to Matthew as the "ecclesiastical gospel," especially in light of the Petrine gift of authority. But France is sober in comparison:

> Ecclesiology is subordinate to christology, and the "church" which emerges is not a shining army with banners, but a relatively unstructured gathering of "little ones" who belong to Jesus, a body which impresses the reader more with its vulnerability and need of correction than with a sense of awe.[17]

The Christocentric nature of the Gospel of Matthew should not be forgotten when we consider the rock upon which the church is built and the role of Simon Peter with regard to the definition of the rock. As noted above, Matthew treats Peter not only as the exemplary personal disciple of Jesus but also as the representative of the disciples and the spokesman for the disciples. The representative nature of Peter on behalf of the other disciples should be recognized. In our subject pericope, the plural pronouns indicate that the questions are addressed to the disciples as a group, and the first set of answers comes from the disciples as a group. Moreover, Peter as the spokesman of the other disciples offers the confession of Christ's person. The representative nature of Peter on behalf of the disciples is a recurrent phenomenon within Matthew, a phenomenon noted by more than one scholar.[18]

May we conclude, therefore, that the blessing of Christ and the gift of authority are given to Peter as the representative of the

---

[16] Ibid., 29.

[17] France, *Matthew: Evangelist and Teacher*, 251.

[18] Ibid., 244–46; Wilkins, *Discipleship*, 211–16; Kingsbury, "The Figure of Peter," 71–76.

other disciples? In other words, is the language of Peter's primacy one that concerns the office of Peter as first among the disciples, or in speaking of Peter's primacy, should we be more concerned with his historical role in the early churches? The New Testament witness affirms the historical role of Peter as a leader in the early churches, and the New Testament does not elevate Peter officially above the other disciples beyond the seminal period.

In the Gospels we learn that Peter's greatest triumph occurred with his confession, and his greatest failure occurred with his denial of Jesus during the latter's trial (Matt 26:69–75). Peter is identified as among the first to see the empty tomb (John 20:6–7) and to encounter the resurrected Lord (1 Cor 15:5). In a painful encounter Christ poignantly reminds Peter of His commission to the apostles to look after the church, restoring the latter to the task that he had forsaken by returning to his boat (John 21:3,15–19).

After the ascension of the Lord, Peter took the lead in the church established by the Holy Spirit at Pentecost, preaching the gospel with powerful effect in Jerusalem alongside the other disciples (Acts 2:14–39). Peter and John extend the healing ministry of Jesus, drawing attention to the power of the risen Lord before the people of Jerusalem (Acts 3:1–11) and the Sanhedrin in particular (4:5–12). Peter also exercised leadership in discerning the spiritual welfare of the church membership and proclaiming the Spirit's judgment (5:1–11) and in the calling of the seven to relieve the twelve so that they might focus on proclaiming the Word (6:1–7). In fulfillment of the Great Commission (Matt 28:16–20) and Christ's program for its spread to the nations (Acts 1:7–8), Peter served the critical role of expanding the membership of the earliest church to include the Samaritans (8:14–15) and the God-fearing Gentiles (10:47–48) through triune baptism. Importantly, he functioned in this critical way while being sent by the Jerusalem leaders and remaining accountable to it (8:14; 11:1–18). So, in the critical phase of the church's expansion in Jerusalem and its extension to the Samaritans and the Gentiles, Peter dispensed the Word of God and interpreted its application. However, by the time of the critical meeting of the Jerusalem church regarding the matter of circumcision, Peter was surpassed by James's leadership in Jerusalem (15:13–22) and by Paul's leadership in the mission to the Gentiles (15:22–28:31).

### The "Foundation" of the Church

Another factor supporting the priority of Christology and the "salvation-historical" nature of Peter's so-called "primacy"[19] is the way in which the concept of the church's foundation is treated in the New Testament. The apostles Paul, Peter, and John have something to say in this regard. We begin with the twofold treatment of the foundation by Paul. First, Paul treats the foundation of the church in such a way that we may not oppose Christ to the apostles, nor oppose the apostles to Peter. Second, maintaining the priority of Christology, Paul states, "No other foundation can anyone lay than that which is laid, which is Jesus Christ" (NKJV). The church, as a "temple," is being built on the foundation of Him alone (1 Cor 3:11,16). But recognizing the place of the apostles as necessary conveyors of the revelation of that foundation, Paul elsewhere includes them within the foundation. The church is being "built on the foundation of the apostles and prophets, Jesus Christ Himself being the chief cornerstone" (Eph 2:20 NKJV). Extending the metaphor further, Paul elsewhere quotes Isa 28:16 so as to emphasize that faith in Christ is the proper foundation, while pursuing the law indicates one has stumbled over the "stumbling stone" of faith in Him (Rom 9:33–34). Paul also refers to Peter and the Jerusalem apostles as the "pillars" of that local church (Gal 2:9).

The apostle Peter himself, however, has a distinctly non-Petrine and nonapostolic understanding of the rock upon which the church is built. B. H. Carroll relates 1 Pet 2:4–8 directly to Peter's "greater confession" in Matthew 16: "[Peter] makes it very

---

[19] Kingsbury, "The Figure of Peter," 71, 81–83.

clear that the foundation of the church is Christ, the rock; he does not understand that the church is built upon him."[20] If Peter is referring back to Matthew 16, and he may be doing so both here and in Acts 4:11, then Carroll is most certainly correct. According to Peter, Jesus Christ is "a living stone, rejected indeed by men, but chosen by God and precious" (1 Pet 2:4 NKJV). And paralleling Paul's more extensive architectural imagery, Peter considers the members of the church to be "living stones," who are being built into "a spiritual house" upon the "living stone," Jesus Christ (2:5). Peter then quotes Old Testament passages that lay in the background of Matthew 16, all of which are referred to God in Christ: Isa 28:16 in verse 6, Ps 118:22 in verse 7, and Isa 8:14 in verse 8. Like Paul, Peter makes Jesus the foundation of the church, but unlike Paul, Peter does not include the apostles in that foundation.

Matthew 16 placed aside for a moment, the New Testament witness with regard to the foundation of the church seems to be clear: According to Peter, Jesus Christ is the "living stone" (*lithon zōnta*, 1 Pet 2:4), "cornerstone" (*lithon akrogōniaion*, 2:6; cf. 2:7), "stone of stumbling" (*lithos proskommatos*, 2:8), and "rock of offense" (*petra skandalou*, 2:8), the last noticeably using the critical Greek term, *petra*. According to Paul, Jesus Christ is the "foundation" (*themelios*, 1 Cor 3:11) and the "chief cornerstone" (*akrogōniaios*, Eph 2:20), but the apostles and prophets share in His "foundation" (*epoikodomēthentes epi tō themeliō tōn apostolōn kai prophētōn*, Eph 2:20) and are reputed "pillars" (*stuloi*, Gal 2:9). The primacy in the non-Matthean passages belongs to Christ, and while Peter participates in the architecture, even in the foundation, he is not individually considered except as a pillar of the Jerusalem church, and even then Peter is listed after James. Finally, according to John, the New Jerusalem has 12 foundations

[20] B. H. Carroll, *The Pastoral Epistles of Paul, 1 and 2 Peter, Jude, and 1, 2, and 3 John*, An Interpretation of the English Bible, ed. J. B. Cranfill (1948; repr., Grand Rapids: Baker, 1973), 173. Cf. P. Patterson, *A Pilgrim Priesthood: An Exposition of the Epistle of First Peter* (Nashville: Thomas Nelson, 1982), 71–80.

that are identified with the 12 apostles, but Peter is not explicitly named (Rev 21:14).

## The Church, the Gates, and the Keys

The bulk of our attention in this chapter has properly focused on the central metaphor of the rock, but other metaphors and terms in the passage must be considered. As noted in our structural analysis, the response of Jesus to Peter's confession has three parts. In the first he pronounces that Peter is blessed because God and not man revealed the confession to him (Matt 16:17). In the second, Jesus proclaims that Peter is to receive a new name, that Jesus will build His church upon the rock, and that the gates of Hades will not overpower it (16:18). In the third, Jesus announces that he will give the keys of the kingdom of heaven to Peter, the representative disciple, and that the decisions of the disciple and heaven will be coordinated (16:19). We must consider the proper interpretation of the words, "church," "gates of Hades," and "keys."

I have elsewhere discussed the biblical definition of the "church" as the gathered congregation and will refer you to that essay[21] and to the chapter in this book by Thomas White on the universal Church and the local church. In Matt 16:18, we note that Jesus Christ is the one who builds the church, although Paul sees Christian ministers as coming alongside to help in that construction (1 Cor 3:9–17). Also, notice that Jesus Christ uses the future tense here: "I will build" (*oikodomēsō*). In light of the New Testament witness, this probably means that Christ began building His church with the first local church's gathering at Pentecost in Jerusalem (Acts 2:1–47), continues building His church with every local church throughout Christian history, and will conclude building it with the universal Church's first complete gathering

---

[21] M. B. Yarnell III, "Article VI: The Church," in *Baptist Faith and Message 2000: Critical Issues in America's Largest Protestant Denomination*, ed. D. K. Blount and J. D. Wooddell (Lanham, MD: Rowman & Littlefield, 2007), 55–70.

at the marriage supper of the Lamb, when all of the servants of Christ will gather to worship Him (Rev 19:5–9).[22]

The "gates of Hades" (*pulai hadou*) is of Old Testament provenance and was likewise common throughout the Near East. "Many peoples in antiquity viewed the underworld as a land, city, fortress, or prison with strong gates which prevented escape and barred access to invaders."[23] References can be found in the mythologies of Babylon, Egypt, Greece, and Persia. Biblically, the phrase "gates of Sheol" is found only in Isa 38:10, where Hezekiah laments his impending death. *Sheol* is the Hebrew equivalent of the Greek word *Hades*, indicating the realm of the dead, rather than "Gehenna," the eternal lake of fire. The related terms of "gates of death" (Pss 9:13; 107:18; Job 38:17), "the gates of darkness" (Job 38:17), and "the bars of Sheol" (Job 17:16) also appear. Joachim Jeremias believed that the gates of Hades were "the aggressors" and "the ungodly powers of the underworld which assail the rock."[24] Moreover, both heaven and hell are considered to have gates, or stronghold entrances, where a city was ruled, defended, and attacked. The collective imagery again evokes a savage war between two great cities protected by their gates manned by stewards with their keys. The point here is that Hades will not be able to overcome the rock.

The word "keys" (*kleis*) has a number of figurative and largely apocalyptic uses in the New Testament, primarily found in the Synoptic Gospels and the Revelation of John. There are keys to Hades (Rev 1:18), the key to the abyss (Rev 9:1; 20:1), the key of knowledge (Matt 23:13; Luke 11:52), keys to heaven (Luke 4:25;

---

[22] H. E. Dana understands the usage here as a generic reference to the local church. H. E. Dana, *A Manual of Ecclesiology*, 2nd ed. (Kansas City, KS: Central Seminary Press, 1933), 38–40.

[23] J. Jeremias, "πύλη," in *TDNT*, vol. 6, 924. "The image in Matthew is of the rulers of the underworld bursting forward *from the gates* of their heavily guarded, walled city to attack God's people on earth." J. Marcus, "The Gates of Hades and the Keys of the Kingdom (Matt 16:18–19)," *CBQ* 50 (1988): 445.

[24] Jeremias, "πύλη," 927.

Rev 11:6), the key of David (Rev 3:7), and the keys of the kingdom (Matt 16:19). These keys belong ultimately to God, who has
power over heaven, who in Christ has regained power over Hades
(Rev 1:18), and who grants these keys to angels (Rev 9:1; 20:1)
and men (Matt 16:19) to employ as He decrees.[25] The keys that are
granted to Peter in Matthew 16 are promised as the future tense of
the verb (*dōsō*) indicates but were not delivered at this time. This
is a point that Luther emphasized, for the keys were only promised
to Peter as the representative disciple but were delivered by Christ
after His resurrection to the disciples as a whole (John 20:23), that
is, to the congregation (Matt 18:18, understood proleptically).[26]

The power of the keys in "binding" and "loosing" have been
interpreted in three senses, each of which seems to be used in the
New Testament. First, the power of the keys has been interpreted as the power to bind demons and free those being oppressed
by the demonic. This power can be found in the intertestamen-
tal tradition and in the New Testament itself (cf. Matt 7:34–35;
Mark 3:27; Luke 10:17; 13:16; Rev 20:1–3).[27] While this sense
deserves more attention, the other two senses are more commonly
discussed among scholars. Second, there is the disciplinary sense
of the keys of binding and loosing. It is important here to define
what discipline here is not. It is definitely not a juridical power,
nor is it a legislative power, and is perhaps best not even described
as an executive power. Rather, the disciplinary use of the keys of
binding and loosing should be described as a pastoral function.
The exercise of discipline by the church is never intended to bring
condemnation but redemption. Although following a careful pro-

---

[25] J. Jeremias, "κλείς," in *TDNT*, vol. 3, ed. G. Kittel, trans. G. W. Bromiley
(Grand Rapids: Eerdmans, 1965), 744–53.

[26] M. Luther, *Against the Roman Papacy, An Institution of the Devil* (1545), in
*Luther's Works*, vol. 41, ed. E. W. Gritsch (Philadelphia: Fortress, 1966), 306,
319.

[27] R. H. Hiers, "'Binding' and 'Loosing': The Matthean Authorizations," *JBL*
104 (1985): 233–50.

cess, the keys as pictured in Matt 18:18 have this pastoral function of redemption in mind.[28]

The third use of the keys, of proclamation and interpretation, is what is being promised in Matthew 16. This sense of the keys goes back to the rabbinic context of normative Judaism from which the terminology likely derived, and is thus used in the teaching of Jesus. In this sense of the keys, binding is the declaration of uncleanness or unrighteousness, while loosing is the declaration of cleanness or righteousness. It is sin that is bound or loosed, and the teacher applies the Scripture as binding or loosing through interpretation.[29] The proclamation by the Jewish teacher of binding and loosing is, moreover, first based on the biblical text. Since the text must be interpreted, the application of the biblical text regarding debated matters must also be considered. According to Mark Allan Powell, this is a continuing function of the church, best understood at the level of the local congregation.[30]

However, although taking the terminology of binding and loosing from the rabbinic tradition, Jesus separated His followers from that legal tradition by pointing to their abuse of the keys of interpretation: the Jewish leaders used the "key of knowledge" to prohibit entrance to the kingdom rather than to grant it (Luke 11:52). Although Jesus did not do away with the law, His burden is light and His yoke is easy, providing rest for weary souls (Matt 11:29–30). The primary emphasis in the use of the keys should, therefore, be upon the extension of grace and not the retention of sins.

Luther, in his exposition of these verses, agrees with this emphasis. The Reformer said that the keys regard the preaching of

---

[28] Bornkamm, "The Authority to 'Bind' and 'Loose,'" 106; France, *Matthew: Evangelist and Teacher*, 249.

[29] J. D. M. Derrett, "Binding and Loosing (Matt 16:19; 18:18; John 20:23)," *JBL* 102 (1983): 115.

[30] M. A. Powell, "Binding and Loosing: Asserting the Moral Authority of Scripture in Light of a Matthean Paradigm," *ExAud* 19 (2003): 81–96.

the Word of God and faith. Through the proclamation of the Word, forgiveness is applied to those who believe and judgment to those who do not exercise faith. "The keys and the power to bind and loose sin was not given to the apostles and saints for their sovereignty over the church, but solely for the good and use of sinners."[31] Although the preacher of the Word is instrumental and necessary, the work of binding and loosing is reserved for God: "To retain or forgive sins is the work of the divine majesty alone."[32]

This emphasis on the primacy of divine grace also coalesces with the unusual syntax employed by Jesus when speaking of "binding" and "loosing." The action that occurs in heaven is described through future perfect passives, both in Matt 16:19 and Matt 18:18. The translation should technically be "will have been bound" (*estai dedemenon*) and "will have been loosed" (*estai lelumenon*), rather than the more common translation as a simple future tense, "will be bound" and "will be loosed." The use of the simple future tense makes it easier to picture Peter (Matt 16:19) or the church (18:18) as somehow automatically obligating heaven for their earthly decisions. The use of the future perfect passive in our translation may emphasize church discipline as originating in heaven rather than upon earth.[33] If a person is loosed from sin upon earth through faith in the proclamation of a Christian disciple, it is because God is applying His grace at a spiritual level.

---

[31] Luther, *Against the Roman Papacy*, 315–16.

[32] Ibid.

[33] Commentators are not entirely agreed on this result. Like this author, France is convinced that the literal tense removes the *ex opere operato* nature of binding and loosing. Carson points out that one could just as easily argue for perfect communication between heaven and earth on the basis of a future periphrastic perfect translation. Carson's point is accepted, but the unusual nature of the verb as expressed in a more literal translation would still mitigate a sacerdotal understanding by opening afresh for the vernacular reader the question of the precise meaning of the sentence, prompting further study. Cf. R. T. France, *The Gospel of Matthew*, New International Commentary on the New Testament (Grand Rapids: Eerdmans, 2007), 626–27; D. A. Carson, "Matthew," in *The Expositor's Biblical Commentary*, vol. 8, ed. Frank E. Gabelein (Grand Rapids: Zondervan, 1976), 371.

It is only the disorderly hubris like that of some medieval popes that would demand that a spiritual leader on earth automatically obligates divine application and human salvation.

## 3. HISTORICAL CONSIDERATIONS: CHRISTIAN INTERPRETATIONS

Our considerations of the history of Christian interpretation of this passage will necessarily be of a summary nature. There are four major periods requiring elucidation: the patristic, the medieval, the Reformation, and the modern.

### Patristic Interpretations

John A. Broadus, in his 1886 magisterial commentary on Matthew, divides patristic responses regarding the identity of the rock into three categories: what he calls the "natural interpretation," and what we will call the confessional interpretation and the Christological interpretation. The natural interpretation, he says, is to regard the rock upon which Christ builds the church as Peter. Among those holding this interpretation were Origen, Cyprian, Basil, Gregory Nazianzus, Ambrose, Jerome, and Cyril of Alexandria. But Chrysostom, Gregory of Nyssa, Isidore of Pelusium, Hilary of Poitiers, Theodoret, Theophanes, Theophylact, and John of Damascus proclaimed the confessional interpretation.[34]

Chrysostom's commentary here is instructive since it recognizes the doctrinal context of the Matthean pericope. Peter is blessed because he holds "no longer a human opinion, but a divine doctrine."[35] As a result, "upon this rock" is another way to say, "on the faith of his confession."[36] Moreover, the commentator who

---

[34] J. A. Broadus, *Commentary on the Gospel of Matthew*, American Commentary Series (Philadelphia: American Baptist Publication Society, 1886), 356. Cf. U. Luz, *Matthew 8–20: A Commentary*, Hermeneia—a Critical and Historical Commentary on the Bible, trans. J. E. Crouch (Minneapolis: Fortress, 2001), 370–72.

[35] J. Chrysostom, *The Homilies of S. John Chrysostom, Archbishop of Constantinople, on the Gospel of St. Matthew*, 2 vols., trans. J. H. Parker (Oxford, 1844), 2: 730.

[36] Ibid., 731.

speculates so as to focus on Peter has begun to "lessen the dignity of the Son."[37] Chrysostom draws a strong line between thinking with heavenly doctrine and thinking with "human and earthly reasoning."[38] The Christian interpreter's mind should be upon the cross and upon heaven. The Christian should no longer be earthly minded, but "set your love on the country above."[39] Augustine's position is perhaps the most sophisticated one, for he early held that the church was founded upon Peter as the rock, but later he came to preach that Christ was the rock, and that the entire church becomes a rock when it confesses Christ. Augustine's canonical approach was eclipsed in the Middle Ages by a juridical approach but would later be restored under the Reformers.[40]

## Roman Catholic Interpretations

The Roman Catholic interpretation of Peter's gift of authority is that it is juridical, doctrinal, and soteriological, and that such total power is granted to the episcopal successors of Peter, who was considered to be the first bishop of Rome. This is why the pronouncements of various popes and Roman councils in history have been so controversial with other Christians both East and West. In November 1302, the bishop of Rome, speaking in the bull *Unam Sanctam*, wrote, "We therefore declare, state, define, and pronounce that it is entirely necessary to salvation for every human creature to be subject to the Roman Pontiff."[41] Vatican I makes similarly broad claims: "In this way, by unity with the Roman pontiff in communion and in profession of the same faith, the church of Christ becomes one flock under one supreme shepherd."[42]

---

[37] Ibid.

[38] Ibid., 735.

[39] Ibid., 737.

[40] Broadus, *Commentary on the Gospel of Matthew*, 356; Luz, *Matthew 8–20*, 373–75.

[41] Boniface VIII, Reg. 5382, cited in James of Viterbo, *On Christian Government: De Regimine Christiano*, ed. R. W. Dyson (Rochester, NY: Boydell & Brewer, 1995), xiv.

[42] Vatican I, Session 4, *Constitutio dogmatica prima de ecclesia Christi*, 3, in

Again, at Vatican I, we hear that when the Roman pontiff speaks *ex cathedra*, "He possesses, by the divine assistance promised to him in blessed Peter, that infallibility which the divine Redeemer willed his church to enjoy in defining faith or morals."[43]

And, in case one believes that Vatican II turned the corner on such grand claims, consider the recent work of the current pope, Benedict XVI, on the apostles. Therein, he focuses in on the role of Peter. Peter is the bishop of the universal Church, and "the Episcopal Succession of the Church of Rome becomes the sign, criterion and guarantee of the unbroken transmission of apostolic faith."[44] Because Peter is called to be "Pastor of the Universal Church," his successors fill the same role.[45] This means that Peter and his successors in the see of Rome possess "primacy of jurisdiction" over all Christians.[46] As a result, "Peter must be the custodian of communion with Christ for all time. He must guide people to communion with Christ; he must ensure that the net does not break, and consequently that universal communion endures."[47] In other words, the Pope believes that the promise of authority to Peter is granted to the bishops of Rome. The problem is that Scripture does not speak of the universal Church as already extant, of Peter as having the power of communion, of Peter ever being the bishop of Rome, nor of a succession of such power to subsequent bishops of Rome.

It is easy to see how such overreaching claims may result in tyranny. Consider the Council of Constance, which met between 1414 and 1418. There, John Wyclif was anathematized for teaching, "That the pope is supreme pontiff is ridiculous. Christ

---

*Decrees of the Ecumenical Councils*, 2 vols., ed. N. P. Tanner (Washington, DC: Georgetown University, 1990), 2:814.

[43] Ibid., 816.

[44] Pope Benedict XVI, *The Apostles and Their Co-Workers: The Origins of the Church* (Huntington, IN: Our Sunday Visitor, 2007), 40.

[45] Ibid., 50.

[46] Ibid., 57.

[47] Ibid., 58.

approved such a dignity neither in Peter nor in anyone else."[48] And because John Hus "declared the said John Wyclif to be a catholic man and an evangelical doctor," he too must be condemned.[49] Wyclif was dead, so they could not punish him. But Hus was alive, so Hus was condemned, relinquished to the state and burned at the stake, for among other things, saying, "Peter neither was nor is the head of the holy catholic church."[50] Bad scriptural exegesis regarding Peter now led to the judicial murder of a Christian theologian. Many more were to follow. The beautiful painting of Christ granting the keys to Peter in the Vatican's Sistine Chapel by Pietro Perugino may seem beautiful in its symmetry, but any who denied its subject matter as a human invention were subject to be killed in the name of an unbiblical orthodoxy.

## The Reformation Revolt

One can perhaps understand why Martin Luther's response to such Roman exegesis was severe. In his book, affectionately entitled *Against the Roman Papacy, An Institution of the Devil* (1545), Luther challenged the poor exegesis of Matthew 16 conducted on behalf of the Roman primacy. The cover illustration, crafted by Lucas Cranach, speaks volumes as to the book's contents. The book itself is rough reading, for Luther was a vulgar man, whose tastes the modern effete scholar may find offensive. And yet his many points about the abuses of the Matthean pericope should be remembered. Perhaps the most germane saying in that book, from the perspective of this conference, concerned the distinction between the churches and the church. "We know that," he said, "it has been so arranged that churches are equal, and there is only one single church of Christ in the world."[51] In other words, the local

---

[48] *Concilium Constantiense*, in *Decrees of the Ecumenical Councils*, 1:423.

[49] Ibid., 427.

[50] Ibid., 429.

[51] Luther, *Against the Roman Papacy*, 358. Cf. B. Lohse, *Martin Luther's Theology: Its Historical and Systematic Development*, trans. R. A. Harrisville (Minneapolis: Fortress, 1999), 118–26.

churches must be kept distinct from one another, and the universal Church should not be uniquely tied to any particular church.

## The Modern Commentators

John A. Broadus has been described as showing "a remarkably current and open attitude toward the more recent science of textual criticism."[52] Although Broadus believed in the inspiration of the Scriptures, he also considered criticism an important tool in exegesis. Unfortunately, Broadus sometimes also used higher criticism, such as the attempt to look behind the text to the original oral traditions that went into the Scripture. This leads to a great deal of speculation, speculation that can harm proper exegesis. Broadus correctly refused to let the Reformation interpretation of Matthew 16 drive his exegesis. But he went too far in peering behind the Greek text to the supposed Aramaic oral sayings. As a result, he returned to the "traditional interpretation" of the rock as Peter himself. Listen to the vehemence of his words, "But there is a play upon words, understand as you may. It is an even far-fetched and harsh play upon words if we understand the rock to be Christ; and a very feeble and almost unmeaning play upon words if the rock is Peter's confession."[53] Broadus did deny the Roman extension of the Petrine interpretation,[54] but he never explained exactly what the "play upon words" was intended by Jesus to mean. Although Oscar Cullmann's 1952 historical-theological study of Peter has been given credit for the development, for Cullmann agrees with Broadus's higher criticism in this regard,[55] it was Broadus who first established in the

---

[52] R. Melick, "New Wine in Broadus Wineskins?" in *John A. Broadus: A Living Legacy*, ed. D. S. Dockery and R. D. Duke (Nashville: B&H, 2008), 107.

[53] Broadus, *A Commentary on the Gospel of Matthew*, 355.

[54] Ibid., 356–57.

[55] Cullmann carefully works his way through the life of Peter, the historical interpretations, and the attempts to dismiss the passage as an interpolation. Like Broadus, he affirms an identification between the two Greek terms on the basis of their Aramaic source. O. Cullmann, *Peter, Disciple—Apostle—Martyr: A Historical and Theological Study*, trans. F. V. Filson (Philadelphia: Westminster, 1953),

English-speaking world the standard interpretation now followed by many evangelicals.[56]

Perhaps with his eye on Broadus's methodology, B. H. Carroll, once a trustee at Broadus's seminary, then the founder of

---

185, 206–7; trans. of *Petrus, Jünger—Apostel—Märtyrer: Das Historische und das Theologische Petrusproblem* (Zürich: Zwingli-Verlag, 1952).

In what is perhaps the most recent substantive study, Gérard Claudel does not challenge the conclusions of Cullmann regarding Peter and the church. Engaging the historical-critical debate, Claudel agrees that the Matthean pericope contains the most primitive confession of the church but that the pericope has been redacted so as to make Peter the connecting point between the later Matthean church's practice of discipline and Christ's original granting of the keys. Beside the problem with his use of the historical-critical method, Claudel unfortunately also sees the focus of the saying as being on the person of Peter: "sa focalisation sur la personne de Pierre." G. Claudel, *La Confession de Pierre: Trajectoire d'une Péricope Évangélique*, Études Bibliques, n.s. 10 (Paris: Librairie LeCoffre, 1988), *passim*, 376, 439.

[56] Among those holding the "traditional interpretation" of Peter as the rock, typically built on the speculative argument from the supposed Aramaic oral form of both terms as *kepha'*, are, besides Broadus and Cullmann: W. F. Albright and C. S. Mann, *Matthew: Introduction, Translation, and Notes*, The Anchor Bible (Garden City, NY: Doubleday, 1971), 195; C. L. Blomberg, *Matthew*, The New American Commentary (Nashville, TN: Broadman, 1992), 251–52; W. D. Davies and D. C. Allison Jr., *A Critical and Exegetical Commentary on the Gospel According to Saint Matthew*, 3 vols., International Critical Commentary (Edinburgh: T&T Clark, 1988–1997), 2: 627–28 (although Davies and Allison allow for a possible distinction beyond the identification with Peter); C. S. Keener, *Matthew*, IVP New Testament Commentary Series (Downers Grove, IL: InterVarsity, 1997), 270–71 (although Keener seems to allow for the composite view); and J. Nolland, *The Gospel of Matthew: A Commentary on the Greek Text*, The New International Greek Testament Commentary (Grand Rapids: Eerdmans, 2005), 667–70 (although Nolland allows for the option of a reference to something else).

Among those holding the confessional or revelational interpretation are: W. C. Allen, *A Critical and Exegetical Commentary on the Gospel According to S. Matthew*, International Critical Commentary (Edinburgh: T&T Clark, 1912), 176; R. H. Gundry, *Matthew: A Commentary on His Handbook for a Mixed Church Under Persecution*, 2nd ed. (Grand Rapids: Eerdmans, 1994), 333–34; R. C. H. Lenski, *The Interpretation of St. Matthew's Gospel* (Minneapolis, MN: Augsburg, 1943), 624–28.

Among those holding some composite view are: Luz, *Matthew 8–20*, 376–77; L. Morris, *The Gospel According to Matthew* (Grand Rapids: Eerdmans, 1992), 422–24; and the present author.

Southwestern Baptist Theological Seminary, responded, in his comments on 1 Peter 2:

> He [Peter] was not bothered as a great many modern theologians in interpreting that passage in Matthew 16, and they would have saved themselves a great deal of trouble if they had allowed Peter, to whom the words are addressed, to give his own inspired understanding of what Christ meant. And it seems always to me that there must be disrespect for the inspiration of Peter when any man says that in Matthew 16:18 the rock upon which the church was built was Peter, and it is disrespect also for Paul, because he is just as clear as Peter: "Other foundation can no man lay than that which is laid, Christ Jesus."[57]

## 4. THEOLOGICAL CONCLUSIONS

With the linguistic considerations, biblical exposition and the history of interpretation surveyed, we offer five preliminary theological conclusions, derived from this theological exposition of Matthew 16:

1.  Although the rock upon which the church is built is not Peter personally or officially, the rock certainly has to do with Peter, specifically with his confession of the divine revelation, which itself points to Jesus Christ.
2.  The foundation of the church is Jesus Christ, and the apostles, including Peter, share in that foundation alongside the prophets as inspired witnesses to the Word that is now our Bible.
3.  Peter was not given primacy over the universal Church in this passage. Authority was given to Peter as representative of all the disciples, that is, to the entire community.

---

[57] Carroll, *The Pastoral Epistles of Paul, 1 and 2 Peter, Jude, and 1, 2, and 3 John*, 173.

4. The gates of Hades indicate both death and the realm of demonic activity, and Christ has conquered both.
5. The keys of the kingdom of heaven include Christian authority to loose those under the influence of demons, to practice church discipline, and most importantly, to preach the saving Word of God, which, when accepted by faith, results in the salvation of the hearer.

# Autonomy of the Local Church: Crucial Baptist Distinctive

*David Allen*

*"O Mamma! Look here! This Bible that brother gave me, is a Baptist Bible. I am sure that brother didn't know it, else he would not have given it to me; and I won't have it. The merchant cheated him; don't you guess he did, Mamma?"*

*"Why, darling, what have you found in it to make you talk so? Don't you know that your brother bought you the nicest Bible he could find, and are you not going to be satisfied with it?"*

*"No, Mamma, because it's a Baptist Bible—I know it is; and I don't want a Baptist Bible. I do wish Buddie hadn't gone to college, so I could have him take it back and get me one of the right kind. O, it is such a nice book, I am so sorry there is a mistake about it. I do wish it was right."*

*"Yes, but it is right dear; I don't understand your crazy notion. Yours is like your brother's Bible that he carried away with him; just like the large family Bible from which I have often read to you; the reading in all of them is just the same."*

"But, Mamma, mine is a Baptist Bible; it is in fact. It tells so plainly about baptizing people in rivers, and places where there was much water, and about going down into, the water, and coming up out of the water, just for all the world like Mr. Coleman, the Baptist preacher, baptizes people. And surely, if the big Bible reads that way, you would not have had Dr. Farnsworth to sprinkle a little water on my face, and to just wet his fingers and rub them on little sister's face, and call it baptism. And, Mamma, if the big Bible does read that way, why did you always skip those places when you were reading to me?"

"O, fie, child! You ask more questions in a minute than I could answer in a day; but there is one thing you may understand, that is, the Baptists, the Methodists and our church, as well as all other Protestant churches, have the same kind of Bibles."

"Why, Mamma, they don't all do alike, yet don't they all say they believe the Bible? I can't see how it is, unless their Bibles are wrong."

"No, my dear, the difference is in the way different people understand the Bible. The Baptists understand it to teach some things just the reverse of what Presbyterians and others do; but this only amounts to an honest difference of opinions, which is, or ought to be, sanctioned by the broadest charity."

"Well, but Mamma, is not Dr. Farnsworth as smart as the Baptist preacher? Mr. Coleman talks just like my little Bible reads, and if he can understand it, I don't see why Dr. Farnsworth can't understand it, too."

The young speaker was little Mellie Brown, a plump, little girl, with rosy cheeks and flaxen hair, who had just passed

*her tenth birthday, on which her brother Frank had given
her a very fine little pocket Bible. At the time the foregoing
conversation occurred, she was sitting in her little rocking
chair at her mother's side, attentively reading the third
chapter of Matthew; and when she had read the account
of John the Baptist baptizing the people in the Jordan,
she was persuaded that the bookseller had practiced a
fraud on her brother by selling him a Baptist Bible. Such
a thought as evading the conclusions that legitimately follow a plain declaration of Scripture, had never entered
her mind. But in her child-like simplicity, she had supposed the Bible to mean what it said, and to say what it
meant.*[1]

Like Mellie Brown, there is a sense in which we Baptists believe that the Bible is a "Baptist Bible." As a people of the
Book, we believe that our understanding of ecclesiology is biblical.
At the center of Baptist ecclesiology is the notion of the believers'
church. As a Baptist distinctive, regenerate church membership
is important to us for biblical reasons, theological reasons, and
historical reasons. Biblically, it is clearly taught in the NT. Theologically, it is the point of departure for congregationalism. Historically, it is the watershed issue behind Baptist origins, and it is
what separates us from Catholicism and the magisterial reformers.
The precious concept of religious liberty, bequeathed to the world
by Baptists, has its fountainhead in the concept of a believer's
church and its concomitant corollary: local church autonomy. The
concept of autonomy is vital to Baptist theology and is in fact part
of the warp and woof of what it means to be Baptist.

The word *autonomous* comes from two Greek words meaning
"self" and "law." Thus, an autonomous entity is a self-governing
or self-directing entity. An autonomous church governs itself

---

[1] J. Martin, *The Little Baptist* (St. Louis: National Baptist, 1886), 5–7.

without any outside control or guidance. Of course every church is under the lordship of Christ and is governed ultimately by the Holy Spirit as it walks in obedience to the Scriptures as the Word of God. A church is technically not a democracy; it is rather a "Christocracy." Jesus rules as Lord over every church. As Paige Patterson correctly noted:

> Congregationalism does not, however, grant absolute autonomy to local churches or establish a "democratic" rule in the assemblies. Authentic New Testament churches will recognize and heartily endorse the absolute lordship of Christ. . . . Churches, then, are autonomous to the extent that no other ecclesiastical body is responsible for their doctrine or practice. But in New Testament churches this autonomy is never interpreted as the right to believe or to do whatever is desired regardless of the will of God as expressed through Jesus and in the Holy Scriptures. And even though in some way New Testament churches are the most thoroughgoing democracies in the world, this democratic process is limited to each member's fervent pursuit of the leadership of the Spirit of God. Overemphasis on this democratic process and on autonomy will lead to the prioritizing of rugged individualism over reverent submission to God, to the exercise of business affairs over ministry, and to the rise of human carnality over humble service to the kingdom.[2]

Malcolm Yarnell put it succinctly: "The New Testament church is *ruled* by Jesus Christ, *governed* by the congregation, *led* by pastors and *served* by deacons."[3]

[2] P. Patterson, "The Church in the Twenty-first Century," in *Baptist Why and Why Not Revisited* (Nashville: B&H, 1997), 111–12.
[3] M. B. Yarnell III, "The Church," in *Baptist Faith and Message 2000: Critical Issues in America's Largest Protestant Denomination*, ed. D.K. Blount and J.D. Wooddell (Lanham, MD: Rowman & Littlefield, 2007), 60.

## LOCAL CHURCH AUTONOMY AND
## BAPTIST CONFESSIONS: A SURVEY

The report from the Southern Baptist Convention Presidential Study Committee of 1994 said with respect to the subject of the autonomy of the local church:

A New Testament church is a gathered congregation of baptized believers who have entered into covenant with Christ and with one another to fulfill, according to the Scriptures, their mutual obligations. Under the Lordship of Christ, such a body is free to order its own internal life without interference from any external group. This same freedom applies to all general Baptist bodies, such as associations and state and national conventions. Historically, Baptist churches have freely cooperated in matters of common interest without compromise of beliefs. We affirm the wisdom of convictional cooperation in carrying out our witness to the world and decry all efforts to weaken our denomination and its cooperative ministries.[4]

The *Baptist Faith and Message* Study Committee was appointed by Convention President Paige Patterson at the Southern Baptist Convention in Atlanta, Georgia, in 1999 with the purpose of reviewing the *Baptist Faith and Message* statement and reporting back to the SBC the following year in Orlando, Florida. The committee's report included reference to the 1963 *Baptist Faith and Message* with the preamble of that confession quoted in full.

Significant for the concept of local church autonomy is this statement: "Baptists cherish and defend religious liberty, and deny the right of any secular or religious authority to impose a confession of faith upon a church or body of churches. We honor the principles of soul competency and the priesthood of believers,

---

[4] "Report from the Presidential Theological Study Committee," in *Annual of the Southern Baptist Convention* (Nashville: Executive Committee for the Southern Baptist Convention, 1994), 117.

affirming together both our liberty in Christ and our accountability to each other under the Word of God."[5] This report and the resultant latest revision to the *Baptist Faith and Message* came in a long line of Baptist confessional statements affirming the autonomy of the local church.

The London Confession of 1644, Article XLVII, stated:

And although the particular congregations be distinct, and several bodies, every one as a compact and knit city within itself; yet are they all to walk by one rule of truth; so also they (by all means convenient) are to have the counsel and help one of another, if necessity require it, as members of one body, in the common faith, under Christ their head.[6]

The Philadelphia Confession of 1742, Chapter 26, "Of the Church" reads in part:

To each of these churches thus gathered, according to his [Christ] mind declared in his word, he hath given all that power and authority, which is in any way needful for their carrying on that order in worship and discipline, which he hath instituted for them to observe. . . . A particular church, gathered and completely organized according to the mind of Christ, consists of officers and members. . . . The officers appointed by Christ to be chosen and set apart by the church so called and gathered. . . . The way appointed by Christ for the calling of any person fitted and gifted by the Holy Spirit unto the office of pastor, teacher, or elder, in a church, is that he be chosen thereunto by the common suffrage of the church itself. . . . Although it be incumbent on the pastors or teachers of the churches to be instant in preaching the word, by way of office, yet the

---

[5] J. Early, *Readings in Baptist History* (Nashville: B&H, 2008), 234.
[6] D. Neal, *The History of the Puritans*, vol. 2 (New York: Harper & Brothers, 1844), 479.

work of preaching the Word is not so peculiarly confined to them but that others also, gifted and fitted by the Holy Ghost for it, and approved . . . and called by the church, may and ought to perform it. . . . In cases of difficulties or differences, either in point of doctrine or administration, wherein either the churches in general are concerned, or any one church, in their peace, union, and edification; or any member or members of any church are injured, in or by any proceedings in censures not agreeable to truth and order: it is according to the mind of Christ, that many churches holding communion together, do, by their messengers, meet to consider, and give their advice in or about that matter in difference, to be reported to all the churches concerned; howbeit these messengers assembled, are not intrusted [*sic*] with any church-power properly so called; or with any jurisdiction over the churches themselves, to exercise any censures either over any churches or persons; or to impose their determination on the churches or officers.[7]

The New Hampshire Confession of 1833, "Of a Gospel Church," stated:

We believe that a visible Church of Christ is a congregation of baptized believers (66), associated by covenant in the faith and fellowship of the gospel (67); observing the ordinances of Christ (68); governed by his laws (69), and exercising the gifts, rights, and privileges invested in them by his Word (70).[8]

Similarly, the 1858 Abstract of Principles section on "The Church" stated:

---

[7] B. Hanbury, *Historical Memorials Relating to the Independents or Congregationalists*, vol. 3 (London: Fisher, 1844), 545–47.

[8] W. Lumpkin, *Baptist Confessions of Faith* (Valley Forge: Judson, 1969), 365–66.

The Lord Jesus is the head of the Church, which is composed of all His true disciples, and in Him is invested supremely all power for its government. According to His commandment, Christians are to associate themselves into particular societies or churches; and to each of these churches He hath given needful authority for administering that order, discipline and worship which He hath appointed.[9]

The first confessional statement drawn up by Southern Baptists in 1925, *Baptist Faith and Message*, said this in its article on "The Church":

A church of Christ is a congregation of baptized believers, associated by covenant in the faith and fellowship of the gospel; observing the ordinances of Christ, governed by his laws, and exercising the gifts, rights, and privileges invested in them by his word, and seeking to extend the gospel to the ends of the earth.[10]

The *Baptist Faith and Message*, revised 1963 edition, stated in the article concerning "The Church": "This church is an *autonomous* body, operating through democratic processes under the Lordship of Christ. In such a congregation members are equally responsible."[11]

The *Baptist Faith and Message*, 2000 edition, stated concerning "The Church":

A New Testament church of the Lord Jesus Christ is an *autonomous* local congregation of baptized believers, associated by covenant in the faith and fellowship of the gospel; observing the two ordinances of Christ, governed by His laws, exercising the gifts, rights, and privileges

[9] J. Leith, *Creeds of the Churches*, 3rd ed. (Louisville: John Knox, 1982), 342.

[10] *Baptist Faith and Message*, "The Church."

[11] Lumpkin, *Baptist Confessions of Faith*, 396. Italics added for emphasis.

invested in them by His Word, and seeking to extend the gospel to the ends of the earth. Each congregation operates under the Lordship of Christ through democratic processes.[12]

Each of these Baptist confessions affirms the autonomy of the local church. However, it was not until the 1963 *Baptist Faith and Message* that the term "autonomous" occurred in one of the confessions. Notice the concept of local church autonomy is further described in the 1963 *Baptist Faith and Message* as "operating through democratic processes under the Lordship of Christ." In the 2000 version, it is significant that the term "autonomous" was shifted to the first sentence in the article and followed by "local congregation." In this way the revised *Baptist Faith and Message* 2000 highlighted the Baptist distinctive of local church autonomy.

### BIBLICAL BASIS FOR LOCAL CHURCH AUTONOMY

The biblical evidence for local church autonomy can be summarized from the following passages of Scripture:

1.  Acts 2:47—Regenerate Membership. All are saved by grace through faith (Eph 2:8–9) and all are believer-priests (1 Pet 2:9) with the freedom to approach God through Jesus Christ unfettered by human intermediaries or human restrictions (Heb 9:11–14; 10:19–25). As members of a local church, each believer shares in the fellowship of the church, a fellowship with Jesus as Lord and with one another.

2.  Matt 18:17; 1 Cor 5:13—Church Discipline. All church discipline issues in the NT apply only to local churches. There is no higher court of appeal than the congregation. Each local church has authority to judge its own

---

[12] Early, *Readings in Baptist History*, 250. Italics added for emphasis.

membership. Neither Paul nor any other apostle attempts to excommunicate a member from the local church, but Paul does instruct the church to do so when necessary.

3. Acts 6:1–6—Church Government. The local church has authority to elect its own officers. The apostles never assume responsibility to choose the pastors or deacons of a local church, but call upon the church to do it.

4. 1 Cor 6:1–5—Church Disputes. The local church has authority to settle its own internal disputes. Paul does not appoint a committee, but directs the local church to look after the matter.

5. Acts 4:18–20; 5:29—Religious Liberty. Christians in New Testament times resisted the efforts of governmental and religious authorities to dictate religious belief and practice. Acts makes it clear the early church insisted on autonomy from both secular and religious authorities.

6. Acts 13:1–3—Church Ministry Decisions. The local church determined who would be commissioned for specific ministry.

7. Acts 15:1–2,22–23,25,30—Church Relations with Other Churches. The local church has authority in matters involving the relations of different local churches. Acts 15 was not a conference of ecclesiastical overlords, but of two local churches, each sovereign in its own affairs, addressing critical issues. Again, even the apostles do not assume exclusive authority in the matter.

8. Revelation 2 and 3—Church Individuality. Each of the seven churches in Asia Minor existed as a unique, separate entity and was under no authority except that of Jesus Christ.

The autonomy of the local church guarantees the spiritual equality of churches to one another. Since no church is superior to another church, no organization of churches is superior to another church. No church or group of churches in any configuration has one ounce of authority over an individual church. Congregational church governance is both the evidence of and a basis for autonomy. Both notions are mutually interdependent.

## BAPTIST VOICES—HISTORICAL SURVEY
## OF BAPTISTS AND AUTONOMY

Recently I read an interesting book by Patrick Granfield, a Catholic scholar, entitled *The Limits of the Papacy: Authority and Autonomy in the Church*. It helped me understand the contemporary Catholic understanding of the church. Citing Alois Grillmeier's assessment of Vatican II's "rediscovery," Granfield pointed out Catholicism's understanding of the universal Church as the sum and communion of the "local Churches." Of course it should be noted here that the Catholic reference to "local Churches" is somewhat distinct from the Protestant understanding. Catholics refer to a diocese as a "local Church." One notes throughout Granfield's book, even in reference to local churches, the word *church* is always capitalized. For Catholicism, "The local Church is the Church, because it possesses the entire promise of the Gospel, the full reality of the faith, and the grace of the Triune God. The local Church is the Church, because in it Christ is wholly present."[13]

As a consequence of this, local churches are not autonomous. Such autonomy would, according to Granfield, jeopardize the unity of both the universal Church and the local church. Since the Church of Rome is considered to be *prima sedes,* that is, "the First See," it possesses "special authority" in the universal Church. Granfield summarizes: "The concept of the local Church, then, is relational; its proper understanding and validity depend on its connection with other local Churches and with the *prima sedes*."[14]

---

[13] P. Granfield, *The Limits of the Papacy: Authority and Autonomy in the Church* (Crossroads: New York, 1987), 112.

[14] Ibid., 114.

Further evidence of the lack of autonomy in Catholic churches may be seen in Granfield's admission that the Pope has the authority to "intervene in the life of the dioceses." The money quote is Granfield's statement: "The local Church should not disregard the universal Church by claiming an unfounded independence and autonomy."[15]

By contrast, Baptists are the polar opposites of Catholics on this issue! The Union Baptist Association's "Bill of Inalienable Rights," Article 1, October 8, 1840, stated: "Each Church is forever free and independent, of any and every ecclesiastical power formed by men on earth, each being the free house-hold of Christ."[16]

Francis Wayland (1796–1865), Baptist pastor and president of Brown University, stated it this way:

> The Baptists have ever believed in the entire and absolute independence of the churches. By this we mean that every church of Christ, that is, every company of believers united together according to the laws of Christ, is wholly independent of every other; that every church is perfectly capable of self-government; and that therefore, no one acknowledges any higher authority, under Christ, than itself; that with the church all ecclesiastical action commences, and with it terminates, and hence, that the ecclesiastical relations proper, of every member are limited by the church to which he belongs.[17]

He further opined:

> We however looked with great disfavor upon any practice which, in the remotest degree, violates the great principle

---

[15] Ibid., 138.

[16] *Minutes of the First Session of the Union Baptist Association* (Houston: Telegraph, 1840), 9–10.

[17] F. Wayland, *Notes on the Principles and Practices of Baptist Churches* (New York: Sheldon, Blakeman, 1857), 177–78.

of the independence of the churches. . . . Throughout the New Testament we can discover not a trace of organization beyond the establishment of individual churches. . . . Is it not probable that as he left it, so he intended that it should continue to the end of time?[18]

In addressing the issue of self-government of the local church, O. C. S. Wallace stated it well:

The church does not need two heads. The church cannot be embarrassed by the laws and regulations proceeding from two sources. A church cannot serve two masters. The gospel church, in order to preserve its integrity, and that it may be truly and completely loyal to Jesus Christ, may recognize no other Head.[19]

Edward T. Hiscox, Baptist pastor, historian, and one of Baptists' chief church polity experts, stated:

As has been said, each particular and individual Church is actually and absolutely independent in the exercise of all its churchly rights, privileges, and prerogatives; independence of all other churches, individuals, and bodies of men whatever, and is under law to Christ alone.[20]

He continued:

There is no such thing as interdependence in the sense of a limitation of the self-governing right and authority of a Church. One Church may be poor and need help from one that is rich; or it may be in perplexity and need advice from one supposed to be more experienced—as the Church at Antioch sought counsel of the older and more

---

[18] Ibid., 182.

[19] O. C. S. Wallace, *What Baptists Believe* (Nashville: The Sunday School Board, 1934), 145–46.

[20] E. Hiscox, *Principles and Practices for Baptist Churches* (Grand Rapids: Kregel, 1980), 145.

experienced Church at Jerusalem, or as the churches in Macedonia and Achaia contributed to the poor saints in Judea. But these facts do not touch the question of polity or government; their relations to each other in these respects remain the same. Fellowship and fraternal accord may be strengthened; the helpfulness of the one and the gratitude of the other may be increased, but the one is none the more independent, nor the other any less so, because of these friendly interchanges.[21]

Isaac Backus, that great Baptist champion of religious liberty during and after the American Revolution, concluded, "The whole power of governing and disciplining their members is in each particular church."[22] Backus himself was reluctant to join the Warren Baptist Association in 1770 until their plan of organization was rewritten to reassure concerned churches about the matter of local church autonomy within the Association. James Manning, president of Rhode Island College later to become Brown University, drew up the document which read in part, "That such an association is consistent with the independence and power of particular churches, because it pretends no other than an advisory council, utterly disclaiming superiority, jurisdiction, coercive right and infallibility."[23]

B. H. Carroll, founder and first president of Southwestern Baptist Theological Seminary in Fort Worth, Texas, argued for individual responsibility as the foundation for local church autonomy and as a distinctive contribution of Baptists to theology:

The sole responsibility of decisions and actions rests directly upon the individual soul. Each one must give

---

[21] Ibid., 148–49.

[22] I. Backus, *A History of New England with Particular Reference to the Denomination of Christians Called Baptists*, 2nd ed. with notes by D. Weston, vol. 2 (Newton, MA: Backus Historical Society, 1871), 232.

[23] W. Hudson, *Baptist Concepts of the Church* (Chicago: Judson, 1959), 124.

account of himself to God. This is the first principle of New Testament law—to bring each naked soul face to face with God. When that first Baptist voice broke the silence of four hundred years it startled the world with its appeal to individuality. . . . If one be responsible for himself, there must be no restraint or constraint of his conscience. Neither parent, nor government, nor church, may usurp the prerogative of God as Lord of the conscience.[24]

These are only a few of the many voices that could be heard on this subject. Clearly Baptists have championed the autonomy of the local church and have viewed this doctrine as biblically and theologically essential to ecclesiology.

## BAPTISTS, AUTONOMY, AND RELIGIOUS LIBERTY

When you look up the term *religious liberty* in anybody's dictionary, there you will find the collective picture of Baptists. Underhill, adding to a quotation of John Locke, said: "The Baptists were the first propounders of absolute liberty, just and true liberty, equal and impartial liberty."[25] The writings of the early Anabaptists bear witness to their commitment to autonomy and religious liberty. In a rather dramatic confrontation between Zwingli and the leaders of the Swiss Brethren, Simon Stumpf objected to Zwingli's deference to the cantonal council in religious matters: "Master Ulrich!

---

[24] B. H. Carroll, *Baptists and Their Doctrines* (Chicago: Revell, 1913), 15, 18.

[25] J. Locke, *A Letter Concerning Toleration*; E. Underhill, *Struggles and Triumphs of Religious Liberty: An Historical Survey of Controversies Pertaining to the Rights of Conscience, from the English Reformation to the Settlement of New England* (New York: Sheldon, Blakeman, 1858), 201. As Jason Duesing correctly pointed out concerning this quotation: "The location of Underhill's inset quotation marks here are of significant historical significance as many later historians and Baptists regrettably failed to notice this distinction and claimed the entire sentence as Locke's" (*First Freedom: The Baptist Perspective on Religious Liberty*, ed. T. White, J. Duesing, M. Yarnell [Nashville: B&H, 2007], 5). This work, *First Freedom*, is an excellent readable account on the subject of Baptists and religious liberty.

You have no authority to place the decision in Milord's hands, for the decision is already made: the Spirit of God decides."[26]

The insistence on autonomy by Baptists has resulted in misunderstanding, criticism, and even persecution. Governments have punished Baptists as traitors, and some denominations have condemned Baptists as heretics. Pope Pius IX in an 1852 papal encyclical condemned the Baptist notion of separation of church and state as pernicious.[27] However, since WWII, things have changed somewhat for the Catholic Church in Italy. As Gianni Long noted concerning the Catholic Church in Italy, since 1947, the Church and the State are completely independent of each other. Other Christian churches likewise possess religious freedom from the state, however, with one clear distinction from the Catholic Church's liberty from the state: said churches must not conflict with Italian juridical order and their relationship with the state must be regulated by law "on the basis of agreements with the respective [church] representatives."[28]

Thus, church autonomy in Italy is based on two different constitutional grounds and two different "measures." Catholic Church independence and sovereignty are matters of international law; with respect to other churches, the autonomy is granted within national law. This means said churches can organize themselves according to their respective beliefs but only insofar as they do not conflict with Italian juridical order. Recall the statement written on the barn wall in George Orwell's *Animal Farm*: "All animals are created equal." Later, when things were going awry, the animals awakened one morning to find this statement scribbled underneath the previous statement: "Some animals are more equal

---

[26] K. Grebel and L. Harder, *The Sources of Swiss Anabaptism*, ed. L. Harder (Scottdale, PA: Herald, 1985), 242.

[27] *Allocution "Acerbissimum"* (Sept. 17, 1852), which was included in the *Syllabus of Errors* of 1864. (See A. Fremantle, ed., *The Papal Encyclicals in Their Historical Context* [New York: The New American Library, 1963], 149.)

[28] *Yearbook on Human Rights for 1956* (New York: United Nations, 1956), 175.

than others." In Italy, it appears the Catholic Church possesses a "more equal" status *vis a vis* other Protestant churches.

By contrast, listen to the earliest Baptists on this subject of religious liberty. In Article 84 of the English version of the Confession of 1612, John Smyth wrote the often quoted words:

> That the magistrate is not by virtue of his office to meddle with religion, or matters of conscience, to force or compel men to this or that form of religion, or doctrine: but to handle only civil transgressions (Rom Xiii), injuries and wrongs of man against man, in murder, adultery, theft, etc., for Christ only is the king, and lawgiver of the church and conscience (James iv. 12).[29]

The first Baptist preacher of record in England died in Newgate Prison in London. His name was Thomas Helwys. Upon his return to London from exile in Amsterdam, he and a handful of followers established their small congregation at Spitalfields in 1612, just outside the walls of London. Soon afterwards, Helwys sent a little book to King James I entitled *A Short Declaration of the Mistery of Iniquity,* with a handwritten inscription in which he boldly proclaimed:

> The king is a mortal man and not God, therefore has no power over the immortal souls of his subjects, to make laws and ordinances for them, and to set spiritual lords over them. If the king has authority to make spiritual lords and laws, then he is an immortal God, and not a mortal man. O King, be not seduced by deceivers to sin against God whom you ought to obey, nor against your poor subjects who ought and will obey you in all things with body, life and goods, or else let their lives be taken from the earth. God save the King.[30]

---

[29] Lumpkin, *Baptist Confessions of Faith*, 140.
[30] T. Helwys, *A Short Declaration of the Mystery of Iniquity*, ed. R. Groves (Macon, GA: Mercer, 1998), xxiv.

King James was not amused and sent Helwys to prison for the rest of his days.

While the Jamestown and Plymouth colonies denied the rights of conscience to their people and punished those Baptists who dissented from the dominant form of Christianity in vogue at the time, Baptist Roger Williams introduced religious liberty to New England in Rhode Island at a place called "Providence." The colony that the Puritans had dubbed "the Garbage Can" of New England became the prototype of a new nation that would be birthed a century and a half later. Exactly 150 years after Roger Williams planted Providence Plantations, Thomas Jefferson's bill for the Establishment of Religious Freedom in Virginia was passed into law. Baptist John Leland's influence on Jefferson in this endeavor is well known.

Hugh Wamble noted:

Leaders of the new colonies left England as critics of the Church of England. In New England they erected their own version of a state church, often called the New England Theocracy; in this system, magistracy (civil officialdom) and ministry (church officialdom) became the twin pillars of the most rigid state churches in the English colonies. Thus, while Congregationalists in England were experiencing the ill consequences of the Clarendon Code enacted in the 1660's, Congregationalists were experiencing the headiness of a state church monopoly in New England.[31]

Wamble continued:

For many decades in England and to the period of the Revolution in America, Baptist were the butt of ridicule and odium emanating from officials of state and church

---

[31] H. Wamble, "Baptist Contributions to Separation of Church and State," *BH&H* 20, no. 3 (1985): 4.

who attacked Baptists as socially insignificant, educationally unlettered, religiously misguided, morally depraved, and politically dangerous. By the 1640's Baptist persons, beliefs, and practices were stock subjects for the gossipy heresiography of the day.[32]

Amidst such opprobrium, from the prolific pens of Baptists came books polemical and historical championing the cause of religious liberty. In 1612, the confession "Propositions and Conclusions concerning True Christian Religion, containing a confession of Faith of certain English people living in Amsterdam" was possibly based on an earlier confession by John Smyth according to Lumpkin.[33] Helwys' *Mistery of Iniquity*, published in 1612, was also a crucial early document. Leonard Busher in *Religion's Peace* (1614) and John Murton in *Objections Answered* (1615) along with his *An Humble Supplication to the King's Majesty* (1620) furthered the Baptist cause of religious liberty. This last work was written in a most unusual manner. Murton was imprisoned for his Baptist views in Newgate. As Roger Williams, who was very influenced by Murton, tells it:

> and having not the use of pen and ink, wrote these arguments in milk, in sheets of paper brought to him by the woman, his keeper from a friend in London as the stopples of his milk bottle. In such paper written with milk, nothing will appear; but the way of reading it by fire being known to this friend who received the papers, he transcribed and kept together the papers, although the author himself could not correct nor view what himself had written.[34]

---

[32] Ibid., 5.

[33] Lumpkin, *Baptist Confessions of Faith*, 123.

[34] R. Williams, *The Bloudy Tenent of Persecution for Cause of Conscience* (London: Classic Textbooks, 1644), 32. Williams followed this with his *The Bloody Tenent Yet More Bloody* (London: Clavert, 1652).

John Clarke's *Ill Newes from Newe England* exposed the episode of persecution that occurred in 1651 at Lynn, Massachusetts, and criticized the colony's oppressive policy in religion.[35] Isaac Backus began research on his three-volume *A History of New England, with Particular Reference to the Denomination of Christians Called Baptists* for the explicit purpose of exposing the union between church and state in most of the New England. The volumes were published in 1777, 1784, and 1796.[36] Toward the conclusion of the eighteenth century, John Leland published his *Rights of Conscience Inalienable* as a rationale for full religious freedom.[37]

Backus received this laudatory notation for his stand for religious liberty:

> In the realm of ecclesiastical polity in the second half of
> the Eighteenth Century, his was perhaps the keenest mind
> in America. . . . Though many others joined in protest
> against civil control of religion and there were other lead-
> ers in the efforts to secure separation of church and state,
> no individual in America since Roger Williams stands out
> so preeminently as the champion of religious liberty as
> does Isaac Backus.[38]

As an agent of the Warren Baptist Association of Massachusetts, which was formed to promote religious liberty, Backus eloquently defended complete religious liberty before the Massachusetts Assembly in 1775 and the Constitutional Convention in Philadelphia in 1787.

---

[35] J. Clarke, *Ill Newes from Newe England* (London: Henry Hills, 1652).

[36] Backus, *A History of New England, with Particular Reference to the Denomination of Christians Called Baptists.*

[37] J. Leland, *Rights of Conscience Inalienable* (New-London [New Haven]: T. Green & Son, 1791).

[38] *Dictionary of American Biography*, vol. 1 (New York: Charles Scribner's Sons, 1928), 470–71.

The fascinating account of John Leland's influence on Thomas Jefferson is crucial to an understanding of Baptists and their contribution to religious liberty in the newly formed republic. Richard Land tells the story well:

> Leland previously had relocated from Virginia in 1791, back to his native Massachusetts, where he became more involved in politics than I believe a Baptist preacher ought to be. He was so involved that when Thomas Jefferson won the incredibly bitter election of 1800 and the Democrats of western Massachusetts wanted to send a token of their regard and esteem for Jefferson, they sent Leland as the spokesperson. Jefferson received Leland at ten o'clock in the morning on the first Friday of January 1802. Leland arrived at the White House accompanied by a wagon holding a several-hundred-pound cheese.
>
> The president personally came outside to receive the gift, and Leland took the opportunity to praise him publicly. Leland told the president the cheese was a token of the regard of the Democrats of western Massachusetts, and he assured the president that no Federalist cows had contributed any milk to this cheese, only Democrat cows. Leland then praised the president as God's great gift to mankind, praying for his leadership and his wisdom. As it was a gift, Leland left the cheese with Jefferson. The cheese was taken into the White House. While Jefferson had lunch soon after, it is not recorded whether cheese was on the menu. After lunch Jefferson took the quill and parchment and penned his letter to the Baptist churches of Danbury, Connecticut, writing, "There is to be a wall of separation between the church and the state."
>
> On the same Friday that a Baptist preacher showed up with an enormous cheese, prayed for the president, and the president thanked him for the prayer, the president later that

day wrote his well-known letter to Baptist preachers of Danbury. Two days later, on Sunday morning, Thomas Jefferson attended a Christian worship service in the House of Representatives. With about half the members of Congress in attendance, as well as the president of the United States, John Leland, a Baptist evangelist, preached a revival sermon from the speaker's rostrum of the House of Representatives.

One account from an Episcopal congressman said Leland preached like an untutored frontier preacher. Yet, no matter his style of delivery, he was afforded the opportunity to preach in what was apparently a regularly scheduled worship service, with Jefferson (who was evidently not a regular attendee) sitting on the front row. Clearly Thomas Jefferson did not intend for a wall of separation between church and state to mean the segregation of religious expression from public life in public places, including the House of Representatives.[39]

It usually comes as some surprise when people learn that Jefferson's father was a Baptist! This fact, along with the influence of Baptists like Leland, contributed to our understanding of Jefferson's championing the separation of church and state.

In spite of this stellar record on religious liberty, one of the great ironies and tragedies of Baptist history is that many of the same Virginia Baptists who went to jail over freedom of religion also owned slaves. Suddenly the same people who demanded absolute religious freedom began to squelch the freedom of other human beings who happened to be of a different skin color. Ironically, the great Baptist William Furman simultaneously sought to retain this heritage of freedom and yet maintain the South's peculiar institution of slavery.

---

[39] R. Land, "The Role of Religious Liberty in the Founding and Development of America," in White, Duesing, and Yarnell, *First Freedom*, 107–8. See also R. Land, *Real Homeland Security* (Nashville: B&H, 2004), 208–10.

W. W. Sweet tells the story of Winney, a black woman and Kentucky slave who belonged to Esther Boulware, a Baptist. Boulware, along with the Forks of Elkhorn Baptist Church in 1807, disciplined Winney for publically stating that "she once thought it her duty to serve her Master & Mistress but since the Lord had converted her, she had never believed that any Christian could own or keep Slaves," and she believed that "there were thousands of white people wallowing in Hell for their treatment to Negroes."[40] Was it any coincidence that the Civil Rights movement against segregation was birthed in the black Baptist churches in Alabama, Georgia, and the other Southern cities? Was it any coincidence that a black Baptist pastor named Martin Luther King should be the Lord's instrument to lead Baptists and a nation to throw off the yoke of injustice that African-Americans had endured for so long?

During the twentieth century there was no more famous display of the meaning of religious liberty and its foundation in Baptist practice than that found in the sermon preached on the steps of the United States capitol on May 16, 1920, by George W. Truett, famed pastor of the First Baptist Church in Dallas, Texas. I quote the relevant portions.

> Baptists have one consistent record concerning liberty throughout all their long and eventful history. They have never been a party to oppression of conscience. They have forever been the unwavering champions of liberty, both religious and civil. Their contention now is, and has been, and, please God, must ever be, that it is the natural and fundamental and indefeasible right of every human being to worship God or not, according to the dictates of his conscience, and, as long as he does not infringe upon the rights of others, he is to be held accountable alone to God for all religious beliefs and practices. Our contention is

---

[40] W. W. Sweet, *Religion on the American Frontier: The Baptist*, vol. 1 (New York: Holt, 1931), 328–29.

not for mere toleration, but for absolute liberty. There is a wide difference between toleration and liberty. Toleration implies that somebody falsely claims the right to tolerate. Toleration is a concession, while liberty is a right. Toleration is a matter of expediency, while liberty is a matter of principle. Toleration is a gift from man, while liberty is a gift from God. It is the consistent and insistent contention of our Baptist people, always and everywhere, that religion must be forever voluntary and uncoerced, and that it is not the prerogative of any power, whether civil or ecclesiastical, to compel men to conform to any religious creed or form of worship, or to pay taxes for the support of a religious organization to which they do not belong and in whose creed they do not believe. God wants free worshipers and no other kind.[41]

Although the Baptist is the very antithesis of his Catholic neighbor in religious conceptions and contentions, yet the Baptist will whole-heartedly contend that his Catholic neighbor shall have his candles and incense and sanctus bell and rosary, and whatever else he wishes in the expression of his worship. A Baptist would rise at midnight to plead for absolute religious liberty for his Catholic neighbor, and for his Jewish neighbor, and for everybody else. But what is the answer of a Baptist to the contention made by the Catholic for papal infallibility? Holding aloft a little book, the name of which is the New Testament, and without any hesitation or doubt, the Baptist shouts his battle cry: "Let all the world go to bits and we will reconstruct it on the New Testament."[42]

---

[41] G. W. Truett, "Baptists and Religious Liberty," *BH&H* 33, no. 1 (1998): 67.
[42] Ibid., 69–70.

Although the battle cry of justification by faith alone was sounded out by Luther and the reformers, yet they retained the doctrine of infant baptism and a state church. They shrank from the logical conclusions of their own thesis. In Zurich there stands a statue in honor of Zwingli, in which he is represented with a Bible in one hand a sword in the other. That statue was the symbol of the union between church and state. Luther and Melancthon fastened a state church upon Germany, and Zwingli fastened it upon Switzerland. Knox and his associates fastened it upon Scotland. Henry VIII bound it upon England. Luther unloosed the dogs of persecution against the struggling and faithful Anabaptists. Calvin burned Servetus, and to such awful deed Melancthon gave him approval.[43]

. . . [A]cross the mighty ocean separating the Old World and the New, we find the early pages of American history crimsoned with the stories of religious persecutions . . . . Yonder in Massachusetts, Henry Dunster, the first president of Harvard, was removed from the presidency because he objected to infant baptism. Roger Williams was banished, John Clarke was put in prison, and they publicly whipped Obadiah Holmes on Boston Common. In Connecticut the lands of our Baptist fathers were confiscated and their goods sold to build a meeting house and support a preacher of another denomination.[44]

Listen to former chief justice of the Supreme Court Charles E. Hughes: "This contribution [of religious liberty] is the glory of the Baptist heritage, more distinctive than any other characteristic of belief or practice. To this militant leadership all sects and

---

[43] Ibid., 75.
[44] Ibid., 76.

faiths are debtors."[45] E. Y. Mullins, while president of the Southern Baptist Convention, addressed the Third Baptist World Congress in Stockholm Sweden, July 21–27, 1923, on "The Baptist Conception of Religious Liberty":

> When a human soul discovers God, the foundation for religious liberty is laid. Men have wandered from the path of duty, civilization has gone astray, because these three realities—the self, the world, and God—have not been properly related. The human problem has been how to relate personality to society, the individual life to the corporate life. But how to relate man to God comes first. It is the key to all problems. The quest for economic liberty, intellectual liberty, civil liberty, all go back to religious liberty as the root. . . . Religious liberty rest upon man's original creation in the image of God.[46]

The "Atlanta Declaration on Religious Freedom" (July 27, 1939) stated in part:

> No man, nor government nor institution, religious or civil, social or economic, has the right to dictate how a person may worship God, or whether he shall worship at all. Therefore, no civil authority may of right make a law, decree or regulation respecting an establishment of religion, or affecting its free exercise. State Churches and Church States are alike in direct conflict with the principle of freedom. A free Church is a free State, each contributing freely and helpfully to the legitimate sphere and functions of the other, is the ideal, but with no financial or

---

[45] C. E. Hughes, "Address of Charles E. Hughes at the Laying of the Corner-Stone of the National Baptist Memorial to Religious Liberty," *Religious Herald*, 90, no. 4 (April 27, 1922).

[46] E. Y. Mullins, "The Baptist Conception of Religious Liberty," *Third Baptist World Congress, Stockholm, July 21–27, 1923* (Nashville: Baptist Sunday School Board, 1923), 67.

administrative dependence of either upon the other. No State may rightly prefer or favour one form of religion above another. In continuance of our consistent Baptist practice, we are imperatively constrained to insist upon the full maintenance of absolute religious liberty for every man of every faith, and no faith.[47]

From the earliest Baptists to today, the concept of religious liberty is endemic to Baptist history, theology and practice.

## CONCLUSION

When Baptists are interviewed on television programs such as *Larry King Live* and affirm that Jesus is the only way to heaven, the response is usually one of offense taken. Baptists do not get offended when someone says that Jesus is not the only way to heaven or that the Baptist "religion" is false. Why is that? The reason is Baptists believe and have always believed strongly in religious liberty and the freedom of anyone to believe what he wishes and worship as he wishes, without coercion. A true convictional Baptist will die for the right of another to believe anything he wants to believe, no matter how theologically incorrect it may be. As a Baptist might say, tongue and cheek of course, "We believe in your right to be wrong."

We believe in tolerance in the correct meaning and usage of that word. Just look at our history. The story is written in milk, ink, and blood. Thousands of us have spilled our blood so that religious tolerance and liberty might be the order of the day, in England, America, and beyond. Mellie Brown, the little Baptist, actually got it right, did she not? When it comes to a believer's church, the autonomy of the local church, the priesthood of believers, and religious liberty, the Bible really is a Baptist Bible.

---

[47] H. Cook, *What Baptists Stand For* (London: Kingsgate, 1974), 182.

# 3

## Covenant or Confusion? "Associated by Covenant in the Faith and Fellowship of the Gospel"

*Emir F. Caner*

In an interview produced by John Piper's Desiring God ministries, Mars Hill Church teaching pastor Mark Driscoll conveyed his flippant opinion about Baptists, stating, "What does it mean to be a Baptist? We dunk adults. Anything else? Uh, no." His diatribe then sought to use the diversity among Baptists as proof of his minimal and relativistic definition: "Some of us are Charismatics. Some of us are Reformed. Some of us are Arminian. Some of us are congregationally-governed. Some of us are elder-governed. What does it mean to be a Baptist? We dunk adults." He concluded that Mars Hill Church is more appropriately defined as an interdenominational church "because we work with a lot of denominations."[1]

It is ironic that such a theologically ill-bred statement could come from a pastor whose church's confessional statement is far more austere than the vast majority of evangelical churches. In order to join Mars Hill Church, one must sign a member covenant, which in part includes the following:

---

[1] Desiring God, "Mark Driscoll on Denominations," http://www.youtube.com/watch?v=oAnGPGd9NyM, accessed October 2, 2009.

- In obedience to Scripture, I have been baptized to personally identify with the death, burial, and resurrection of Jesus, and to publicly demonstrate my commitment as a disciple of Jesus.
- I have read and understood the Mars Hill doctrinal statement and will not be divisive to its teaching. I also understand the importance of submission to church leadership and will be diligent to preserve unity and peace.
- I covenant to submit to discipline by God through his Holy Spirit, to follow biblical procedures for church discipline in my relationships with brothers and sisters in Christ, to submit to righteous discipline when approached biblically by brothers and sisters in Christ, and to submit to discipline by church leadership if the need should ever arise.[2]

The faithful Mars Hill member must adhere to believer's baptism by immersion and some type of church discipline, and that member must not be divisive, that is, disagree with the leadership's beliefs.

However, Mark Driscoll himself explicitly partners with those who disagree with him, though these partners might find it difficult or impossible to join his fellowship. Driscoll's Acts 29 Network, wanting to be ecumenical in its scope, advocates a doctrinal statement that adheres to the classic doctrines of the faith found within the Nicene and Apostles' creeds. Additionally, the network is self-described as "Evangelical" (affirming doctrines like the infallibility of Scripture, the deity of Christ, and regeneration by the Holy Spirit), "Missional" (affirming the need to reflect the "continually changing context of culture") and "Reformed" (emphasizing "God's saving grace is ultimately irresistible").[3] Notably absent from the confession is any mention of believer's baptism, a

---

[2] Mars Hill Church, "Member Covenant," http://www.marshillchurch.org/about/member-covenant, accessed October 2, 2009.

[3] Acts 29, "Doctrine: What Does Acts 29 Believe," http://www.acts29network.org/about/doctrine/, accessed October 2, 2009.

memorial Lord's Supper or regenerate church membership. How incongruous that a pastor would require one belief system for his members and another weaker system for church leaders who will be planting fellowships across the country. That paradox is only exacerbated by the fact that Acts 29 loudly denounces separation over secondary doctrine yet inflexibly advocates Reformed doctrine in order to join the network.

It is apparent that one of the most "successful" Christian pastors in reaching out to postmodern Americans has himself succumbed to postmodern ideology. Ultimately, a proper definition of being Baptist—of being a New Testament church—would go a long way in correcting his inconsistent practices.[4] While Driscoll is to be highly commended for requiring a confession of faith for his church members, he must be admonished for the lax doctrinal standards imposed on church planters. If theology is integral to his vision, as he claims and in part has demonstrated, then ecclesiology must be brought to the fore of today's discussions. Simply put, being Baptist is not merely the dunking of adults; it is a fully orbed biblical system founded upon the "covenant in the faith and fellowship in the gospel." Anything short of this comprehensive statement will lead to a church that lacks biblical precision.

## ECCLESIAL CONFUSION AND CLARIFICATION: THE INFLUENCE OF THE NEW HAMPSHIRE CONFESSION ON THE *BAPTIST FAITH AND MESSAGE*

The *Baptist Faith and Message* in its 1925, 1963, and 2000 forms, borrowed its basic structure from the New Hampshire Confession of Faith of 1833 and took Article VI nearly verbatim, including its statement on our covenant association. Note the parallel between the 1833 New Hampshire Confession and the 1963 *Baptist Faith and Message*:

---

[4] To be fair, Driscoll is updating his doctrinal statement at the present time. M. Driscoll, "A Word on Our Doctrinal Statement," http://www.marshillchurch.org /about/a-word-on-our-doctrinal-statement, accessed October 2, 2009.

[We believe] that a visible Church of Christ is a congregation of baptized believers, *associated by covenant in the
faith and fellowship of the Gospel*; observing the ordinances of Christ . . . [emphasis mine].

A New Testament church of the Lord Jesus Christ is a
local body of baptized believers who are *associated by
covenant in the faith and fellowship of the gospel*, observing the two ordinances [emphasis mine].[5]

For nearly two hundred years belief in being "associated by covenant" has held its sway over the hearts of millions of Baptists in
America. Baptist groups such as the American Baptist Association
and the General Association of Regular Baptists, alongside many
local Baptist churches, adopted the confession without revision.[6]
Walking in lockstep with the phraseology, Southern Baptists have
also chosen to leave the wording unchanged, recognizing its biblical acumen.

The wide-ranging adoption of the statement illustrated how
well the confession answered the problematic ecclesial climate of
its own contemporary culture. Indeed, the New Hampshire Confession of Faith became the most widely disseminated confession
in the history of American Baptist life due to its judicious theological principles. Like today, nineteenth-century American Baptists were dealing with an ecclesiological upheaval within church
bodies. These problems included:

- *Rampant ecumenism*, represented by Protestant groups
  such as the Evangelical Alliance and London Missionary Society,[7] advocated interdenominational unity above
  theological integrity.

---

[5] W. L. Lumpkin, *Baptist Confessions of Faith* (Valley Forge: Judson, 1959),
364.

[6] Ibid., 361. Some groups added a supplement doctrinal statement as well.

[7] Evangelical Alliance, "About Us," http://www.eauk.org/about/, accessed October 2, 2009.

- *Rising liberalism*, grounded in the historical-critical method, made its way from German schools such as the University of Berlin.
- *Eschatological fanaticism* was found within the theology of William Miller and, subsequently, the Great Disappointment (1843–44).
- *Soteriological and ecclesiological perversion* arose in the views of Alexander Campbell and the embryonic Church of Christ movement.

J. M. Pendleton (1811–91), known as a Landmarker due to his allegiance to the local church and its autonomy as well as emphasizing proper baptism and the Lord's Supper, gained significant appreciation for the New Hampshire Confession of Faith and soon published it in his popular *Church Manual* (1867). Due to the influence of Pendleton, who arguably was the most prominent American Baptist theologian of the nineteenth century,[8] the confession gained more notoriety and persuasion over the average Southern Baptist than the newly formed flagship seminary of the Southern Baptist Convention, Southern Baptist Theological Seminary (Greenville, SC, later Louisville, KY). As Southern Baptist historians Russ Bush and Tom Nettles point out, "The laity in the churches throughout the South were often taught more effectively by the writings of Landmarkism than by the seminary leadership in Louisville."[9]

Although pockets of Landmarkism would lead to isolation from other ecclesiastical bodies, the influence of the movement encouraged Southern Baptists to stay theologically distinct. Additionally,

---

[8] For a succinct biography of Pendleton, see K. Eitel, "J. M. Pendleton," in T. George and D. S. Dockery, eds., *Baptist Theologians* (Nashville: Broadman, 1990). Unfortunately, the revised edition of this work, *Theologians of the Baptist Tradition* (B&H, 2001), inexplicably removes the chapter on Pendleton, even though his influence is unquestionable.

[9] L. R. Bush and T. J. Nettles, *Baptists and the Bible*, rev. ed. (Nashville: B&H, 1999), 198.

while other denominations were minimizing the importance of the local church, Landmarkers cherished the importance of the local body of believers. That emphasis resulted in Southern Baptists experiencing exponential growth well into the twentieth century while other Protestant denominations, capitulating to ecumenism and liberalism, began the gradual decline that continues to this day. Contemporary Southern Baptists would do well to learn the difficult lesson of yesteryear and stand firm on our Baptist distinctives. While alarmists warn us of drastic numerical decline if we do not relinquish our beliefs to a moderate ecumenism, we must learn the lessons of history and not cede biblical territory to those whose intentions may be proper but whose prognostications are unfounded within our story.

## COVENANTS AND CONFESSIONS: THEIR NECESSARY CORRELATION

The affirmation of a newly revised *Baptist Faith and Message* in 2000 by an overwhelming majority of Southern Baptists gathering in Orlando, Florida, has reignited debate over the worthiness of creeds/confessions and the extent to which they should be followed. Writing on the subject of covenant in Article VI of the *Baptist Faith and Message*, Southern Baptist professor Greg Wills explained, "Each congregation is responsible under Christ to interpret Bible truth, proclaim it and defend it. This is not possible unless they agree together on the central truths of Scripture and gather these truths into a confession of faith."[10] Wills succinctly articulates the traditional Baptist conviction that a covenant must have confessional clarity in order for unity to be maintained.

Juxtaposed to this conservative position, Mercer University professor Walter Shurden, in his work *The Baptist Identity: Four Fragile Freedoms*, articulates:

---

[10] G. Wills, "The Church: Baptist Faith and Message, Article 6," http://baptisttobaptist.net/b2barticle.asp?ID=249, accessed October 2, 2009.

> BAPTISTS ARE A NON-CREEDAL PEOPLE! There is
> no The Baptist Creed or The Baptist Confession of Faith
> or The Baptist Church Covenant. . . . Baptists have feared
> creeds because of the seemingly inevitable tendency to
> make the creed the norm and then to force compliance to
> the creed.[11]

One cannot help but find marked inconsistencies within Dr.
Shurden's argumentation. First and most obvious, his book is entitled *The Baptist Identity*—note the use of the definite article—
even though he asserts that there is no such thing. Second, his
conclusion magnifies this contradiction, stating, "The historical
Baptist identity, therefore, has been chiseled primarily from freedom rather than control, voluntaryism rather than coercion, individualism rather than a 'pack mentality,' personal religion rather
than proxy religion, and diversity rather than uniformity."[12] In a
nutshell, he confesses both that there is no confession and that
Baptists must confess such or we will lose our confessional identity, which eludes us in the first place. Third, Shurden implies that
the *Baptist Faith and Message* (2000) was bullied upon average
Southern Baptists. However, this cannot be the case. No person
or committee has the authority to force Baptists to believe anything. We are a free people who come together on a voluntary basis.
Southern Baptists could have easily rejected the revised confession, yet they chose to accept its tenets by more than a 95-percent
majority. Fourth, Shurden's argument falls apart on historical
precedent. Baptists have always been a confessional people, a fact
that is evidenced by the innumerable confessions we have passed

---

[11] W. B. Shurden, *The Baptist Identity: Four Fragile Freedoms* (Macon, GA: Smyth & Helwys, 1993), 14. The BFM Report (2000) video is available through the Executive Committee of the SBC and provides the viewer with a priceless historical encounter between liberals/moderates and conservatives/fundamental-ists over this very issue.

[12] Ibid., 59.

locally, regionally, nationally, and globally.[13] Additionally, these confessions were passed and enforced, as can be seen by the discipline of church members from a believer's fellowship or the removal of a church from an association or convention.

Finally and most importantly, the dispute between the two parties does not find its sole or primary basis in the realm of confessionalism but in the authority of Scripture. Those who limit confessional accountability also argue for "Bible freedom,"[14] that is, the freedom to interpret biblical doctrines according to one's own opinion. If confessions are viewed as a diverse array of different beliefs and interpretations, the Bible follows suit as fundamental doctrines are thereby discarded for the freedom of the individual to believe whatever he wishes. Such was the case with Matthew Caffyn (1628–1714), a British Baptist pastor who denied the Trinity and, subsequently, the divinity of Christ. When fellow Baptist Joseph Wright called for Caffyn's removal from the General Assembly, his colleagues chided him for lacking Christian love. The result of such nonaction was the spread of heresy across the General Baptists in Great Britain. By the time the debate was

---

[13] It should be noted that Shurden argues that the plethora of confessions throughout Baptist history is evidence of the diversity of Baptist beliefs and the lack of a Baptist identity. However, even a superficial glance at the confessions of faith, such as are found in William Lumpkin's *Baptist Confessions,* illustrates the commonalities within the confessions, not diversity. Although Anabaptists and Baptists may differ on issues such as pacifism or serving in government, the overwhelming support demonstrates that Baptists have, with little variance, agreed upon issues including the authority and inerrancy of Scripture, the deity of Christ, exclusivity of salvation through Christ alone, a believer's church, and religious liberty. It is quite remarkable that a people so free have remained so unified theologically over the years. It is only in recent years, post-1925, that the onslaught of modernism and postmodernism has changed this general theological confluence.

[14] The Cooperative Baptist Fellowship, an organization of moderate and liberal Southern Baptists begun in 1991, has made this freedom one of the four freedoms of faith. The others include soul freedom, religious freedom, and church freedom. The four can be found on the official CBF Web site. Cooperative Baptist Fellowship, "About Us: Who We Are," http://www.thefellowship.info/About-Us/Who-We-Are, accessed October 2, 2009.

over and Caffyn was dead, few General Baptists were willing to defend the doctrine of the Trinity. This was evidenced in the now famous Salter's Hall Debate (1719), a meeting of Presbyterians, Congregationalists, and Baptists over the issue of the Trinity and other crucial doctrines. The spread of Caffyn's heresy found culmination in the fact that only one General Baptist pastor signed a document affirming the Trinity. The rest either remained silent or had fallen prey to theological error.

Yet Baptists have always been a confessional people. One must remember that the purpose of a confession is not to force a belief upon other Baptists—that is not possible within the realm of congregational polity—but to tell the world what we believe together. Those beliefs do not serve to usurp biblical authority but serve to uphold biblical authority. The alternative is to tell an unbelieving world that we have no set of fundamental beliefs we all agree upon, that our core belief is at best relative and, at worst, unbelief.

### BACK TO THE BASICS: THREE LESSONS FROM OUR "COVENANT IN THE FAITH AND FELLOWSHIP OF THE GOSPEL"

We may learn today three relevant lessons from examining this confessional affirmation that Baptists have a "covenant in the faith and fellowship of the gospel." First, the magnitude of a covenant in the faith is necessarily seen in the New Testament polity of congregationalism. Whereas Catholic and Protestant denominational bodies are hierarchical in structure and thereby can compel parishioners to comply by a set of principles, the believers' church movements in which Baptists are rooted believe the New Testament verifies congregational polity and thereby choose for themselves the extent of their beliefs. The body of Christ is governed by Christ through the entire body. As one scholar noted:

> In Congregationalism, the granting of authority is by Christ to the apostles rather than to one apostle; indeed,

the gift of authority is from Christ to the entire congregation (cf. John 20:19–23; Matt 18:15–20). . . . Baptist congregationalism is deeply founded in the New Testament witness. In Matthew 18:15–20, final temporal authority for excommunication resides within the congregation. . . . In Acts 6:3 the Jerusalem congregation itself was charged with choosing seven men who were obviously Spirit-filled. . . . In Acts 13:2–3, the Holy Spirit led the Antioch congregation to set apart Barnabas and Saul for missionary work by laying hands on them.[15]

Thus, for a covenant actually to represent a particular, local New Testament fellowship, three principles about the church must be intact. First, the New Testament church must be made up of a regenerate church membership. The "covenant in the faith" of a local church can only be entered if a person has experienced the promise of the New Covenant (Jer 31:31–34). Furthermore, covenantal agreement is impossible if one has not had his wicked heart changed by the riches of God's grace. B. H. Carroll (1843–1914), founder of Southwestern Baptist Theological Seminary, in a section entitled "Salvation is essential to baptism and church membership," wrote the following:

Here, if nowhere else, Baptists stand absolutely alone. The foot of no other denomination in Christendom rests on this plank. Blood before water—the altar before the laver. This principle eliminates not only all infant baptism and membership, but locates the adult's remission of sins in the fountain of blood instead of the fountain of water.[16]

Second, for a church covenant to be authentic, the church

---

[15] M. B. Yarnell III, "Article VI: The Church," in *The Baptist Faith and Message 2000: Critical Issues in America's Largest Protestant Denomination,* ed. D. K. Blount and J. D. Wooddell (Lanham, MD: Rowman & Littlefield, 2007), 61.
[16] B. H. Carroll, *Distinctive Baptist Principles*, http://www.baptisttheology.org/documents/DistinictiveBaptistPrinciples.pdf, accessed October 2, 2009.

must be voluntary and free in its expression. Churches must not partner with any political organization in order to accomplish the purposes God gave to them. Indeed, the church that ensnares itself with the state has perverted itself until such time that those fetters are removed. As Carroll himself contended:

> United with the state, the church can never obey Christ: "Be ye not unequally yoked with unbelievers. What part hath he that believeth with an infidel? Come out from among them and be ye separate." There cannot be union of church and state without persecution for conscience' sake.[17]

A church will not be able to speak freely and believe freely if encumbered with state regulations and political correctness. No group understood this better than the Anabaptists[18] of the sixteenth century who were considered heretics and anarchists due to their allegiance to Christ and their rejection of political authority in spiritual matters. Yet they would rather endure persecution for the sake of a pure church than enmesh themselves within the confines of a sacralist system. At stake was the very life of the churches.

According to the Anabaptist view, the merger of the state with the church under Constantine (d. 337) doomed the organized church, as opposed to the Free Churches, such as the Donatists, into darkness for more than a millennium.[19] With the amalgamation of the two organisms, every aspect of a Christian's discipleship was corrupted. The father of modern Anabaptists, Conrad Grebel (1498–1526) wrote, "Our forebears fell away from the true God and from the one true, common, divine Word, from the

---

[17] Ibid., 7.

[18] The term *Anabaptist* or *rebaptizer* is used as far back as the fourth century AD and is equated with those who rejected infant baptism and required another baptism subsequent to one's conversion.

[19] For an invaluable discussion on the Donatists and the Free Church movement beginning in the fourth century AD, see L. Verduin, *The Reformers and Their Stepchildren* (Paris, AR: Baptist Standard Bearer, 2001), 118.

divine institutions, from Christian love and life, and lived without God's law and gospel in human, useless, unchristian customs and ceremonies."[20] The essence of Christianity can and will be compromised if our souls are rendered to Caesar.

Third and finally, for a covenant to be effective, the church must be seen in light of New Testament evidence that primarily defines the church as the visible body of Christ in a certain locale. It is, of course, true that on occasion the New Testament speaks of the church as the body universal, but the vast majority of instances the church is referred to as a particular body of believers.[21] Historically, the church only began defining itself as primarily universal in scope after its merger with the Roman Empire. The Protestant reformers piggy-backed upon the sacralist notion.

Churches that partnered with the state wrongly defined the universal Church as the remnant among the institutional church instead of seeing the universal Church as the body of all who have been regenerated and will meet one day together. The Protestant definition, wrought with problems including an unregenerate view of the visible church, was used by Lutheran and Calvinistic reformers, one of whom stated, "Nevertheless, there have always been some true Christians in the masses, and we hope that they are present also with us."[22] As can be seen by this statement, this improper definition of the church created not only unfamiliarity with the true church but also uncertainty of salvation. Whereas entrance into a Free Church fellowship was based on one's confession in Christ and certainty of his relationship with Christ, the state church based one's entrance on an impersonal ritual of infant baptism.

---

[20] W. R. Estep, *The Anabaptist Story* (Grand Rapids: Eerdmans, 1975), 183.

[21] B. H. Carroll argued that all references to the church as universal or invisible were eschatological in scope. See his work, *Ecclesia*, available online at www.BaptistTheology.org.

[22] Verduin, *The Reformers*, 118. The quotation comes from Urbanus Rhegius (1489–1541), a Lutheran reformer who traveled throughout Germany.

No one could be denied entrance since it was a birthright. How ironic that the guarantee of church membership in the Roman Empire, and later the Holy Roman Empire, had the ability to remove security which could be grasped only when one was called from death to life. In this way Christianity was reduced to an initiatory act presumed upon everyone. No one could be separate from the world as the world was given membership into the church.

## RECAPTURING OUR DISTINCTIVES: COVENANT RELATIONSHIP THROUGH INITIATION (BAPTISM) INTO PERPETUITY (DISCIPLESHIP)

Many Christians believe that Baptists have overemphasized the importance of baptism and the Lord's Supper. Indeed, on one occasion a colleague of mine at a Southern Baptist seminary stated as much, arguing that baptism is secondary in importance and that I should not major on a minor doctrine. My response was straightforward: in the Great Commission passage of Matt 28:18–20, the Lord Jesus Christ correlated baptism with evangelism ("make disciples") and continuing discipleship ("teaching them to obey all things I commanded you," a statement that includes the Lord's Supper) until the culmination ("I am with you always, even to the end of the age"). The Great Commission teaches not a quick fix for one's soul but conveys a fully developed theology that cares for someone from regeneration to glorification. Through becoming a disciple we enter into a covenant relationship with the Lord that is eternal in nature, and we publicly testify to this by entering into a covenant with the local church through baptism.

### BAPTISM: THE ENTRANCE INTO THE VISIBLE COVENANT

Knowing the scope of the covenant, a biblical view of baptism, the initiatory rite into the local church, becomes all the more important. New Testament baptism is the public proclamation that one has died to the former self and now walks in "newness of life" (Rom 6:4). They have "gladly received his word" to be saved (Acts

2:41), "believed with all [their] heart" (Acts 8:37), and "have received the Holy Spirit" (Acts 10:47). All the relevant biblical citations, of course, give clear indication that one must first publicly profess their faith in Christ before true baptism can occur. The public proclamation was also a public promise—a covenant—that the new believer was dedicating himself to obedience to the Lord, "continuing steadfastly in the apostles' doctrine and fellowship, in the breaking of bread, and in prayers" (Acts 2:42). This victorious declaration recognized that "abundant life" (John 10:10) was to be the norm, not the exception, and that Christ promised that no one can "snatch them out of My hand" (John 10:28).

New Testament baptism therefore included the promise of eternal security in Christ, a doctrine that must once again thrill the souls of Southern Baptists. As baptism has slowly lost its meaning over the past century among many Southern Baptists, the first doctrine to be squandered was the guarantee of glorification which accompanies true baptism. Christ promised His eternal presence after the symbolic picture of baptism in the Great Commission passage: "I am with you always." We were not only "baptized into his death" (Rom 6:2) but "believe that we shall also live with Him" (Rom 6:8). Believers are "buried with Him in baptism" (Col 2:12a) and "raised with Him through faith in the working of God" (Col 2:12b); so that we can be assured the Lord has "wiped out the handwriting of requirement that was against us . . . having nailed it to the cross" (Col 2:14).

Henceforth, baptism cannot merely be seen as a duty to be fulfilled after one's salvation; it is a symbol that carries far more meaning. Balthasar Hubmaier (1480–1528),[23] the most influential theologian of the formative Anabaptist movement, articulated a more comprehensive meaning of baptism in his classic work, *A Christian Catechism*:

---

[23] For further information on Hubmaier, see H. Vedder, *Balthasar Hubmaier* (Valley Forge: Judson, 1905), and T. Bergsten, *Balthasar Hubmaier: Anabaptist Theologian and Martyr* (Valley Forge: Judson, 1978).

[Baptism] is an outward and public testimony of the inner baptism of the Spirit, which a person gives by receiving water, with which one confesses one's sins before all people. One also testifies thereby that one believes in the forgiveness of his sins through the death and resurrection of our Lord Jesus Christ. Thereupon one also has himself outwardly enrolled, inscribed, and by water baptism incorporated into the fellowship of the church according to the institution of Christ, before which the person also publicly and orally vows to God and agrees in the strength of God the Father, Son, and Holy Spirit that he will henceforth believe and live according to his divine Word.[24]

Here baptism is a covenant between the Lord and His elect and between the elect themselves. The baptismal covenant included at least three vows:

- A promise that one had already been born again.
- A promise that one is assured of his salvation.
- A promise that one is accountable to other believers through the avenue of the local church.

This final stipulation troubles many modern and postmodern Christians. The vast majority of contemporary Christians, regardless of their denominational affiliation or lack thereof, have not been taught that baptism, being the proper venue for one's public confession in Christ, was not a private act but was intimately linked with church discipline.

Believers were not merely accountable to God but to one another (Matt 18:15–20). This is just as true for the churches today, for the authority of the Scripture must reign supreme in the life of believers (Gal 6:1–2). Accountability begins at the moment

---

[24] B. Hubmaier, *A Christian Catechism*, in *Balthasar Hubmaier: Theologian of the Anabaptists,* ed. H. Wayne Pipkin and John H. Yoder (Scottdale, PA: Herald Press, 1989), 349.

of regeneration and, subsequently, baptism, and then continues perpetually through the ordinance of the Lord's Supper (1 Cor 5:1–13).

That being the case, one cannot assume that either of the ordinances is divorced from the local body of believers. If it were indeed the case that the universal body assumed the ordinances, would it not also be appropriate that church discipline fall under the authority of the "universal Church"? Ultimately, the idea of a visible covenant lends itself to a visible community. And the visible covenant of water baptism—indicative of a promise between two parties—finds its abode in the visible community of believers.

Some Baptists worry that a stricter requirement for baptism will further facilitate the numerical decline of baptisms experienced recently in the Southern Baptist Convention. In actuality, a strong case can be made that baptismal numbers have declined due in no small part to our laxity in maintaining the biblical and doctrinal parameters of the ordinance. When Southern Baptists hoped for "a million more in '54," we did so with little preparation of what to do with the new candidates. While we enjoyed a substantial increase in baptisms short-term, we did not always disciple the new disciples to carry on the task of evangelism. We did not, in large part, teach new believers the significance and meaning of baptism but simply dunked them in haste. On the other hand, Hubmaier, believing God was powerfully at work in the small town of Nikolsburg, Moravia, prepared each individual candidate for baptism. Every new believer was required to sign a covenant of faith before he or she entered the baptismal waters. All new believers pledged themselves to the Lord and His church. Every new believer was trained in the meaning and significance of baptism, the Supper, church discipline, and other foundational doctrines of the faith. And, in the end, Hubmaier baptized between six and twelve thousand new believers in a span of just over a year. Once Baptists rediscover the New Testament meaning of baptism and covenant—a doctrinal foundation we must admit we have neglected over the past two generations—God will honor our obedience and once again restore the house that He has built.

## DOCTRINE AND DISCIPLESHIP: PERPETUATING
## THE PRINCIPLES OF THE VISIBLE COVENANT

Southern Baptists have, in their national convention, halted the doctrinal decay of liberalism within our own ranks. While other mainline denominations have consumed the poisonous water of secularism and naturalism, God has smiled on our efforts to stand secure in the infallible Word of God. However, the Conservative Resurgence remains incomplete. We who have stood on the inerrancy of Scripture must now walk in the sufficiency of Scripture. For that to occur, the belief in what the Baptist confessions call "association by covenant" must be thoroughly embraced. Our covenant is based in the blood of the Lord Jesus Christ (Heb 9:22), yet many of our church members believe their good works will allow them to enter heaven. Covenant obligation begins through the door of baptism and is perpetuated through the ordinance of the Supper, yet few Baptists can articulate clearly the meaning of either ordinance. Our covenant brings responsibility to "bear one another's burdens" (Gal 6:1), yet the majority of our members are absent without leave and, thereby, cannot fulfill this essential duty.

Southern Baptists must realize that for our belief in covenant to be restored, discipleship and doctrine must be seen as twin brothers who walk together in tandem. In no place is this better illustrated than behind the pulpits in our local assemblies. The banner of covenant is lifted most high at the point of the reading and preaching of God's Word. And there is no substitute for the clear proclamation of the Word of God, the exposition of the text. The grandfather of the Conservative Resurgence, W. A. Criswell, stated it best, "What is the sorriest way to preach? It is the spiritualizing, allegorizing way. What is the sublimest way to preach?

It is the grammatical-historical way, the expository method. It is proclaiming the message as it is in the Holy Scriptures."[25]

A covenant cannot be obeyed if it is not understood. Southern Baptist pastors cannot expect laypeople to engage in a covenant that has not be properly introduced to them. Perhaps the reason Southern Baptists have largely forgotten our covenant with one another is because pastors and teachers have forgotten their covenant to preach the Word. As pulpiteers fulfill their covenant to preach the Word (2 Tim 4:1) and teachers fulfill their covenant to expound the Word (Luke 24:25), parishioners will fulfill their promise to obey the Word.

Truth is immortal.

---

# 4

# Observing Two Ordinances—
# Are They Merely Symbols?

*Paige Patterson*

A sincere young pastor stood in the baptistry of a flagship Baptist church on a recent Sunday night and prepared to baptize the first of numerous candidates. The young minister provided explanation for several thousand gathered saints as he said, "Baptism does not save anyone. It is merely a symbol of the salvation that has already occurred." Approximately 15 new believers were then baptized with theological appropriateness and aesthetic impressiveness. In addressing baptism as "merely a symbol," the young minister parroted what he had heard uttered by a plethora of ministers before him. In fact, the majority of contemporary Southern Baptist "baptizers" would in all probability echo a similar sentiment. This perspective is further advocated by the many pastors who never administer the ordinance itself but simply delegate the baptismal task to others.

To the young minister's credit, neither his motive nor his soteriology can be faulted. Clearly enough, his motive was to be obedient to the Great Commission of Christ, baptizing the new converts in the name of the Father, the Son, and the Holy Spirit. Soteriologically, he understood correctly that baptismal waters do not and cannot impart salvation and thus must be entered subsequent to an experience of godly sorrow, which brings repentance and salvation by faith in the Lord Jesus Christ (2 Cor 7:10). In Acts 10:47, Peter asks concerning Cornelius and his house, "Can anyone forbid water that these should not be baptized who have received [aorist tense] the Holy Spirit just as we have?"

Michael Walker opens his work on the Lord's Supper by observing:

> The path followed by any theological journey is determined by the place from which it begins. Baptists did not begin with the Lord's Supper. Unlike Roman Catholics and many Anglicans they did not make it central either to their understanding of salvation or to their religious experience. They came to neither font nor table believing that there God's grace was channeled to them in the setting of a sacramental church served by a sacerdotal ministry. They did not believe that the bread and wine of the communion was a real feeding upon the ubiquitous body and blood of a Christ in whose nature true humanity shared in the attributes of divinity and divinity had surrendered itself to a true humanity, as did the Lutherans. They did not see themselves as a church body both reformed and faithful to the ancient and catholic tradition of the church, as did the Anglicans. Their starting point was neither a sacramentally mediated grace, nor a sacramentally embodied word, nor an unbroken Christian tradition spanning the centuries. Lest one should be misled by the name by which they were happy to be known, they did not even begin with baptism. They began with the men and women whom, they believed, Christ had called to be his church on earth.
>
> The early Baptists, who broke away first from the Church of England and then from the rest of the Puritan separatist movement, believed that they were establishing

a church that was faithful to the teaching of the New Testament. Fundamental to that conviction was their belief that the church should consist of those only who had in the freely chosen, conscious assent of faith, surrendered their lives to the lordship of Jesus Christ.[1]

So why am I troubled by the expression "merely a symbol"? The substance of this chapter invites a reexamination of the purpose of the two ordinances of the church. In stressing two ordinances of the church, there is explicit rejection of Roman sacramentalism in both the number and nature of the ordinances; and there is also a rejection of pedilavium as a bonafide ordinance of the church. Without doubt the washing of the saints' feet is commanded by Christ and in the church should take multiple forms of expression, through which saints meet every need within the body of Christ. However, the present thesis denies foot-washing the status of an ordinance because, unlike baptism and the Supper, the washing of the saints' feet carries no picture of the atonement, which, together with the incarnation, provides the foundational theology of redemption for the church of the living God.

The faith of the churches of the New Testament was largely a nonritualistic faith. In Israel the faith of the people of God worked itself out in repeated ceremony—the Passover, the Day of Atonement, and the other feasts and fasts of Judaism as well as the daily liturgy of the temple. Even this highly ritualized faith expression, however, eventually resolved itself into the two great commandments—"You shall love the LORD your God with all your heart, with all your soul, and with all your mind.' And the second is like it: 'You shall love your neighbor as yourself'" (Matt 22:37,39; Deut 6:5 NKJV). Nevertheless, the outward expression of the faith of the average Israelite exemplified itself much more heavily in ritual.

In contrast, the faith of the church of the New Testament

---

[1] M. Walker, *Baptists at the Table* (Oxford: Baptist Historical Society, 1992), 1.

saints was relational—an ardent two-way communication with God in which Gentiles were no longer separated by a wall, beyond which only priests from the tribe of Levi were allowed to a holy place, and a veil hiding the *qōdeš haqqŏdāšîm* from all but the high priest, who could enter only on one particular day of the year. Accessibility directly to God through the permanent indwelling of the Holy Spirit was the "mystery" of the church age (Eph 1:9), which came through the rending of the veil of the body of Christ so that the two-way communication between God and man (Heb 10:20) was radically enhanced. Thus, the worship of the early church was characterized by the communication of the Spirit within the congregation through the dramatic reading of the Word of God and the vivified preaching of that Word, which were encompassed in the people's heartfelt expression directly to God through both Spirit-directed prayer and Spirit-inspired singing. As such, the worship of the early church was little involved with ritual and much involved with the Spirit and with truth. The call of the New Testament church was to radical conversion, and this again called the attention of the early church both to the Word of God and to preaching infused by the power of the Holy Spirit.

Only two approaches to worship, which could be described in some sense as "rituals," were given to the church; and the fact that there are only two dramatically emphasizes the charismatic (in the best sense of the word) nature of the worship of the early church. Further, the relative paucity of such "rituals" also coincidently establishes the strategic importance of the exercise of the two ordinances prescribed for those early assemblies.

If baptism and the Supper are of such singular importance to the worship of the Church, then surely there must be more here than "mere symbol." The thesis of this chapter is that finding sacramental significance in the ordinances is not necessary in order to rediscover in them purposes that transcend the "merely symbolic." The argument that follows shows that the two ordinances cooperate together to enforce the biblical teaching of sanctification in all of its aspects. If the church were able to recover a significant understanding of the ordinances, the author is persuaded that both ordinances would receive enhanced significance in their practice within the churches, and the legitimately changed lives of those who make up the fellowship of the local congregation would bring a corresponding revival of credible witness to a watching world.

## THE SIGNIFICANCE OF SANCTIFICATION

As is commonly known, the word *sanctification* (Gk. *hagiasmos*) refers essentially to that which is "set apart." What is "set apart" is holy, not simply in contrast with that which is wicked but even in stark contrast to that which is common.[2] In so far as can be known, Nadab and Abihu did not pilfer gold shavings from the table of shewbread in the tabernacle to enrich their own financial substance, nor did they engage in forbidden sexual liaisons with male or female. They simply failed to distinguish between that which was holy and that which was common, and that failure resulted in an astonishing judgment of God (Lev 10:1–11).

Achan was not guilty of murder, nor was he convicted of peddling heresy before his death by stoning. Rather, he took what was identified by the Hebrew term *chērem*, coming from the same Semitic concept of *harem*, referencing something that is refused to all others and devoted only to one person because of its devotion to that one. A harem belonged to a single city-state king or ruler and was, therefore, off-limits to anyone else. Jericho's possessions were *chērem*, devoted to the Lord God of Israel; and, therefore, no Israelite was to take any of it for himself. Achan's mistake was in thinking that God would not miss a Babylonian garment, some shekels of silver, and a wedge of gold included in Jericho's properties devoted in entirety to God. This blunder cost him and his

---

[2] For extended discussion of the concept, see TDNT vol. 1, 88–115. Procksch notes that the oldest meaning of the word ἅγιος signifies an object of awe whether in a sense of reverence or of aversion, while the adjective ἁγνός approximates the sense of καθαρός, or clean.

entire family their lives (Josh 7:1–26). Distinguishing between the holy and the mundane appears to be far more serious in biblical theology than can be appreciated by the present generation. For this reason the expression "some are sick and many have died" in 1 Cor 11:30, noted in light of the abuses of the Lord's table in the church at Corinth, seems utterly strange and foreign to contemporary codes of holiness, which run the gamut from virtual nonexistence to a postmodern embrace of the mores of the world.

Theologians have frequently addressed sanctification in terms of positional and progressive sanctification. By positional sanctification, one understands that a person is sanctified or placed in Christ Jesus as a part of the benefits of salvation. Biblical references to being "in Christ" abound and vividly place each believer as a part of the body of Christ. There is no condemnation for a believer who is "in Christ Jesus" (Rom 8:1) because Christ, being without sin, has transferred to each believer His own holiness.

Progressive sanctification is the recognition that a believer should grow in his faith and in the deportment of his life. A careful examination of the uses of the word *sanctification* in the New Testament will confirm that the vast majority of these occurrences unquestionably allude to positional sanctification. But even if it is difficult to construe the word *sanctification* in its progressive significance, this is only a question of nomenclature. For example, though sanctification is not mentioned as such, believers are told to "desire the sincere milk of the Word in order that they may grow thereby" (1 Pet 2:2). We are, after all, at the time of conversion mere "babes in Christ" (1 Cor 3:1), having been forgiven and placed in Christ Jesus but with only a limited grasp of how such a commitment should affect us, change our belief systems, and redirect our thought lives and our activities. So progressive sanctification is an appropriate way to speak of an individual's growth to full Christian maturity, which ought to be occurring in each genuine believer.

The third aspect of sanctification is known as "glorification." This is the final strophe in the soteriological plan of God whereby even the believer's body is sanctified and made holy unto God in glorification. The thesis, which I would like to advance, is that both baptism and the Supper not only provide a remarkable picture of the atoning sacrifice of Christ for our salvation but also move beyond that picture having to do with the historic act of God in Christ and picture perfectly for the church the three tenses of sanctification, which I shall call positional, progressive, and ultimate sanctification. I would further suggest that in the church's recovery of this understanding of the ordinances such ordinances will be revitalized in their practice and meaning and will provide motivation for purifying and sanctifying the life of the congregation in the midst of a secular world and further broadcast the hope for the future intervention of God, which ought to be a primary motivator for the church in this age.

## POSITIONAL SANCTIFICATION IN
## BAPTISM AND THE SUPPER

Both baptism and the Lord's Supper focus on the intervention of God in history. At God's chosen *kairos*, the second person of the Trinity became incarnate in Christ and is unique, among other things, in that He is the only individual ever born to die. While the rest of humanity is born to live but die because of sin, Jesus was born for the express purpose of dying a death He did not deserve for the liberation of those who would place themselves in Christ Jesus.

The Supper bears eloquent testimony to both the incarnation and the death of Christ. The elements of the Supper, consisting of bread and the fruit of the vine, fairly shout from the table that God became man in the person of Jesus Christ, actual flesh and blood, without divesting Himself of His deity (John 1:14; 1 John 1:1). Never should one approach the table without emphasizing the grace of God as seen in the incarnation itself.

Christ, the second person of the Trinity, maintained perfect fellowship with Father and Spirit, the heavenly relationship without limitation. Nevertheless, the agreement in the counsels of eternity was that the Son would empty (Gk. *kenōsis,* Phil 2:7) Himself temporarily of some divine prerogatives in order to experience humanity, "being tempted in all ways as we yet without sin" (Heb 4:15). This remarkable incarnation would be for the purpose of being broken and shedding his blood on the cross as atonement for sin because "the life of the flesh is in the blood and I have given it to you to make sacrifice on the altar" (Lev 17:11). The body of Christ given and the blood of Christ shed for all are thus remembered symbolically in the elements of the supper as historic moments.

In the metaphor pictured in the baptismal waters, the "baptized" one who walks into the water and is immersed is recounting that Jesus died for the convert's sin in that *kairotic* moment and was buried; but as the candidate emerges from the watery grave, he is reminded that on the third day the Lord was raised for our justification. Thus, together baptism and the Supper recreate in the minds and hearts of all who observe, as well as for the participant, a vivid understanding of the cruciality, indeed the very focus of biblical testimony of the incarnation and the atoning death of Christ.

In terms of positional sanctification, Romans 6 avers that as many of us as were baptized were baptized "into His death." And if you have been immersed into His death, you can then be confident that you will also be in the likeness of his "resurrection." Positional sanctification, the forgiveness and safety that believers have in Christ Jesus, is the first focus of baptism. A death has occurred. You die to the old way of life and are then safely in Christ Jesus.

By the same token, not everyone is invited to the Lord's table. In the prolonged debate among Baptists over open communion, some have occasionally noticed that there really is no such thing in Christian history as "open Communion." There are simply varying degrees to which one may choose to be a closed communionist. Only true believers could hope to grasp any real significance in the Lord's Supper. Obviously in a Roman system, the Supper is a sacrament and in some way imparts grace to the participant. This sacrament would then separate him from the rest of the world, which would have no access to this grace. In a free-church conception, those who would come to the Lord's table, at the very least, would have experienced the Lord salvifically through repentance toward God and faith in the Lord Jesus Christ. The fact that believers are at the Lord's table speaks of the fact that they are positionally sanctified (i.e., they are in Christ Jesus).

Now here is the significance of what I am attempting to argue. If baptism is a "mere symbol," then the participant or the observers will find difficulty seeing anything more than the historical referent to what happened at Golgotha 20 centuries ago. If the two ordinances did no more than that, they would still remain critically important and worthy of practice. My contention, however, is that the failure of the church to testify to the enhanced symbolism of positional sanctification has led to a devaluing of the ordinance.

Sometimes baptism has been referred to as the "Ordinance of Initiation," as in White's book, *The Biblical Doctrine of Initiation*.[3] This is a wholesome understanding focusing on positional sanctification. This approach underscores the significance of one's experience of the death, burial, and resurrection of Christ, resulting in a new status before God, which is portrayed in baptism and in the Lord's Supper.

A rough equivalent then of what is happening in baptism and the Supper could be derived from the British practice of knighthood. A noble soldier bows and is touched on the shoulders by the sword of the sovereign, granting to him a totally new status. From that time forward he is a knight. The ceremony itself does

---

[3] R. E. O. White, *The Biblical Doctrine of Initiation* (Grand Rapids: Eerdmans, 1960).

not establish his knighthood. Knighthood is received by virtue of the command of the sovereign, but it is pictured in the ceremony. So the believer's new status in Christ Jesus is pictured initially by baptism and then repeatedly in coming to the Lord's table.

## PROGRESSIVE SANCTIFICATION

In regard to progressive sanctification, the most substantive loss has occurred both at the Lord's table and in baptism; and yet in both cases the ordinances vividly portray a commitment on the part of the believer to spiritual growth and to a new kind of existence. In baptism the old man is buried and the new man rises to walk in newness of life (Rom 6:4). Note first the emphasis on the walk. To walk refers to the way you live, to the way you act, to the way you perceive, and to the way you think by virtue of the power of the indwelling Holy Spirit. You rise from the waters of baptism, symbolizing that resurrection has brought forth a new man to walk with altered thinking.

No longer does he think the way the world thinks; he now is committing himself to learn how to think the way Christ thinks and then to conform his ways to that noble thought. He is confessing in his baptism that he will no longer act the same way he has acted as a child of the world. Now, as a child of God, his actions, his motives, his thoughts, and his intentions will be governed by the leadership of the Holy Spirit as the Spirit of God makes clear the revelation of the Word of God to the heart of that new believer.

The Anabaptists objected to infant baptism partly because there could be no declaration on the part of the infant. First, the infant was not yet capable of distinguishing between a worldly walk and a godly walk. Second, in the life of the infant, nothing had yet happened that could be construed as saving faith or repentance toward God and faith in the Lord Jesus Christ. That being the case, to baptize the infant was without significance.

Unfortunately, in Baptist life today the emphasis on baptism as a "mere symbol" inadvertently fails to call attention to the church itself, and more especially to the convert who follows Christ in baptism, who is making a public statement in baptism about his commitment to Christ. Baptism, and not walking the aisle, is the public profession of his faith. He is stating that he has died to the old way of life and is now going to be walking in a totally different way with Christ.

Arriving at the table of the Lord, that same progressive sanctification ought to be the order of the day. Jesus, in one of His "hard sayings," which the disciples had difficulty comprehending, said that they "must eat the flesh of the Son of Man and drink His blood" (John 6:53–56). This eating of the body of Christ and drinking of His blood surely intends to teach the assimilation of the life of Christ into the life of the believer. When you come to the Lord's table, you should be reminded that you are inevitably in the process of assimilating the life of Christ into your own life.

Whereas you *walk* out of the baptistry to continue *walking* in newness of life, so you come repeatedly to the Lord's table to remind yourself that you have an ongoing, progressively sanctifying task of assimilating the Lord's life into your own. The recovery of the emphasis on progressive sanctification in the Supper and in baptism once again will revivify the emphasis of the ordinances and affect the life of the believer and of the body of Christ.

Recent assemblies of the Southern Baptist Convention have made considerable efforts to reestablish responsible membership in the churches through the reinstitution of church discipline.[4] In 2008, the efforts featured both Calvinist and non-Calvinist Baptists reaching across the aisle in friendly, though tentative and cautious, cooperation.[5] But for all of the efforts some have

[4] See June 2008 Southern Baptist Convention Resolution, "On Regenerate Church Membership and Church Membership Restoration," http://www.sbc.net/resolutions/amResolution.asp?ID=1189, accessed September 8, 2009.
[5] See M. Kelly, "Resolution on 'regenerate church membership' adopted by SBC Messengers," in *Baptist Press* (June 11, 2008), http://www.bpnews.org/bpnews.asp?id=28262, accessed September 8, 2009.

expanded through the last quarter of a century, why has so little apparent progress been made toward this goal of meaningful church membership?

Recently an incident brought to my mind at least one reason for this lack of progress: We have been working on the wrong end of the train. Focusing on the repair of the caboose deserves little commendation if the locomotive will not run or at least will not run efficiently. Indeed, attempting to repair the caboose in light of a runaway engine may be more destructive than helpful.

In our Texas parlance: "One can never make a cow pony out of a mule by demanding that the Ferrier shod the mule with a new set of horseshoes." The new iron may be needed, but it will not help until you change the mule into a cow pony and get him trained to do what cow ponies are supposed to do.

The further question of the Lord's table as the appropriate place for the exercise of church discipline is not the subject of this chapter; but if the Anabaptists were correct in associating church discipline with the Lord's table, then this adds even further evidence for the emphasis on progressive sanctification—spiritual growth that is pictured through the exercise of the Supper itself. The ultimate response of the church to a rebellious and recalcitrant member is not erasure from the roll but exclusion from the Lord's table. Fellowship has been broken by known, unconfessed sin.

## ULTIMATE SANCTIFICATION

Salvation has not reached its ultimate goal until the believer is glorified. Here one labors under conditions that are sometimes frustrating to the believer. The things you wish you would do, you do not; and the things you wish you would not do, those things you do. You and I are frequently forced to join the apostle Paul in crying out, "O wretched man that I am! Who shall deliver me from the body of this flesh" (Rom 7:24). Our weakness and propensity toward sin manifests itself repeatedly in the present bodies, which show the effects of the fall.

Though we are in Christ Jesus (positionally sanctified) and though we are growing in our set-apartness to Christ (progressive sanctification), yet "we groan in this body earnestly desiring to be clothed with our heavenly body" (2 Cor 5:2). That hope for ultimate sanctification is perpetually witnessed through the practice of baptism and the Supper. In baptism one acknowledges the inevitability of physical death. Although this may take a different form, if you are fortunate enough to live until the *parousia*, you still must lay aside the present, limited, earthly tabernacle and take on the heavenly body, which is anticipated in both baptism and the Supper. In baptism, buried in a watery grave is explicit. Thus, the certainty that it is "appointed to a man once to die and after that the judgment" is symbolized. But you also are raised from that grave and that which was dead is made alive in Christ. The life you have is not merely life you have known experientially on earth but life as God has in mind for you in heaven.

One may then ask, "How does the Lord's table depict this final form of sanctification?" The answer resounds in 1 Corinthians 11 when Paul says that in the Supper you "do show the Lord's death until He comes." In other words, the Lord's table is itself a testimony to the fact that this is something the church does in memory of the Christ who is going to come and once again sit down at the table with believers in the kingdom of heaven. "But I say to you, I will not drink of this fruit of the vine from now on until the day I drink it new with you in my Father's kingdom" (Matt 26:29). Consequently, the eschatological hope of the church is also symbolized in the Supper even as in baptism.

## CONCLUSION

A recovery of the intention of the two rituals given by our Lord to the church to be practiced until He comes would, I think, revolutionize church life. If no candidate who did not comprehend that he was making a statement of positional, progressive, and ultimate sanctification were to be admitted to baptism and if no one invited to the Lord's table was not aware that his participation there emphasized positional, progressive, and ultimate sanctification, the motivation for godly living and for church life honoring God would be greatly enhanced. The abuses of aberrant congregationalism, which have resulted in church squabbles and all kinds of nefarious abuses, to say nothing of the general worldliness of the churches, could in part be averted by an emphasis upon the significance of the confession given by every believer as he participates either in baptism or the Lord's table.

Sometimes it is said that baptism is a one-time event, but I would like to suggest that the church, in witnessing the baptism of new believers, becomes a repeated participant in that event itself. So in both ordinances the church is continually involved in the significance of progressive sanctification, as well as in the hope for ultimate sanctification, rather than emphasizing only positional sanctification. This can and should be accomplished without attributing any sacramental significance to either ordinance. Neither is talk of the "real presence" of Christ in the Supper essential. Symbolic it is. "Mere symbol" it is not. Rather, both baptism and the Supper constitute a repeated confession and declaration of intent on the part of the individuals who make up the body of Christ as a whole. Understood in this way, a new day could be coming in the church of God. While repairing the caboose, let us move to the engine and see that the locomotive functions right. Then our people in the churches will understand why they need to repair the caboose.

# 5

## Under the Lordship of Christ through Democratic Processes[1]

*James Leo Garrett Jr.*

B aptists have for four centuries claimed to be practitioners of what has traditionally been called "congregational polity." Differentiated from papal, episcopal, and presbyterial polities, congregational polity is

> that form of church government in which final human authority rests with the local or particular congregation when it gathers for decision-making. This means that decisions about membership, leadership, doctrine, worship, conduct, missions, finances, property, relationships, and the like are to be made by the gathered congregation except when such decisions have been delegated by the congregation to individual members or groups of members.[2]

Such congregationalism means externally the denial of the authority of any "superior or governing ecclesial bodies (autonomy)" and internally the affirmation that every member of

---

[1] These words are taken from the SBC's *Baptist Faith and Message* (2000), Article VI.

[2] J. L. Garrett Jr., "The Congregation-Led Church: Congregational Polity," in *Perspectives on Church Government: Five Views of Church Polity,* ed. C. O. Brand and R. S. Norman (Nashville: B&H, 2004), 157.

the congregation has "a voice in its affairs and its decisions (democracy)."[3]

If these words address the human dimension in congregational decision-making, then what about the divine dimension? I would propose two answers as appropriate: "under the lordship of Jesus Christ (Christocracy) and with the leadership of the Holy Spirit (*pneumatophoria*)."[4]

Although Baptist historians during the twentieth century were not agreed on the origins of Baptists, especially the diversities of Anabaptist kinship and English Separatist descent, one can affirm, without fear of serious denial, that on the single theme of congregational polity Separatist Puritans constituted the matrix for Baptists in ways not clearly attributable to the Anabaptists. For Anabaptists, whose congregations did choose their leaders, advocacy of congregational polity is hardly to be found, it seems, whereas such polity was endemic to and advocated by the Separatist Puritan movement,[5] at a time when England was "a monarchy in transition"[6] and the Church of England, of course, had episcopal polity. Hence Separatists in advocating congregational polity were truly countercultural.

But, one may ask, does congregational polity have a basis in the New Testament? In a 2004 debate with Daniel L. Akin, Robert L. Reymond, James R. White, and Paul F. M. Zahl,[7] I argued in detail, with heavy investment in commentary study, that six texts are capable of being interpreted as indicative of the practice of congregational polity:

Matthew 18:15–20 (Congregational Discipline)
Acts 6:3 (Selection of the Seven)

---

[3] J. L. Garrett, *Systematic Theology: Biblical, Historical, and Evangelical,* 2nd ed. (North Richland Hills, TX: BIBAL, 2001), 2:644.

[4] Ibid.

[5] Garrett, "The Congregation-Led Church," 174–76.

[6] According to J. W. Vardaman.

[7] In Brand and Norman, *Perspectives on Church Government.*

Acts 13:2–3 (Commission of Barnabas and Saul)
Acts 15:22 (Jerusalem Council)
1 Corinthians 5:2 (Excommunication of an Incestuous Man)
2 Corinthians 2:6 (Sufficient Majority Punishment)[8]

The results of the exegesis cannot be reviewed in detail here, but the conclusion that these texts "are capable of being interpreted as supportive of congregational polity" can be correlated with the view that the New Testament affords a general pattern or principle of congregationalism rather than with either of the alternative views, namely, the view that the New Testament does not speak about or describe church polity or the view that the New Testament specifies a detailed and inflexible model of polity.[9]

The earliest Baptist confessions of faith did not include full-orbed statements about congregational polity. The confessions attributable to John Smyth did affirm the "congregational selection and dismissal of ministers," a confession related to Thomas Helwys found that "every congregation is said to have the Word of God and the obligation of discipline," and the First London Confession (1644) of Particular Baptists stressed "congregational financial support of officers and the need for help and counsel among congregations."[10] One might "surmise that in the context of American political democracy" Baptist confessions in the American colonies and in the later United States "would have been more explicit than the English" regarding congregational polity, but the opposite has actually been true in that American confessions "have generally been less explicit," perhaps because such polity was assumed.[11]

The most explicit American [confessional] statements have been in [1] the Doctrinal Statement of the American

---

[8] Garrett, "The Congregation-Led Church," 158–70.
[9] Ibid., 171–72.
[10] Ibid., 176, based on William L. Lumpkin, *Baptist Confessions of Faith*, rev. ed. (Valley Forge: Judson, 1969), 101, 109, 120–22, 165–69.
[11] Ibid., 177.

> Baptist Association (1905), which specified the "equal
> authority and responsibility" of churches and the role
> of denominational bodies as being "the servants of the
> churches," [2] the Articles of Faith of the Baptist Bible
> Union of North America (1923), which affirmed the
> "self government" of the local church as superintended
> by Christ, its final authority in decision-making, and the
> cooperation of "true churches," and [3] the Baptist Faith
> and Message Statement of the Southern Baptist Conven-
> tion (1963), which defined a "New Testament church"
> as "an autonomous body, operating through democratic
> processes under the Lordship of Jesus Christ," in which
> "members are equally responsible."[12]

All three of these statements were framed during the twentieth century. Continental European Baptist confessions have also addressed
the subject of congregational polity, especially "the congregational
selection of church officers." Noteworthy are (1) "the statement of
the Evangelical Association of French-speaking Baptist Churches . . . (1879, 1924) . . . involving autonomy, church officers, and
discipline," (2) the 1977 confession for all German-speaking Baptists asserting that "the priesthood of all believers is 'the basic
structure' of the church and that 'pastoral care of the members is
entrusted to the entire congregation,'" and (3) the Romanian Baptist confession (1974) declaring "that 'local church organization is
based on the principle of autonomous democracy.'"[13]

Treatises on ecclesiology by Baptist authors have been another "indicator of Baptist teaching and practice of congregational
polity." Before the American Civil War, John Leadley Dagg affirmed that churches in the New Testament "were both organized
and independent" and that today's churches should choose their

---

[12] Ibid., based on Lumpkin, *Baptist Confessions of Faith,* 379, 388, 396.
[13] Ibid., based on G. K. Parker, *Baptists in Europe: History and Confessions of Faith* (Nashville: Broadman, 1982), 141–44, 64–69, 221–23.

pastors and deacons and administer church discipline.[14] According to Edward Thurston Hiscox, "independent" polity is grounded in "divine authority and New Testament teaching." Each church "governs itself, manages its own affairs, admits, disciplines, and dismisses its members, and transacts any and all other business'" in such a way that "no one [member] possesses a preeminence, but each enjoys an equality of rights."[15]

> James Madison Pendleton taught three "truths" related to congregational polity: (1) "the governmental power is in the hands of the people"; (2) "the right of a majority of the members of a church to rule [is] in accordance with the law of Christ"; and (3) "the power of a church cannot be transferred or alienated, and . . . church action is final."[16]

Contending that the Bible is "the only authority for church polity," Hezekiah Harvey opposed "two contrary views: the authority of the patristic age and the argument from expediency."[17] "Edwin Charles Dargan concluded that 'the local church of the New Testament appears as a self-governing unit, and yet as having important relations to its sister churches and imperative duties to mankind.'" Finding "no trace whatever of any organization beyond the local church," Dargan "interpreted Baptist history in the United States as indicating that 'the almost uniform traditional practice of the Baptists' has been 'the independency of the churches.'"[18]

---

[14] Ibid., based on J. L. Dagg, *A Treatise on Church Order* (Charleston, SC: Southern Baptist Publication Society, 1858; rpt. ed., Harrisonburg, VA: Gano, 1982), 80–83, 163–74.

[15] Ibid., based on E. T. Hiscox, *The Baptist Church Directory: A Guide to the Doctrines and Discipline, Officers and Ordinances, Principles and Practices of Baptist Churches* (New York: Sheldon, 1860), 56, 240.

[16] Ibid., based on J. M. Pendleton, *Church Manual: Designed for the Use of Baptist Churches* (Philadelphia: American Baptist Publication Society, 1869), 101–17.

[17] Ibid., based on H. Harvey, *The Church: Its Polity and Ordinances* (Philadelphia: American Baptist Publication Society, 1879), 13–20.

[18] Ibid., 178–79, based on E. C. Dargan, *Ecclesiology: A Study of the Churches* (Louisville: Dearing, 1897), 46, 34, 107.

"William Roy McNutt applied" E.Y. Mullins's concept of "soul competency" "to church polity, joining it with 'the free association of believers as a church,' and asserted that '[d]emocracy and independency are the two chief planks in the platform of Baptist polity.'"[19] According to Norman H. Maring and Winthrop S. Hudson, Baptists have advocated congregational polity not

> "because it offered a convenient administrative procedure by which decisions could be reached easily by a show of hands" but "because they believed that Christ intended the full participation of the members of the church in its total life, as implied in the doctrine of the priesthood of all believers."

Denying that congregational decisions are infallible, Maring and Hudson regarded a church as "'a sensitive and delicate instrument' for searching out the will of God" and "a check to the distortion occasioned by self-regard, human limitation of knowledge, and vested interests."[20] Very different was the assertion of a recent English Baptist, Alec Gilmore: "The Church is not, and must never be regarded as, a democracy, for the power is not in the hands of the *demos* but of the *Christos*; it is a Christocracy."[21]

But Baptist advocacy of congregational polity in the United States has run the risk of excessive claims vis-à-vis political democracy. A classic example of this may be found in the leading Landmarker, James Robinson Graves (1820–93), and his polemic against the Methodist Episcopal Church, South. In his *The Great Iron Wheel* Graves critiqued Methodist polity as "the antipode of the American political system."[22] Then in his *The Little Iron*

---

[19] Ibid., 179, based on W. R. McNutt, *Polity and Practice in Baptist Churches* (Philadelphia: Judson, 1935), 21–37.

[20] Ibid., based on N. H. Maring and W. S. Hudson, *A Baptist Manual of Polity and Practice* (Valley Forge, PA: Judson, 1963), 52–53.

[21] Ibid., quoting A. Gilmore, "Baptist Churches Today and Tomorrow," in *The Pattern of the Church: A Baptist View,* A. Gilmore, ed. (London: Lutterworth, 1963), 143.

[22] J. R. Graves, *The Great Iron Wheel; or, Republicanism Backwards and*

*Wheel*, with the Methodist author Henry Bidleman Bascom, he scored Methodism's "despotism" as being much like 12 centuries of papal-epispocal dominance and as being contrary to the republican government of the United States as well as contravening the New Testament.[23] For Graves, Methodist polity was primarily un-American and secondarily unbiblical.

But Baptists have never been able to claim rightly congregational polity as a pure distinctive, as they did with believer's baptism by immersion, for from the seventeenth century Congregational churches also taught and practiced congregational polity, even though in early New England they modified it by a synodical structure.[24] In the mid-twentieth century most of the Congregational churches in the United States merged with the Evangelical and Reformed Church to form the United Church of Christ with little residue of congregational polity. But there were at least 33 non-Baptist denominations in the United States at the beginning of the twenty-first century that claimed to practice congregational polity.[25]

Having identified the principal New Testament texts relative to congregational polity and having reviewed Baptist confessions of faith and the writings of leading Baptist ecclesiologists, we must now address congregational polity in the contemporary context. As Baptists have developed from their seventeenth-century and eighteenth-century roots to the advent of the twenty-first century, what factors seem to have influenced their exercise, both as to use and to abuse, of congregational polity?

---

*Christianity Reversed* (Nashville: Graves and Marks, 1855), 289–306, 308–26 (esp. 319).

[23] Garrett, *Baptist Theology: A Four-Century Study* (Macon: Mercer, 2009), 219–20, based on H. B. Bascom, *The Little Iron Wheel: A Declaration of Christian Rights, and Articles Showing the Despotism of Episcopal Methodism* [with] *Notes of Application and Illustration by J. R. Graves* (Nashville: South Western, 1857), 56–59, 70–71, 77–78.

[24] W. Walker, *The Creeds and Platforms of Congregationalism* (repr., Boston: Pilgrim Press, 1960), 185–86, 212–14, 217–20, 246–50.

[25] Garrett, "The Congregation-Led Church," 180–81.

First, the development of congregations with a large membership (i.e., more than 1,000 members) has made the practice of congregationalism more difficult. With the exception of C. H. Spurgeon's Metropolitan Tabernacle in London, this was largely a twentieth-century phenomenon. Congregationalism assumed that church members, especially when they had together affirmed a church covenant and were still practicing corrective church discipline, knew one another personally and reckoned a church meeting more as a family gathering than as a political convention. Knowing other members personally was more difficult in large congregations, which made greater use of committees that were accountable to the congregation.

Second, the twentieth century witnessed among Baptists in the American South and America's major cities the advent and the increased number of full-time, employed ministers assisting the pastor of large congregations. The Dallas-Fort Worth area and Southwestern Seminary with its schools of religious education and sacred music (1921) contributed significantly to this trend. Constituting what came to be known as a "church staff," these ministers, whether ordained or not but often seminary trained, frequently exercised functions or made decisions that in smaller congregations were being carried out by deacons or decided in church meetings. Likewise these ministers often rendered service or ministry that in smaller churches was being rendered by the pastor, deacons, or individual members.

Third, the latter third of the twentieth century brought especially in the United States and among Baptists the phenomenon of the megachurch. Although there are differing definitions of this term,[26] I shall employ it to refer to churches having more than 10,000 members. Such churches not only seldom have

---

[26] C. P. Wagner and P. Heibert differentiated the "metachurch" (with "several ten thousands" of members) and the "megachurch" (with "several thousands of members"), as cited by J. N. Vaughan, *Megachurches and America's Cities: How Churches Grow* (Grand Rapids: Baker, 1993), 34, 54.

congregational meetings but also can scarcely arrange for the seating of such a gathering. Wilson Hull Beardsley in his study of First Southern Baptist Church, Del City, Oklahoma, offered some generalizations about the megachurch. It is

"heavily pastor centered." The selection and the termination of the employed church staff is "at the direction of the pastor and in consultation with the personnel committee." The pastor is expected to speak first in most church meetings, the role of deacons is altered, and the pastor and the staff become "less accountable to the congregation for the details and plans of the ministries." Members "tend to be 'more willing to be observers than . . . participants.'"[27]

Fourth, the history of congregational polity among Baptists contains examples of its misuse or abuse as well as its more proper use. Examples of such include: (1) usurpation by the body of deacons of authority that belongs to or at least should be shared with the congregation; (2) usurpation by the pastor of authority that belongs to or at least should be shared with the deacons or with the congregation; (3) usurpation by some or all members of the church staff of authority that belongs to the congregation (or adoption of a system of ordained elders who function not only as preaching-teaching elders but also as ruling elders); and (4) usurpation by a clique within the church, by an "in-group," or by families with lengthy membership of authority that belongs to the pastor, the deacons, or the congregation. Although such abuses call for corrective action, their occurrence should not be used to build a case for the abandonment of congregational polity.

Fifth, church "business meetings" (the British prefer "church meetings") have been greatly influenced by such models as

---

[27] Garrett, "The Congregation-Led Church," 190, based on Beardsley, "The Pastor as Change Agent in the Growth of a Southern Baptist Mega Church Model" (D.Min. diss., Fuller Theological Seminary, 1991), 194, 200, 200, 267, 278, 309, 310, 315.

legislatures and political conventions. The use of parliamentary procedure for the sake of good order has served to accentuate this trend. The partisan rivalry of competing parties or factions, the desire to win a majority vote despite a considerable minority, and the relatively low regard for the unity of the church have often characterized such business meetings.

Sixth, present-day Southern Baptist churches exercise church governance with many of their members having served outside the church community in short-term mission projects both in North America and overseas. Fisher H. Humphreys perceptively noted in 2001 that the most important change in Southern Baptist life during the latter twentieth century was "the sweeping introduction of short-term missions (defined as from a few days to a few years by volunteers)."[28] Whereas earlier Southern Baptists had prayed for, studied about, and contributed to the support of career missionaries at home and abroad, many of today's Southern Baptist church members also come to their church meetings having had hands-on experience of sharing the gospel across cultural divides and language barriers. Is it "tenable" that such members "should be deprived of meaningful participation in the decision-making of their local churches" because congregational polity has been replaced in fact by another mode?[29] Rather, "Baptist laypersons from the various professions, businesses, and trades and of various ages and both sexes must have a voice in the decision-making and mission-projection of their Baptist congregations, for their churches need their wisdom and experience."[30]

With these factors influencing Baptist congregational polity in mind, let us turn to the crucial question of the relationship of church polity and church leadership. Some seem to regard the two terms as synonyms.[31] I would argue to the contrary, urging that the

---

[28] "The Most Important Change in Baptist Life," *Baptists Today* (July 2001): 8.

[29] Garrett, "The Congregation-Led Church," 187.

[30] Ibid., 189.

[31] Contributors to *Perspectives on Church Government,* ed. Brand and Norman,

two are closely related but not synonyms and that they also should not be posed as either/or alternatives. The earliest Congregational and Baptist documents "affirmed the essential roles of ordained ministers as well as congregational polity." Since the first Great Awakening "Baptists in the United States" have had a strong conviction as to "the indispensability of a divinely called and gifted pastoral ministry."[32] In addition to and prior to the external call of the congregation to a specific pastorate there must have been the internal call of the Holy Spirit to a specific believer to the pastoral ministry; a call to be differentiated from the call to repentance, faith, and discipleship. The pastor is to preach/teach, engage in pastoral care, and lead in church administration.

The exercise of his preaching/teaching function derives from his dual calling and from his preparation for ministry rather than from repeated decision-making by the congregation. The selection of sermon texts and subjects and the ordering of worship services are not decisions to be made at the congregational meeting but rest with the pastor and ministers who serve with him. The preaching of the gospel and indeed of "all the counsel of God" (Acts 20:27 KJV), within the boundaries of the congregation's confession of faith, is not subject to congregational vote, unless the pastor should be deemed to be utterly derelict in his entire exercise of preaching. The congregation does not vote on the preaching agenda of the pastor as it does on the selection of church officers, the congregational borrowing of money, or the reception and dismissal of members. By the exercise of his preaching/teaching function the pastor can greatly influence the thinking and the behavior of church members. He can help to predispose members to a larger vision of the ministry and mission of the church.

---

were invited to write on polity without any specification as to leadership, but in the table of contents and the chapter titles polity and leadership were used as synonyms.

[32] Garrett, "The Congregation-Led Church," 187.

It must then be asked: Does the pastor lead by his office or by his influence? The answer is both.[33] By the fact that this particular congregation has called him to be its pastor and he has accepted the call, he is entitled to function as the elder-bishop-pastor of this congregation. But the mere fact of being pastor alone may not be sufficient to convince a majority of the congregation of the tenability of what he advocates in a church meeting, especially if it should be expressed in terms of "do this because I as your pastor say so."

The pastor's leadership by influence is also important. "He who has baptized and instructed the newly converted, married the young, visited the sick, counseled the troubled, and buried the dead" is likely to have an enormous influence on the decisions by the congregation.[34] Hence congregational polity and pastoral leadership are not either/or but both/and. A church with congregational polity but poor pastoral leadership may founder or limp along, unable to fulfill its mission. A church with strong pastoral leadership but bereft of congregational decision-making may see its members become compliant observers or see the congregation splinter with dissatisfied dissidents. Together congregational polity and pastoral leadership, properly bonded, can give strength and stability for the fulfillment of the church's mission. Such congregational-pastoral collaboration can thrive only if the pastor himself is committed to basic congregational polity. Pastor search committees sometimes fail to ascertain whether a potential pastor under consideration is so committed, only to discover later that he is committed to the rule of a body of elders or to single-pastor rule, thus leading to a congregational crisis.

On the other hand, we must be sure to recognize that congregational decisions are not infallible. What the Congregational

---

[33] Daniel Akin has incorrectly assumed that the present author holds only to pastoral influence. "Response by Daniel L. Akin" to Garrett in *Perspectives on Church Government*, ed. Brand and Norman, 197.

[34] Garrett, "The Congregation-Led Church," 188. See also F. M. Segler, *A Theology of Church and Ministry* (Nashville: Broadman, 1960), 73.

Church in Northampton, Massachusetts, did in terminating its pastor, Jonathan Edwards Sr., may be a sober reminder as to how congregations may err in their decisions. Moreover, some of us may be keenly and painfully aware of more recent examples.

With a view to the future, let us consider what is needed for and possible in the transformation of church business meetings. Unfortunately, many Baptists have a negative attitude toward or perception of such meetings, often because of bad memories of contentious and strife-filled meetings or the feeling that such meetings are not relevant or necessary or meaningful. Such memories and feelings make imperative a reconceptualization of church meetings. Some of the problem lies in the tendency to look upon church meetings as something other than a spiritual exercise or experience. In contrast to the fond memories by senior adults of a life-changing revival service in their youth, or to the recent enthusiasm kindled among youth by a Christian music festival, or to the blend of Christian and patriotic emotions evoked after September 11, 2001, church business meetings often evoke a verdict by memory: bland, controversial, mundane, or less than edifying.

Consider again the New Testament witness. First, Christians have the promises of Jesus that the Holy Spirit "will teach you all things and will remind you of everything I have said to you" (John 14:26 NIV) and "will guide you into all truth" and "will tell you what is yet to come" (John 16:13). Paul's prison epistles afford guidance for church members when they gather for decision-making. As church members, we are "in humility [to] consider others better than" ourselves (Phil 2:3 NIV). We are to "get rid of all bitterness, rage and anger, brawling and slander, along with every form of malice" (Eph 4:31 NIV) and "not be foolish, but understand what the Lord's will is" (Eph 5:17 NIV). We are to "clothe" ourselves "with compassion, kindness, humility, gentleness and patience" and "put on love, which binds" these virtues "together in perfect unity" (Col 3:12,14 NIV). Having "encouragement from being united with Christ," we are to be "like-minded, having the same love, being one in spirit and purpose" (Phil 2:1–2 NIV). We are to "stand firm in one spirit" (Phil 1:27 NIV) and "make every effort to keep the unity of the Spirit through the bond of peace" (Eph 4:3 NIV). Church members in the spirit of a loving family should look forward with prayer and anticipation to their congregational meetings, in which together they are to seek the mind of Christ and the guidance of the Holy Spirit.

Paige Patterson has aptly stated that congregations are to seek to arrive "at a *spiritual consensus*."[35] This is not to say that every single congregational decision will be unanimous but to affirm that united and agreed-upon decision-making is to be the goal. As church members, we should go from our congregational meetings praising and thanking our living Lord Jesus, worshipping the Holy Spirit even as we worship the Father and the Son, and celebrating our Christian fellowship in the congregation, ever conscious of our responsibility as well as our privilege within the family of believers.

Church polity is once again on the front burner of theological debate and discussion.[36] Anglicans defend Episcopal polity. Peter Toon argues that the Holy Spirit who oversaw the canonization of the New Testament books must surely have approved the episcopal polity under which it was actualized and decries congregationalism as a seventeenth-century innovation.[37] Whereas Paul F. M. Zahl argues for episcopacy and a threefold ministry from the *bene esse* (for the "well-being") of the church,[38] Toon argues for

---

[35] P. Patterson, "Single-Elder Congregationalism," in *Who Runs the Church? 4 Views on Church Government,* ed. S. B. Cowan (Grand Rapids: Zondervan, 2004), 140.

[36] *Perspectives on Church Government,* ed. Brand and Norman; *Who Runs the Church?,* ed. Cowan.

[37] P. Toon, "An Episcopalian's Response" [to Taylor], in *Who Runs the Church?,* 99–100, 103; idem "An Episcopalian's Response" [to Patterson] in ibid., 157; idem, "An Episcopalian's Response" [to Waldron] in ibid., 223–26.

[38] P. F. M. Zahl, "The Bishop-Led Church," in *Perspectives on Church Government,* 213–16.

it from the *plene esse* (for "fullness of being") of the church.[39] Zahl insists that "there is no one governing New Testament ecclesiology," so that New Testament exegesis offers no answer, and then complains that whenever polity becomes a "driving" issue, thereby the church is to be reckoned as "decadent."[40] Toon notes that episcopal polity for Roman Catholics, Eastern Orthodox, Anglicans, and Scandinavian Lutherans requires acceptance of apostolic succession, whereas for United Methodists and Lutherans in the United States, it does not.[41]

Presbyterians and Reformed, as expected, defend presbyterial polity, both within and above the congregation. L. Roy Taylor is confident that all New Testament churches had a plurality of elders built on the model of synagogue eldership.[42] Robert L. Reymond argues at length that the church at Jerusalem was "the prime example" with Acts 15 descriptive of an elder-led, connectional council.[43] Clearly, for Reymond, the elders are to "rule" and "oversee" the congregation.[44] "All elders rule, but some elders also have special responsibilities in preaching and teaching."[45] Whereas Louis Berkhof[46] has insisted that each "court" (presbytery, synod, general assembly) in the Presbyterian system derives its authority from "the session of the local church," Reymond holds that each court has "its own intrinsic authority peculiar to itself."[47]

Congregational polity has its own present-day advocates in various forms. Some argue for a plural-elder-led congregationalism. James R. White is sure that "plural elders in each church" was "the apostolic pattern," and elders are equal in office but diverse as

---

[39] P. Toon, "Episcopalianism," in *Who Runs the Church?*, 36–38.

[40] Zahl, "The Bishop-Led Church," 212, 210.

[41] Toon, "Episcopalianism," 21.

[42] L. R. Taylor, "Presbyterianism," in *Who Runs the Church?*, 78–80

[43] R. L. Reymond, "The Presbytery-Led Church," in *Perspectives on Church Government*, 95–109; Taylor, "Presbyterianism," 80–81.

[44] Reymond, "The Presbytery-Led Church," 134.

[45] Taylor, "Presbyterianism," 81.

[46] Berkhof was following William Cunningham and James Bannerman.

[47] Reymond, "The Presbytery-Led Church," 124–25.

to "ministry and gifts" with each church's elders deciding how to divide their duties.[48] For Waldron all elders "must have the gifts of leadership and teaching," but they may differ as to "spiritual gifts, financial support, and actual influence."

Elders "are not *mere* representatives" of the congregation, for "they have an authority far greater."[49] But Mark E. Dever advocates plural elders among whom one is the preaching/teaching senior elder or pastor.[50] Others espouse a single-elder system. Akin, acknowledging that a biblical case can be made for plural elders, makes the cases for a senior elder (or pastor) and for a single elder (or pastor) but leaves that issue unresolved and advocates a "representative" congregationalism in which there are annual, not monthly or quarterly, church meetings.[51] Paige Patterson, conceding that there is no "hands down" New Testament case for a single elder (or pastor), nevertheless favors such "from observing leadership practice throughout the Scriptures."[52] In summary, congregationalism can be explained and defended without settling all the leadership issues.[53]

Baptists need to be fully represented and active in the current debates about church polity, most of which are being carried on outside particular congregations. But even more crucial is the question as to whether Baptist congregations of the twenty-first century can and will rediscover a healthy and balanced congregationalism by having their culture-tainted, overindividualized, widely suspect, and joyless practice, or their loss of congregationalism in the world of the megachurch, transformed by the risen,

---

[48] J. R. White, "The Plural-Elder-Led Church," in *Perspectives on Church Government*, 280–81.

[49] S. E. Waldron, "Plural-Elder Congregationalism," in *Who Runs the Church?*, 216, 219.

[50] M. E. Dever, "The Church," in *A Theology for the Church*, ed. D. L. Akin (Nashville: B&H, 2007), 802–5.

[51] D. L. Akin, "The Single-Elder-Led Church," in *Perspectives on Church Government*, 64–69, 73, 70.

[52] Patterson, "Single-Elder Congregationalism," 150–52.

[53] Garrett, "The Congregation-Led Church," 157–94.

authoritative Lord Jesus through the teaching-guiding Holy Spirit into a hopeful quest for the mind of Christ for the sake of the church's mission to all humankind and for the glory of the triune God.

6

# A Denomination of Churches:
# Biblical and Useful

*Bart Barber*

In 2009 North Carolina megachurch pastor J. D. Greear bluntly decreed, "Denominations are not biblical institutions," seemingly settling in a single clause the question allocated an entire chapter in this book. Greear's declaration gives every appearance of arising out of the noblest of Baptist motivations—an enthusiastic defense of the unique authority of the local congregation. Denominations are not to usurp the divinely ordered role of the congregations. Those doing so have devolved into Greear's "BAD parachurch" model, while those that successfully restrain themselves to the mere facilitation of "the ministry of the church" have clung to the higher "good parachurch" model.[1]

Greear's words are timely and significant. Usurpation of the local church's unique authority is indeed an ever-present danger. In no epoch has it not served the churches well to remain wary of this threat. Pastors like Greear, who keep the local church diligent

---

[1] Greear further clarified that he did not regard denominations as "unbiblical institutions" either. See J. D. Greear, "Great Commssion [*sic*] Resurgence Task Force," jdgreear.com, available at http://jdgreear.typepad.com/my_weblog/2009/08/great-commssion-resurgence-task-force.html, accessed October 1, 2009.

in her responsibilities and vigilant toward her unique prerogatives, are a blessing from the Lord.

Nevertheless, one wonders whether the entirety of Christian experience can be subsumed neatly into the categories of "church" and "parachurch"? Something of a false dichotomy seems to be afoot here. When First Baptist Church of Farmersville (where I serve) assembles on Sunday for corporate worship, corporate exhortation, and our collective seeking for the will of God in the conduct of the church's ministries, this is obviously an activity of the church. When James Dobson sat down in the Colorado Springs studios of Focus on the Family to record a radio program that was the fruit of his own entrepreneurial vision and labor, this was obviously the activity of a parachurch organization.

However, to which category belongs the gathering where deacons and pastors from a variety of congregations meet to examine me and to consider ordaining me to the gospel ministry? This was not merely the action of a single congregation (neither in its individual composition nor in its effects), but neither does it seem to belong to the realm of "parachurchism" (to borrow a word Greear has favored elsewhere). What does one call ministry when it is neither the ministry of a nonchurch organization nor the ministry of a single local church—when it is neither more nor less than the cooperative ministry of multiple congregations? If this kind of ministry indeed qualifies as a *tertium quid*, is it possible that a "denomination of churches" could belong to the same category?

## WHAT MAKES A DENOMINATION?

Complicating careful analysis of this topic is the bewildering variety of denominations and the difficulty in defining with any precision what makes a denomination. Webster's *Ninth New Collegiate Dictionary* reports that a denomination is "a religious organization uniting in a single legal and administrative body a number of local congregations."[2] This definition does not suffice.

It is too narrow to apply to the Church of Christ denomination here in the United States, which has no "single legal and administrative body" but is definitely a denomination. Indeed, their own history evinces the difficulties of knowing when a group of churches become a denomination. Lacking any headquarters, bureaucracy, or annual convocation of churches to aid them in the matter, historians have frequently identified the birth of the Church of Christ denomination with a 1906 decision by the United States Census Bureau first to tabulate denominational affiliation with the Churches of Christ separately from the Disciples of Christ.[3] A denomination "founded" by the Census Bureau! Yet who can deny that the Church of Christ churches make up a legitimate denomination? On the other hand, Webster's definition is so broad as to include the North Texas Baptist Association or the Founders Conference.

One group of Baptist churches has sought to differentiate "denominationalism" from "associationalism," affirming the latter while decrying the former. The distinctive criteria of a denomination, by their reckoning, consists in the facts that:

> An association has absolutely no power or authority over any local church, except to break fellowship with a disorderly church over doctrine or practice and to make known to others its actions toward the erring church and why its actions were taken. Its capacity and function is only advisory. There is no impingement upon the autonomy or independency of any local church. Also, an association does

---

[2] *Merriam-Webster's Collegiate Dictionary, Ninth Edition* (Springfield, MA: Merriam-Webster, 1983).

[3] U.S. Department of Commerce and Labor, Bureau of the Census, *Special Reports: Religious Bodies: 1906, Part II, Separate Denominations: History, Description, and Statistics* (Washington, DC: Government Printing Office, 1910), 235–44.

not have any authority to ordain or appoint pastors, elders or deacons over any church. A denomination, on the other hand, can have varying degrees of authority and power over a local church such as owning a local church's property, owning the church name, ordaining and appointing church officers and changing and enforcing church doctrine or practice.[4]

Using this definition alone, one must conclude that the Southern Baptist Convention is in no way a denomination and agree wholeheartedly with Greear that denominations are not biblical institutions.

Atwood reported in the preface to the eleventh edition of the *Handbook of Denominations in the United States* that he had employed in the compilation of his volume a statistical definition—a minimum threshold of 5,000 adherents in order to constitute a denomination worthy of inclusion in the book.[5] This rule would exclude the General Six-Principle Baptists, although they are among the longest-surviving denominations of Baptists in the United States.[6]

A better and more practical definition would tie denominational barriers to the boundaries of ministerial service and mem-

---

[4] E. M. Blackburn, "A Biblical Basis for Associations of Churches," in J. M. Renihan, ed., *Denominations or Associations? Essays on Reformed Baptist Associations* (Amityville, NY: Calvary, 2001), 27.

[5] F. S. Mead and S. S. Hill, *Handbook of Denominations in the United States*, 11th ed., rev. by C. D. Atwood (Nashville, TN: Abingdon, 2001), 15.

[6] That they are a venerable and aged association of Baptists is demonstrably true, even if they cannot document that their denomination is as old as they allege. See *Minutes of the General Six Principle Baptist Conference of Rhode Island* (Newport, RI: Rhode Island Historical Society, 1835–1955), 1862, for their claim to be the oldest organization of Baptists in America. The claim of the Philadelphia Baptist Association is much better attested by historical record. See A. D. Gillette, ed. *Minutes of the Philadelphia Baptist Association, from A.D. 1707, to A.D. 1807; Being the First One Hundred Years of Its Existence* (Philadelphia: American Baptist Publication Society, 1851; repr., Otisville, MI: Baptist Book Trust, 1976), 6.

ber migration. A denomination, by this proposed definition, is a realm of churches within which pastors and congregants move from church to church freely and beyond which they do not.[7]

This familial definition of a denomination best accounts for the fact that, were each one of the offices and apparatuses of our joint institutional ministry to pass into oblivion tomorrow, the Southern Baptist Convention would yet remain the Southern Baptist Convention, albeit a Southern Baptist Convention weakened by the loss. Churches, sharing important things in common, swap people in certain circumstances and interact with one another in certain circumstances. This is a universal component of the meaning of *denomination*, and among Baptists it exhausts the topic. Is this interaction biblical and useful? Absolutely it is.

## TWO DIMENSIONS OF AND TWO REACTIONS TO DENOMINATIONALISM

Denominationalism has both an inclusive aspect and an exclusive aspect. It is inclusive in that any denomination represents individual local congregations connecting with one another and creating a denominational community. It is exclusive in that some congregations are not welcome to enter the community, whether by virtue of their doctrine, their geographical location, or some other factor. To defend the existence of any denomination is to fight the war on both of these fronts.

The proponents of a radical congregational independency will oppose denominationalism for its inclusiveness.[8] One apocryphal Baptist announcing a change in denominational affiliation

---

[7] *Facts & Trends* reported on a 2005 study by Ellison Research demonstrating that only 9 percent of Protestant pastors had left a congregation in one denomination to serve in a congregation of another denomination—this in a sample that did not exclude nondenominational pastors. See R. Sellers, "Pastors think pastors should stay put," *Facts & Trends* 51, no. 5 (September/October 2005): 6.

[8] See Renihan, *Denominations or Associations*, for a book almost entirely devoted to answering this objection by positing an ostensibly more acceptable "associationalism."

declared: "I have decided to become an Independent Baptist, and the first thing that I have determined to be independent of is all other Independent Baptists!" In reaction against such radical independency, proponents of denominationalism will attempt to demonstrate that connective relationships among local congregations are a biblical, useful, and nearly unavoidable phenomenon.

Those who have been convinced that denominational divisions are contrary to Christ's command for Christian unity will sometimes critique denominationalism for its exclusivity. To be obedient to Christ's call for unity, they would say, one must abandon one's denomination and its prejudices. Consider this statement issued by a group of churches:

> We wish for this denominational institution to die, be dissolved, and sink into union with the Body of Christ at large; for there is but one Body and one Spirit, even as we are called in the hope of our calling. . . .
>
> We wish for our power of setting doctrines and policies for the government of the church, and enforcing them upon the Christian members of our congregations, to end forever; that every believer may have the liberty to follow the Bible, and follow *the law of the Spirit of life in Christ Jesus.* . . .
>
> We wish for preachers and people to cultivate a spirit of tolerance; to pray more and to fight less. . . .
>
> We wish for our weaker brethren, who may have been wishing to make an empire of their denomination, and now do not know where to turn at its demise, to place their hope in the Rock of Ages, and follow Jesus for the future. . . .
>
> Finally, we wish that all our sister churches will . . . see the ultimate fate of denominations and prepare for their death before it is too late.[9]

---

[9] Adapted and modernized by the author from B. W. Stone, et al., *Last Will and Testament of the Springfield Presbytery* (28 June 1804).

The preceding quote may sound like the declaration of some radical group of twenty-first-century postdenominationalists, but it is actually a modernization of excerpts from the *Last Will and Testament of the Springfield Presbytery* written by Barton W. Stone in 1804. Stone's life and the tradition that he birthed illustrate the grand historical irony of nondenominational movements—if they endure at all, they tend to accomplish not the unification of the Body of Christ but instead the fragmentation of Christianity into even more denominations. Whether it operates by attempting to expand the denomination to encompass the entire church or by whittling down the entire church to fit within the denomination, no ecumenical movement has yet succeeded.

Against the ecumenical critique, some denominationalists emphasize the inclusive aspect of denominationalism. To obey Christ's call for unity, one must embrace one's denomination and its mutual relationships, they say, contending that any passion for Christian unity will make a local congregation more faithful to a denomination and more diligent for the sound doctrine that promotes unity, as President George Allen Yuille argued before the Baptist Union of Scotland in 1902:

> It is our conviction that the ordinance of Christian baptism, being designed for believers only, was intended to guard the entrance to the Church from those who have not genuine faith in Christ. The churches of the second century ceased to be congregational because large numbers were in fellowship who held no personal faith. They were children or grandchildren of the original Jewish or pagan converts, had inherited Christian customs and creed but the vision of God in Christ which had caused their fathers to break away from their old life had never come to them. We must guard against that danger.
>
> Beyond the individual church unity is *a wider unity*, the unity of all such churches in a common brotherhood to

further God's kingdom. It is what the Spirit of Christ requires and creates. As Baptists we need to learn that the corporate union of all our churches for Christian purposes is not only an advantage, an expedient, but a sacred duty which we owe to Christ whose Spirit dwells in us. We must make more room for the Spirit of Christ, trust one another more, seek each others' good as churches and give ourselves to one another for Christ's sake.[10]

So, which is it? To be faithful to Christ, are we obligated to regard denominations as walls to be torn down or as partnerships to be built up? Arising out of the conviction that both radical independency and doctrinally erosive ecumenism are unbiblical and useless, an argument follows that we are faithful to the teachings of the Bible and useful in the kingdom of God when our local congregations seek to connect and cooperate with one another denominationally to whatever degree that we can do so without compromising biblical truth.

## IS DENOMINATIONALISM BIBLICAL?

Some previous generations of Baptists have not only concluded that a healthy denominational life is biblically permitted or described but have further claimed that denominational fellowship is biblically commanded.[11] The biblical ideal is that we "be diligent

---

[10] C. Lumsden, *George Yuille: Grand Old Man of Scottish Baptists* (2005), in *Baptist History Collection* (CD-ROM).

[11] The First London Confession of Faith reads in Article XLVII, "And although the particular Congregations be distinct and severall Bodies, every one a compact and knit Citie in it selfe; yet are they all to walk by one and the same Rule, and by all meanes convenient to have the counsel and help of one another in all needfull affaires of the Church, as members of one body in the common faith under Christ their onely head (1 Corinthians 4:17, & 14:33,36 & 16:1. Matthew 28:20; 1 Timothy 3:16 & 6:13, 14. Revelation 22:18, 19. Colossians 2:6,19, & 4:16.)." See "The First London Confession of Faith," in *The Baptist History Collection* [CD-ROM] (Paris, AR: The Baptist Standard Bearer, 2005), 19. Sharing in this opinion was Benjamin Griffith in his "Short Treatise Concerning a True and Orderly Gospel Church" (1743) and a number of subsequent works. A little

to preserve the unity of the Spirit in the bond of peace," gathering around the singular body, Spirit, calling, hope, Lord, faith, baptism, God, and Father that collectively define our faith (Eph 4:3–6 NASB). The biblical paradigm is unity and peace within parameters of orthodoxy. But what happens when congregations violate those parameters? The Bible provides support for both the inclusive and the exclusive dimensions that have created modern denominationalism.

## COOPERATIVE CONNECTION AMONG
## NEW TESTAMENT CONGREGATIONS

The connection between local churches in the New Testament was more subtle than it was overt and more familial than it was institutional. We read of no headquarters or executive secretaries. No annual convention graces the pages of the New Testament. Very few New Testament commandments may be construed to direct the congregations in how to interact with other congregations. Yet spread throughout the pages of the New Testament we find these local congregations doing just that—interacting with other local congregations.

### Generational or Familial Connection

In the New Testament era, denominational connection among churches arose inevitably from the mere fact that the vast preponderance of Christian congregations existed as the spiritual offspring of some other congregation. The same is often true of modern denominational connections. The nineteenth-century Sandy Creek family of Baptist churches, for example, was heavily

---

more than a century later, this earlier biblical basis for a duty of denominational participation had begun to give way, such that P. H. Mell could write, "The Scriptures recognize no such bodies as Associations and Councils. . . . Some have endeavored to find the germ of Associations and Councils [in the New Testament]. But this only shows how easy it is to pervert the plain and common-sense transactions of apostolic times to the purposes of superstition." See *Corrective Church Discipline* in *Polity: Biblical Arguments on How to Conduct Church Life*, ed. M. Dever (Washington, DC: Nine Marks Ministries, 2000), 472.

populated with the daughter and granddaughter congregations of
Shubal Stearns's Sandy Creek Baptist Church in North Carolina.
Denominational histories commonly trace the ancestry of congregations back through a "Father" or "Fathers" of the denomination
who founded a "Mother" congregation.

In the New Testament the original matriarchal congregation
existed in Jerusalem. A great many of the New Testament congregations we know by name were grandchildren of the Jerusalem
congregation by way of the church in Antioch and the ministry
of its great missionary, the apostle Paul. Furthermore, after the
establishment of the daughter and granddaughter congregations,
persecution, missiological strategy, and other migratory pressures
caused individual believers to transfer occasionally from one congregation to another. Thus we find Priscilla and Aquila mentioned
in connection with initial membership in the church at Corinth
and later membership in the church at Rome (Acts 18:2–3; Rom
16:3–4).

Intercongregational association and cooperation have been
inevitable throughout Christian history for this very reason: The
allure of familial fellowship draws us together. Sprinkled throughout the epistles are words of warm greeting conveyed between
congregations separated by great distance and hardship in travel
but connected by a common experience of the Lord Jesus Christ.

## Doctrinal Connection

The congregations of the New Testament pursued an informal
yet robust relationship of doctrinal accountability with one another. Upon the anomalous founding of the church at Caesarea, Peter
sought doctrinal harmony between the Caesarean congregation
and the Jerusalem congregation (Acts 10:1–11:18). Paul reported
to the church in Antioch on behalf of his congregations planted in
Asia Minor (Acts 14:26–28), and then duplicated Peter's earlier
pilgrimage to Jerusalem to reassure Jewish believers as to the sin-
cerity and morality of Gentile Christians (Acts 15:1–35).

Even in the absence of any evidence of institutional inequality between the Jerusalem congregation and her spiritual descendants, the younger congregations clearly exhibited a deferential respect for the original church. Greater parity was evident among the churches of the Lycos Valley in Phrygia, who swapped their respective Pauline letters in order to cooperate in the transmission and teaching of sound doctrine (Col 4:16). Arising out of this practice, the compiled New Testament itself represents a cooperative effort among many congregations to pool doctrinal resources and to develop a comprehensive doctrinal repository of the definitive documents of the Christian faith. Thus, not only is intercongregational connection biblical, but the Bible itself is also a product of intercongregational connection.

The New Testament also gives evidence of an informal positive peer pressure by which congregations encouraged one another toward sound doctrine. While writing to the church at Corinth, Paul confronted both the aberrant abuse of the spiritual gift of tongues and the aberrant gender egalitarianism in Corinth by appeal to the practice of other churches:

> God is not a God of confusion but of peace, *as in all the churches of the saints*. The women are to keep silent *in the churches*; for they are not permitted to speak, but are to subject themselves, just as the Law also says (1 Cor 14:33–34 NASB, emphasis mine).

Likewise, Paul had previously challenged the presence of uncovered women in the Corinthian church by appeal to the example of other congregations, declaring, "But if one is inclined to be contentious, we have no other practice [than the covering of women in corporate prayer and worship], *nor have the churches of God*" (1 Cor 11:16 NASB, emphasis mine). In neither case does the apostle represent the pattern of sister churches as a foundational argument in favor of his theological position, but he seems quite willing to employ to advantage a desire among Corinthian believers to retain a faith and practice in harmony with that of the sister congregations with which the Corinthian congregation was affiliated.

If denominations exist as nothing more than functional tools that churches can use to accomplish the mission given to them, then denominations certainly are not biblical and are not as useful as they could be. Such denominations are nothing more than vendors in which the primary relationship is between church and "headquarters" rather than between church and other churches. The concept of denominations of churches (including the Southern Baptist Convention) as fellowships of mutual doctrinal accountability among churches is an aspect of New Testament intercongregational relationships worthy of invigoration or recovery.

## Pastoral Connection

The exchange of pastors/elders/overseers among congregations also connected individual congregations with one another. Paul considered it within the scope of his authority as an apostolic church planter commissioned by the Antiochene congregation to direct the appointment of elders for the congregations in Crete (Titus 1:5). Although there is no further suggestion in the New Testament of the formal selection of church leadership by parties external to the local congregation, there may be evidence of one local church encouraging and exhorting to the ministry a member of another local congregation. If the congregational recipient of Paul's letter to Philemon is any congregation other than the recipient of Paul's letter to the church at Colossae, then Paul's instruction to the Colossian church to "say to Archippus, 'Take heed to the ministry which you have received in the Lord, that you may fulfill it'" (Col 4:17 NASB) represents the deliberate involvement of one congregation in the encouragement of one young Christian from another congregation into some divine ministerial calling.

In the New Testament era Christian teachers arriving at unfamiliar congregations began to carry with them letters of commendation from congregations that knew them to congregations that did not (2 Cor 3:1). The Philadelphia Baptist Association acted in this biblical tradition when, in 1707, "it was then agreed that a person that is a stranger, that has neither letter of recommendation, nor is known to be a person gifted, and of a good conversation, shall not be admitted to preach, nor be entertained as a member in any of the baptized congregations in communion with each other."[12] Several years later, in 1723, the association reiterated along these same lines: "Agreed, that the proposal drawn by the several ministers, and signed by many others, in reference to the examination of all gifted brethren and ministers that come in here from other places, be duly put in practice, we having found the evil of neglecting a true and previous scrutiny in those affairs."[13]

### Fiduciary Connection

New Testament churches further united with one another in the fiduciary governance of Paul's missionary enterprise. Alongside Titus, Paul sent two other unnamed men to Corinth to collect the offering for the saints in Jerusalem. One of these Paul explicitly identifies as having been "appointed by the churches to travel with us in this gracious work" (2 Cor 8:19 NASB). The purpose of this companion on Paul's team the apostle connected with "our readiness, taking precaution that no one will discredit us in our administration of this generous gift, for we have regard for what is honorable, not only in the sight of the Lord, but also in the sight of men" (2 Cor 8:19–21 NASB). A conglomeration of churches in Paul's missionary context had banded together not only to provide financial support to another local congregation but also to appoint (pardon the anachronistic wording) trustees to oversee and administer the finances of their cooperative endeavor.

So these congregations of the New Testament cultivated a warm fellowship among one another; pressured one another toward

---

[12] Gillette, *Minutes of the Philadelphia Baptist Association*, 15.
[13] Ibid., 17.

orthodoxy; planted and supported new work, carefully selecting leaders to work in new church plants; vouched for the giftedness and orthodoxy of teachers sent out from one congregation to another; shared financially with Christians of other congregations who were in financial duress; and collectively appointed individuals to positions of trust overseeing their cooperative ministries. Although they may not have employed our precise terminology, certainly the germ of our present-day denominational activities is present in the New Testament.

## DOCTRINAL EXCLUSIVITY AMONG NEW TESTAMENT CONGREGATIONS

If the New Testament depicts local congregations interacting with one another, does it portray any limits to that interaction? Certainly it does. It demonstrates an aloofness from congregations that had departed doctrinally from Christian orthodoxy. John referred to a group that had departed a local congregation, identifying them as "antichrists" (1 John 2:18–19). John also conveyed Christ's warning against the reception of false apostles or teachers (Rev 2:2), a warning echoed by Paul (Gal 1:8–10) and by Peter (2 Pet 2:1–3), who further asserted that false congregations would accompany false teachers.

Also pertinent is the biblical aversion to those who are factious (Titus 3:10, for one example). A great many churches and groups of churches have as their origin some past schism in which they separated from other Christians. For the Southern Baptist Convention this is quadruply true—various Reformation groups separated from Roman Catholicism; separating from those separated groups were a more stringent group of dissenters (equally true regardless of whether one traces a Baptist family tree through Anabaptists or English Separatists); separating next from those dissenters were the Baptists; and finally Southern Baptists separated from another group of Baptists. We are great-great-grand-schismatics.

It takes two to split, but the blame for separation does not always distribute evenly. In the New Testament example cited above, the blame for separation lies not at all upon Titus for his "rejection" but entirely upon the "factious man" for being one who "is perverted and is sinning, being self-condemned" (Titus 3:10–11 NASB). In Christian schisms it is possible for both parties to be at fault, and it is possible for one party to be at fault, but Christian intercongregational relationships have no authority to adopt a notion of no-fault divorce.

Thus, even if the preceding section has demonstrated that it is biblical to have *a denomination*, it has nevertheless not put forward any good case that there should be *some denominations*. The notion of multiple equally valid denominations of Christianity is foreign to the New Testament—antithetical to it, even. That this unbiblical state is the present reality of the Christian faith cannot accurately be described as anything less than the sinful result of a sinful mixture of grave doctrinal errors and stubborn schismatic attitudes. Every Christian's best solution to this problem is to woo errant fellow believers to the truth and to implore the wrongly factious that "the fellowship of [Christian] faith [toward the Lord and toward one another] may become effective through the knowledge of every good thing which is in [Christian believers] for Christ's sake" (Phlm 6 NASB). Preceding and pending the successful outcome of that enterprise, each believer, each church, and each association of churches must look inwardly with fear and trembling to make certain that they are neither the heretics nor the unjustifiably factious ones.

Is denominationalism biblical? A denomination may have biblical grounds both for its gathering together of sister congregations and for its exclusion of other churches for their grave doctrinal errors or their stubborn schismatic attitudes. At the same time multiple denominationalism, or the idea that equally valid arms of the body of Christ might normatively exist in some unreconciled state, is not a biblical concept.

## IS DENOMINATIONALISM USEFUL?

One might be tempted to assert *ipso facto* that whatever is biblical is inherently useful—that being biblical is use enough in itself. Failure to follow the biblical pattern for denominational relations can result in diminished usefulness of the denomination of churches. As denominations lose familial cohesion among the congregations, they become less biblical and less useful.

At the turn of the twentieth century, Southern Baptists altered their structure and practices in a quest for greater professionalism.[14] This change in direction among Southern Baptists was consonant with a cultural shift from the frontier values of individualism, nationalism, mobility, and egalitarianism to the industrial values of efficiency, ambition, professionalism, and futurism. Whatever values industrialism brings, familial intimacy is not among them. By the turn of the twenty-first century, have Southern Baptists come to regard their associations and conventions more as an office and a staff than as families of churches? If so, this is to the detriment of these institutions and their usefulness. For example, if the local association is to compete with publication houses and specialized parachurch ministries as a vendor of church services, it is likely to find itself outmanned, underfunded, and endangered. As a family of local like-minded congregations, however, it is irreplaceable.

As denominations lose doctrinal cohesion among the congregations, they likewise become weaker. The English General Baptists quarreled, divided, and then reunited and reorganized while trying to determine whether they would enforce basic Trinitarianism as a test of fellowship for their affiliated churches. They eventually eschewed most doctrinal tests and refused any creed but the biblical text of Heb 6:1–2 (the "six principles" passage).

---

[14] C. B. Barber, "The Bogard Schism: An Arkansas Baptist Agrarian Revolt" (Ph.D. diss., Southwestern Baptist Theological Seminary, 2006), 39. See also F. J. Turner, *The Frontier in American History* (New York: Holt, 1920).

This experiment with associational life *sans* doctrinal parameters marked one of the weakest seasons in Baptist history.

The doctrinal connection of Southern Baptist churches was once strongest in the sphere of the local association and was only infrequently a topic of discourse at national convention meetings. Such no longer seems to be the case. Where are the doctrinal circular letters of a bygone era of Baptist associational life? Where are the queries from churches to sister churches seeking solutions to perplexing theological, moral, and practical questions?[15] Have Southern Baptists come no longer to regard doctrinal cohesion as a ground of unity among congregations, and if so, how may we recover a concept so prevalent in the New Testament?[16]

Evidence suggests that the Southern Baptist Convention retains some pastoral connection among its member churches since Southern Baptist pastors tend to stay within the Southern Baptist Convention at a higher rate than do Protestant clergy at large.[17] Scholarly analysis of trends regarding the level of intercongregational participation in ordinations would provide another helpful batch of data for evaluating denominational health in this area. Nevertheless, deplorable lapses in the duty to warn local congregations of predatory pastors show the way to an avenue of greater usefulness for Southern Baptist associations and conventions.

The fiduciary connection among Southern Baptists has perhaps received more attention in the past century than has any of the other emphases and is consequently strong. An epidemic of

---

[15] Readers may contrast contemporary denominational proceedings with the annals available in A. D. Gillette, *Minutes of the Philadelphia Baptist Association: From 1707 to 1807, Being the First One Hundred Years of Its Existence* (Paris, AR: The Baptist Standard Bearer, 2000), or in other associational minutes from previous centuries.

[16] D. Kingdon has reached this conclusion regarding initially British Reformed Baptists and subsequently American Reformed Baptists. See D. Kingdon, "Independency and Interdependency," in Renihan, *Denominations or Associations?*, 27.

[17] Southern Baptist pastors leave the SBC at a rate one-third less than the national average. See chart in Sellers, "Pastors think pastors should stay put."

appalling fiduciary failures blighted the first half of the twentieth century for Southern Baptists. After several years of unwise and aggressive borrowing on the part of Southern Baptist entities, the convention faced the shocking revelation that top financial personnel at both the International Mission Board and the North American Mission Board had been embezzling funds undetected and had absconded from the boards with a cumulative sum of nearly two million dollars. That this nadir of Southern Baptist fiduciary oversight came during the Great Depression only made matters worse. Individual Southern Baptists were so greatly scandalized that one Georgia man actually composed a song lamenting the situation![18]

In the aftermath of these scandals, Southern Baptists rededicated themselves to more careful systems of fiduciary oversight. Although the turn of the twenty-first century has witnessed two major financial scandals in state conventions,[19] although Southern Baptist financial generosity toward SBC cooperative enterprises seems to be waning somewhat from our apex,[20] and although Southern Baptists seem always to imagine better and more efficient ways of doing more ministry with less money, the fiduciary connection among Southern Baptist congregations is at present the strongest connection holding Southern Baptists together.

## CONCLUSION

Certainly denominational life has contributed its share of embarrassing moments to Baptist history. Devoid of a warm, cooperative spirit and a broad and collegial agreement on important

---

[18] D. Hornsby, *The Story of C. S. Carnes*, Columbia Records (October 23, 1928), http://www.archive.org/details/DanHornsby-TheStoryOfC.S.Carnes, accessed October 1, 2009.

[19] T. Starnes, "A Look Back at the Arizona Baptist Foundation Struggle," *Baptist Press* (December 17, 1999); S. Smith, "Details of Church Funds Scandal Recounted in BGCT Report," *Baptist Press* (November 2, 2006).

[20] *Baptist Press*, "SBC 2008–09 Fiscal Year: Below Budget 2.87%; Cooperative Program Down 2.32%" (October 2, 2009).

doctrinal matters and operational goals, denominational life can degenerate into something that hinders the kingdom rather than advancing it—just as there is bad church life and bad parachurchism, there is indeed such a thing as bad denominationalism.

These vulnerabilities notwithstanding, the most amazing and glorious triumphs in evangelism, church planting, discipleship, and apologetics, among other things, have come not as the work of an individual church but as the fruit of churches working together.

# 7

# The Church and Its Officers:
## A Pastor's Perspective

*Byron McWilliams*

In the spring of 1997, I answered God's call to become pastor of a Southern Baptist congregation in rural East Texas. As this was my first vocational ministry experience, and having been called from a large metropolitan church, I was unsure of protocol and polity in this smaller rural congregation. The church, however, received me wonderfully, and God affirmed His call with a unanimous congregational vote from this sweet fellowship of believers. I will always treasure fond memories of this church and our work together for God's kingdom. I will also be thankful for the training I received on how to be a pastor.

My training in local church ecclesiology began just days after arrival when I spent time with a gentleman in his early 80s. His small, somewhat frail, physical size gave no hint to his large stature within the church family. He had a friendly smile and seemed a stately representative of what I could expect from these wonderful people. Little did I realize that from his hands I would soon receive an "advanced degree" in leadership and church government.

As the learning curve was steep, I methodically began to decipher the necessary steps for success. I examined the organizational structure, observed the community, sought to understand the committees and identify key individuals involved in leadership—both out front and behind the scenes. I found the elderly man described above to be a long-tenured deacon, current chairman of the finance committee, current chairman of the personnel committee, church trustee, current church treasurer, and the primary signatory on the church checking account.

He and his family had been entrenched as leaders of the congregation for decades. They were such strong leaders that for years he and his wife had taken the tithes and offerings home each Sunday for counting at their convenience. Thankfully this practice had ceased before I arrived on the field. Nonetheless, with decades of strong influence upon this congregation, it became apparent that if I was to accomplish God's plan for this church I would either obey established precedent and receive direction from this man or face the power struggle that would most assuredly ensue. Over a decade later I remain confident that choosing to allow God to be Lord and leader of His church was the only viable option. As the months passed this young pastor and an established congregation sought answers to the age-old question of "Who runs the church?"

Drawing from this and other pastoral experiences, I will share the "real" story behind the church and its officers from one pastor's perspective. Volumes have been penned related to this subject, and I seek not to be redundant. This paper will briefly explore various models of church government, followed by a look into the church and its officers from a scriptural, historical, and relational perspective.

## CHURCH GOVERNMENT MODELS

Scripture establishes Jesus Christ as Lord of His church. The church is the bride of Christ, purchased with His blood. He is the ruling head of the universal Church and should be the ruling head of every local congregation as well. Only Jesus is divinely entitled to "run and rule" His church in the manner He deems best for the advancement of His kingdom. No subordinating officer is ever justified in usurping the leadership and authority of Jesus as Lord of His church.

This being true, why does conflict related to church government exist? Why are power struggles between ordained offices the norm in many churches? Did God create a less-than-perfect system of church government, doomed to failure from the start? Absolutely not! In fact, Scripture holds insight regarding ecclesiology with the purpose of maximizing the influence and effectiveness of the church. In order to increase understanding in this area, we must therefore examine some of the ecclesiological claims of the New Testament and the offices found therein.

When studying church government, it is apparent one size does not fit all as Christian denominations come in many different shapes and sizes. There is no singular form of church government that receives exclusive treatment in Scripture. Had God sovereignly appointed the apostle Paul to include a standard model for church operations in his writings to Timothy all confusion would be eliminated. However, in His sovereignty, God did not do so. George Eldon Ladd, longtime professor of New Testament at Fuller Theological Seminary, submits, "It appears likely that there was no normative pattern of church government in the apostolic age, and that the organizational structure of the church is no essential element in the theology of the church."[1] Daniel Akin, president of Southeastern Baptist Theological Seminary, seems to agree with Ladd by stating, "The New Testament does not provide a precise manual on how the structure of church government should be organized."[2] Although Scripture does not provide a step-by-step process for the organization and governing of a New Testament church, from this writer's perspective, evidence points to one model naturally rising to the surface, primary-elder congregationalism. This being said, a review of the existing

---

[1] As quoted by G. P. Cowen, *Who Rules the Church?* (Nashville: B&H, 2003), 2.
[2] C. O. Brand and R. S. Norman, eds., *Perspectives on Church Government: Five Views of Church Polity* (Nashville: B&H, 2004), 25.

governmental models is in order before exploring the officers and their responsibilities.

The contemporary church has no less than six models of church government found in practice today. The first, the Episcopal model, is a hierarchical system of church government. An archbishop resides over bishops who have authority over rectors, the local priests or congregational leaders within the congregation. Decisions descend from the archbishop to the bishops who then communicate with the rectors with little or no congregational input regarding how the church should operate. Roman Catholics, Episcopalians, and United Methodists use this model.

The Presbyterian model practices an elder-rule ecclesiology. Each local church elects elders to a "session" with the pastor being one of the elders making up this ruling body. They report to a presbytery made up of selected elders having authority over several churches in a region. This model uses minimal congregational input in selection of elders but should not be considered a congregational rule form of government. Most decisions are made by the selected board of elders who subsequently communicate them to the congregation as needed.

National state churches follow an Erastian model of government. Thomas Erastus founded this model in the sixteenth century. Erastus argued that the state had the right and responsibility to oversee the churches within its geographical domain, thus allowing for strong influence by the civil government in the affairs of the church.[3] The Church of England is a practicing example of this model with the monarchy being the supreme ruler of the church.

The Quakers and Plymouth Brethren used the Minimalist or Nongovernmental model. The name is indicative of the loose form of polity found in these congregations.

Some churches use a CEO model of church government. This model employs a corporate "chief executive officer" form

---

[3] Ibid., 300.

of autocratic, top-down rule with minimal congregational input. Many of these churches will have both offices in the church, pastor and deacon, but deacons will have little or no administrative oversight, functioning as servants only. The pastor is the leader who makes decisions and determines strategy for the church.

As will be shown, the form of church government most clearly delineated in the New Testament is the Congregational model. James Leo Garrett defines congregational polity as "that form of church governance in which final human authority rests with the local or particular congregation when it gathers for decision-making."[4] Through this model the local autonomous congregation seeks the will of God and makes decisions accordingly. Rather than a small ruling board, the congregational church supports decision making by the body as a whole under guidance from the Holy Spirit. Congregational churches can be primary elder or plural elder. Regardless of which, the entire congregation plays a direct role in the welfare and direction of the church.[5]

## NEW TESTAMENT BASIS FOR OFFICES IN THE CHURCH

There are two offices in the New Testament church: pastor and deacon. Other "unofficial" offices exist, for example, treasurer, trustee, or perhaps Sunday school director, but the New Testament specifies only two.[6] The following explores the definition and responsibilities of each.

### Office of Pastor

Five different English titles from three different Greek words are used to denote the office of pastor in the New Testament.

---

[4] Ibid., 157. See also chapter 5 in this volume.

[5] For a more thorough presentation of the various forms of church government see, for example, S. B. Cowan, ed., *Who Runs the Church?* (Grand Rapids: Zondervan, 2004); G. P. Cowen, *Who Rules the Church?*; W. Grudem, *Systematic Theology* (Grand Rapids: Zondervan, 1994); or Brand and Norman, eds., *Perspectives on Church Government: Five Views of Church Polity.*

[6] Cowan, *Who Runs the Church?*, 134.

These five are used interchangeably, and all point to the same office. They are elder, bishop, overseer, pastor, and shepherd.[7]

The term elder, or *presbuteros* in the Greek, the most common title for the office of pastor, is used 66 times in the New Testament.[8] Several usages denote those of advanced age; however, on at least 18 different occasions, the term is specifically applied to an officer of the local church.

The Greek word *episkopos* refers to two words in the English translation of the New Testament—bishop and overseer. It is derived from two Greek words, *epi* and *skopos,* and means "one who watches over." This word is found five different times in Scripture.

*Poimēn* describes the pastor or shepherd of the church. This word is used 18 different times in the New Testament and is the most commonly used term to describe the office of pastor in the contemporary church. In Acts 20 and in 1 Peter 5, all three Greek terms are used interchangeably indicating that the same office is intended. The remainder of this document will use "pastor" to denote any of the three terms described above.

What are the responsibilities of the pastor? He is the under-shepherd of the church as Christ is the Chief Shepherd (1 Pet 5:4). He submits to the direct authority and leadership of the Lord Jesus Christ as Chief Shepherd. Even in a congregational environment, the pastor works for and receives ultimate guidance from the Lord Jesus. Paige Patterson submits, "Pastors were [are] expected to be decisive spiritual leaders and interpreters, with accountability first to God and then to the autonomous congregation."[9] This is not an entitlement to ignore the desires of the congregation to which he has been called. To do so would be foolish indeed. It does imply

---

[7] See previously cited works for additional information related to the names associated with church offices. See also W. A. Criswell, *Great Doctrines of the Bible: Ecclesiology* (Grand Rapids: Zondervan, 1983), 96–104.

[8] Cowen, *Who Rules the Church?,* 9.

[9] Cowan, *Who Runs the Church?,* 134.

that the congregation should not seek to usurp the authority of Jesus Christ by restraining the pastor from fully executing his duties and responsibilities as the undershepherd appointed by God.

The pastor's chief responsibility as undershepherd is to preach the Word of God. He is wisely and diligently to seek guidance from the Holy Spirit to know what the Lord desires communicated to His people. In Acts 2:42 the priority of preaching is seen as the congregation in Jerusalem was "continually devoting themselves to the apostles' teaching." This devotion centered on the clear communication of sound doctrine for the edification and strengthening of the church to the praise and glory of Jesus.

Acts 6:2 emphasizes the apostles' priority not to "neglect the Word of God in order to serve tables." The pastor is to do no less. He must preach the Word of God, or he abdicates his charge from God. This charge, as communicated by Paul to Timothy, applies to every local man of God as he is to "preach the Word; be ready in season and out of season."[10] To demote the call to preach to a lesser status in the church is to fail the calling of God as pastor. Every man of God, called to the office of pastor in one of the Lord's churches, is uncompromisingly to preach the Word! I like what the now heaven-residing evangelist Vance Havner once said, "God is on the lookout today for a man who will be quiet enough to get a message from Him, brave enough to preach it, and honest enough to live it."[11]

The pastor is also called to shepherd God's people. This responsibility pays particular attention to the discipling, nurturing, comforting, and protecting of the congregation. In John 21, Peter, who recently denied the Lord, is told three times by Jesus to take care of His children. Jesus tells Peter to tend His lambs, shepherd (*poimaine*) His sheep, and tend His sheep. The term *tend* is a basic word that means simple feeding. Shepherding, however,

---

[10] 2 Timothy 4:2

[11] V. Havner, cited in Denis Lyle, "A Man Just Like Us," http://www.lurganbaptist.com/sermons/Elijah12.htm, accessed June 19, 2010.

is directed more to the office of pastor and the responsibility to the flock of the Lord. The shepherd provides guidance, comfort, discipline, feeding, and protection of the flock.[12]

Evangelism is a responsibility of the office of pastor. The apostle Paul encouraged Timothy to "do the work of an evangelist."[13] Every pastor does not possess the New Testament gift of evangelism, but he is to seek fulfillment of the Great Commission nonetheless. God's call to pastor brings with it the inherent calling to lead in the evangelism efforts of the local church. The church will not naturally be drawn to this element of kingdom service apart from being challenged through the example and teaching of the pastor.

The other areas of pastoral responsibility revolve around receiving and imparting God's vision, providing leadership in decision making, and providing an appropriate amount of administrative oversight in the operation of the church. These three areas are essential responsibilities. The New Testament gives ample indication that those who are pastor-elders must provide leadership and administrative guidance to the congregation. Does the pastor rule the church? No. Must the pastor lead the church he has been called to pastor? Emphatically, yes!

## Office of Deacon

The term *deacon* comes from the Greek word *diakonos* and is used 29 times in the New Testament.[14] Not every occurrence refers to the official office of deacon as is understood today. The term *diakonos* is commonly used as the ordinary word for "servant" in a context unrelated to church offices. Therefore, when you see

---

[12] Cowen, *Who Rules the Church?*, 38.

[13] 2 Timothy 4:5.

[14] The various forms of *diakonos* are used over 100 times in the New Testament. For more information concerning the use of *diakonos* throughout the New Testament, see J. S. Hammett, *Biblical Foundations for Baptist Churches: A Contemporary Ecclesiology* (Grand Rapids: Kregel, 2005), 191–92.

the term *servant* in the New Testament, you cannot automatically interpret it as the ordained or official office in the church.

An example of this would be the oft-quoted passage of Rom 16:1 wherein Phoebe is called a "deaconess" by some and used to support the ordination of women to the office of deacon. This verse declares Phoebe "a servant (*diakonos*) of the church which is at Cenchrea" (Rom 16:1 NASB) but does not stipulate her to be a deacon in the proper sense of the word as related to the church office.[15] To understand more fully the responsibilities of the office of deacon, a brief review of Acts 6:1–6 is in order. Admittedly a minority of Baptists do not see this to be the calling of the first deacons. I disagree and hold with a long history of theologians and pastors affirming this to be the establishment of the office of deacon in the New Testament church. As such, this passage gives us a strong indication as to the responsibilities that come with this office in the church.

Due to a disagreement within the local congregation, the apostles requested the selection of seven men "of good reputation, full of the Spirit and of wisdom" (Acts 6:3 NASB) to be given the task of soothing the conflict that fueled the disagreement. This is a powerful indication that a form of congregationalism was being practiced even in the earliest days of the New Testament church. The apostles did not personally appoint the seven; they requested the congregation make the selection. Ultimately there was unanimous approval within the "whole congregation" or multitude of believers in Jerusalem. Had God sought the creation of a hierarchical system of church government, would He not have had the apostles choose the men from among themselves and excluded the congregation from any decision-making responsibility?

The seven, chosen by the multitude, were called upon to be servant leaders. Their service reduced the administrative demands

---

[15] A more thorough discussion of deaconesses can be found in the chapter of this work dedicated to this subject.

of the apostles so they could devote themselves "to prayer and to the ministry of the Word." The seven were appointed to resolve conflict and restore harmony to the fellowship. They were called upon to serve the body of Christ by aiding in the restoration of the peace and unity of the church.

Contemporary deacons are likewise charged with the responsibility of being a peacemaker, an instrument of unity, a healer of broken relationships, and one who is a protector of the fellowship within the body of Christ. In purest form, all of these responsibilities incorporate servant leadership using preemptive measures for conflict resolution before irreparable damage occurs within the congregation. When this is understood correctly, it is seen that the primary role of deacon is not to "rule" the church or pastor but to aid the pastor by standing in the gap as a servant.

Theologian Wayne Grudem points out a commonly overlooked fact related to the issue of deacons who seek to rule the church. He states that it is "significant that nowhere in the New Testament do deacons have ruling authority of the church as the elders do, nor are deacons ever required to be able to teach Scripture or sound doctrine."[16] If this premise were held among all deacons, it would be easy to imagine a rapid reduction of conflict in many local churches.

The deacon is also called to evangelize the lost, care for widows and orphans, and assist in carrying out God's vision within the local congregation. All of these are important, but none grant undue authority to the office of deacon that should allow him to preclude himself to be anything other than a servant within the church.

## HISTORICAL BACKGROUND FOR OFFICES IN BAPTIST LIFE

The following is a short review of Baptist history to determine if a Baptist distinctive related to church government exists. Has

---

[16] Ibid., 920.

there been a normative pattern established in Baptist life that indicates a primary form of church government? When Baptist history is examined, it becomes difficult to dismiss a pattern of government that emerges and develops for centuries.

In 1609 John Smyth, a separatist exhausted with the Established Church, was living in Amsterdam when he penned the first Baptist confession in the English language. "A Short Confession of Faith in Twenty Articles" reflects a developing ecclesiology that is distinctively Baptist. Article 16 states that "the ministers of the church are, not only bishops ('Episcopos'), to whom the power is given of dispensing both the word and the sacraments, but also deacons, men and widows, who attend to the affairs of the poor and sick brethren." Although primitive in some respects, Smyth's confession reflects a commitment to congregationalism and appears to be directed toward a primary-elder form of church government.[17]

Thomas Helwys, a wealthy contemporary of John Smyth, in disagreement with Smyth's leadership wrote "A Declaration of Faith of English People Remaining at Amsterdam in Holland" in 1611. Articles 20, 21, and 22 relate to church government and declare two valid offices: elder and deacon. The declaration is unreserved in support of congregational polity. No reference is given to the number of elders or deacons to be selected; however, the selection process is to be entirely congregational under the leadership of God as outlined in Scripture.[18]

Article 36 of "The First London Confession" in 1644 states, "Every church has the power given them from Christ for their better well-being, to choose to themselves meet persons into the office of Pastors, teachers, elders, Deacons."[19] This particular confession was fine-tuned in 1646 and became known as "The Second

---

[17] W. L. Lumpkin, *Baptist Confessions of Faith,* rev. ed. (Valley Forge: Judson, 1969), 97–101.
[18] Ibid., 114–23.
[19] Ibid., 166.

London Confession." The revision removes ambiguity as related to those serving in official capacity as officers of the church. It established the two offices to be elders and deacons. Again a Baptist distinctive emerges as related to the two offices of the church and congregational rule. Early Baptists clearly sought autonomy from the Church of England and seemed determined to govern according to New Testament teaching.

"The Standard Confession of General Baptists" in 1660 also supported two offices to govern Christ's church. These are elders or pastors and deacons. Congregationalism is again evident as the church is to be governed under the rule of Christ by the people of Christ.

The first American confession was "The Philadelphia Confession of Faith" of 1742. This document was authorized for print by the Philadelphia Baptist Association on September 25, 1742, and subsequently printed by Benjamin Franklin. The confession supports two offices in the Lord's church: bishops or elders and deacons. The Baptist distinctive of congregational rule and two authorized and ordained offices became the accepted pattern for church activity in America.[20]

Article XIII of "The New Hampshire Confession of Faith" supports only two offices in the church: bishops or pastors and deacons. This document served as the foundational resource for the first Southern Baptist confession, the *Baptist Faith and Message* of 1925. Since that time the Southern Baptist confession has been revised on three different occasions with the final revision being approved by the Convention at its annual meeting on June 14, 2000. In relation to the church, Article VI of the *Baptist Faith and Message* declares, "Its scriptural officers are pastors and deacons."[21] All ambiguity is removed. This confession provides no room for debate as to how Southern Baptists in majority view

---

[20] Ibid., 347–53.

[21] The *Baptist Faith and Message*, adopted June 14, 2000, Article VI.

Baptist ecclesiology. Church government is distinctively congregational and supportive of only two ordained offices.

The conclusion can easily be drawn from this review of Baptist history that autonomous congregations played a distinct role in the development of ecclesiology in the Baptist tradition. There are no references to a hierarchical bishopric structure, nor is there evidence that a presbytery was involved in Baptist life to any large degree. A multitude of elders is a possibility, but with the interchangeable nature of the titles for this office, a profound case for the dominant governmental model during this period to be congregationalism is a reality.

Understanding this as such, a question is in need of reflection: After 400 years of Baptist tradition, why are some Baptist churches—particularly Southern Baptist churches—dismissing the Baptist distinctive of the two offices of pastor and deacon as less than best? Why depart from a method of church government that has weathered the storms of persecution, conflict, and challenge for four centuries of Baptist witness? Why depart from what is distinctively Baptist toward that which appears to be "un-Baptist" in origin and function? In other words, why change ecclesiology midstream? The following are possible reasons for this unnecessary departure.

From this pastor's perspective the Reformed movement in some Southern Baptist churches is one cause for this shifting ecclesiology. In recent history the Southern Baptist Convention has experienced a rise in the advocacy of Reformed theology.

As a Southern Baptist pastor, I certainly see a movement by "some" of our Baptist brethren away from primary-elder congregationalism toward a Reformed ecclesiology. Yet this trend in Baptist life seems rather small numerically in comparison to the convention as a whole. Most Southern Baptists remain unconvinced of a need to change traditional Baptist ecclesiology and view the modified form of Presbyterianism advocated by the Reformed camp as distinctly "un-Baptist."

Centralization of authority is another factor leading some to move away from traditional Baptist ecclesiology. Perhaps the adage that decisions are more easily made when less are involved is true, but that is not necessarily Baptist. Simply referring back to Acts 6 and the selection of the original seven deacons would support a decentralized authority in church government. The apostles wisely, and most assuredly under God's leadership, dispersed authority to the congregation rather than seeking to establish a hierarchical form of government wherein they would rule.

Protectionism by insecure Southern Baptist pastors has led some to attempt to insulate themselves from the congregation in matters of leadership. The enlisting of elders to assist in governing allows for a "buffer" to surround the pastor from hardship arising from leadership decisions. But is this necessary? The office of pastor sometimes requires the man of God to endure hardship if he is to lead effectively. Protectionism does little to strengthen his ability to lead.

Another factor leading to a shift in ecclesiology is the minority status this important topic receives in many, if not most, Southern Baptist pulpits in America. Sermons related to Baptist history and church government are virtually nonexistent. Pastors simply do not preach on how the church is to be operated and who is responsible within each local congregation. Perhaps it is to be assumed that these topics are understood by all and therefore need no attention. With an increasing number of individuals declaring the church to be moving in a postdenominational direction, additional understanding regarding Baptist distinctives could aid in alleviating the disengagement from our heritage.

The final possibility for a shift in ecclesiology centers upon relational tension between the two offices in the church. The remainder of this article will explore this issue and provide ideas for enhanced cooperation.

## THE RELATIONAL REALITY OF CHURCH
## OFFICES IN GOD'S SERVICE

John Bisagno was the pastor of First Baptist Church in Houston for 30 years. He has long been known as "the pastor's pastor" due to his love for his fellow servants seeking to do God's will. In his book *Inside Information* Bisagno reveals that during his ministry 95 percent of all calls received from fellow pastors seeking advice involved "conflict between pastors and deacons over authority and leadership in the church."[22] With such a staggering statistic one might question whether the two offices are on the same team or opposing sides.

Why does so much tension exist between these two groups of individuals? Again, God's system is not less than perfect; He did not create a flawed system of church government in spite of outward appearance. What are some reasons for conflict and tension between the two church offices?

Referring back to the introduction of this article, it is apparent that power struggles wreak havoc on local congregations far too often. With this particular deacon becoming increasingly frustrated because I sought God's leadership above his, I realized as pastor that the situation must be dealt with to protect the fellowship of the church. Upon advice from a longtime pastor and trusted mentor, the decision had to be made as to who was going to lead the church: the deacon or God? It was nonsensical for me to imagine any structure where God would not be allowed to lead His church. To this end, on a Wednesday night the church gathered and handled the situation related to this power struggle in a manner conducive to unity within the body. God's people were thankful for my leadership to protect the fellowship at all costs. Although it was unnecessary to name specific names during this gathering, the deacon who sought to retain authority understood

---

[22] J. R. Bisagno, *Inside Information* (Longwood, FL: Xulon Press, 2008), 25.

that his powerful antics were unacceptable by the congregation. The church had spoken.

Power plays of this type come in all size churches. Upon arrival at my current church, I found a similar situation where a deacon chaired both the finance and personnel committees simultaneously. This was in direct violation of the bylaws of the congregation, but nothing had been done to address the matter. Under God's leadership and in His timing, this power struggle was dealt with, and others were selected to serve in these positions. Again, God's grace and wisdom were sufficient to lead me through a difficult time even when the power-hungry deacon sought intentionally to divide the church over denominational politics. Again the church as a congregation had spoken.

Personal agendas are also conducive to conflict and tension between the two offices. I was not at my current church long when I received an invitation to lunch from a prominent man in the city who was also a church member. He had tread in some lofty Baptist circles in his life and yet was not a deacon. With me being his new pastor, he thought this apparent oversight might be rectified. As we got to know each other over a sandwich, he revealed the agenda for the meeting. Boldly and without hindrance, he requested he be made a deacon and asked me to see if I could take care of that situation. Apart from nearly choking on my food, I made a mental note of caution. This man sought the prominence of the office of deacon not for service sake but for appearance. His motives were incorrect, and his agenda was personal advancement.

There is only one agenda in the church our Lord finds acceptable—His. If God wanted His servants to "run" the church, He would have been far more explicit about responsibilities in this area. That does not dismiss a pastor's necessity for providing godly leadership. The pastor-leader must spend time before the Lord in prayer to determine the direction for the local congregation. Nowhere in Scripture do I find a vision committee established to hear from God. God expects His called servants to receive the vision from Him and then to impart that vision to the people under his charge. God provides a vision through His undershepherd. He can certainly speak to others in the congregation and use them to aid in understanding the fullness of the vision, but God communicates vision to His pastor first. Again, prayer and diligent study of Scripture are keys to hearing God's voice of leadership regarding vision.

Blurred vision contributes to conflict and tension when the deacon body and the pastor are not on the same page as to the direction of the church. Proverbs 19:18 reveals what occurs when the congregation cannot see God at work as the people "are unrestrained." This leads to the application of worldly wisdom and practice in the operation of God's church.

Other problems emerge when communication collapses between the offices. Tension is minimized when communication is clear and all involved know what is transpiring. The wise pastor will be forthright with deacon leadership to ensure that a lack of communication does not evolve into conflict and crisis.

Integrity failures of both offices lead to conflict and tension. When trust becomes a factor, problems in the fellowship are the natural outcome. Integrity failures, regardless of size, result in a diminished ability to lead.

I have labeled the final cause for tension and conflict between the offices as ministry malfunctions. Every church that strives to advance the kingdom with passion faces ministry malfunctions at certain times. And yet, sometimes, in ministry what was thought would go well seems to malfunction and is less than effective. That which was prayed and planned for just does not work out as expected. Some seek to place blame when this occurs—creating tension that is oftentimes unnecessary. Grace should be imparted by all as a new direction from God is sought on how ministry effectiveness can be enhanced.

## STEPS TOWARD ENHANCED COOPERATION
## BETWEEN CHURCH OFFICES

With the stories shared above that reveal times of conflict between the two offices in the church, you may be thinking, *But pastor, I thought we were all on the same team.* As believers in Christ, we certainly are supposed to be. A natural cooperation between the two offices should be the norm rather than the unnatural conflict that often surfaces. When the pastor and deacon body work in unison for the advancement of the kingdom, God is honored and His hand of blessing is apparent through unity, fellowship, and especially through baptisms. His will is accomplished, and the church is advanced forcefully against the darkness of evil. Bearing this in mind, I conclude by submitting the following steps toward an enhanced cooperation of the two offices for kingdom advancement purposes.

*1. An emphasis on increasing the biblical understanding of the roles and responsibilities of the two offices should be applied.* Rarely does change occur overnight in church work. Patterns of confusion and conflict between pastors and deacons have existed for centuries. But in a congregational environment, the more the church understands what the Bible teaches related to the two offices the better the understanding of each role and function. Members who understand the pastor to be the undershepherd of the local church, answerable to Christ first and foremost, are more likely to follow his leadership when he serves in a trustworthy manner. His work is much more enjoyable, and the congregation receives the blessing of God when they honor their pastor. W. A. Criswell strongly advocated this:

> Any church that loves and honors its pastor, whatever its size, is a wonderful church. The obverse of that is also true. Any church that looks upon its pastor as a hireling

is a weak and unblessed church. There is no exception to that in the ecclesiastical world.[23]

When cooperation and honor exist in the congregation for their pastor, Heb 13:17 becomes a living truth for the local body of Christ. This verse encourages the congregation to "obey your leaders and submit to them, for they keep watch over your souls as those who will give an account. *In order that they may do* this with joy and not *groaning*, for this would be unprofitable for you" (NASB, emphasis mine).

Deacons who understand their primary roles as peacemaker and servant leader will also honor God as they humble themselves to the task to which they have been ordained. Their responsibility is immense as they assist in the ministry endeavors of the local body of Christ through service and self-denial. When they embrace the biblical role to which they have been selected, the ongoing strength and viability of the local church is bolstered. The kingdom of God will be advanced in the local community through the witness of a church determined to follow the biblical mandate of the two church offices.

*2. The use of wise participatory leadership should be embraced.* With primary-elder congregationalism being the Baptist distinctive promoted in this paper, I wish for no person to conclude falsely that I support autocratic rule with little or no lay participation. The wise pastor will use every opportunity available for congregational participation in leadership in the church. Many lay leaders desire God's kingdom to move forward as strongly as the pastor. These men and women must be used for efficacy in ministry to result.

There are two times when wise participatory leadership is particularly essential. First, when the new pastor arrives at an old, established Baptist church, many will view him as brilliant if he

---

[23] Criswell, *Great Doctrines of the Bible,* 101.

immediately seeks participation in leadership decisions. To fail to do so in some churches will almost automatically ensure a brief tenure in that pulpit. Second, incorporating the wisdom of trusted deacons who have a strong love for Jesus and His church is always a good idea when decisions of consequence affecting the entire church must be made. This does not negate the pastor's leadership but reveals his proficiency in this area. I hold to the belief that if I cannot lead the deacons to see God's vision unfolding, I would be unwise to attempt to convince the church of the same without their support. The real world of church service in many locations demands a similar methodology be employed.

Some would deem this shared responsibility of leadership to be a valid reason for the use of a plural-elder form of church government as the use of wise participatory leadership. Perhaps, but the absolute necessity for pastoral leadership in the congregation remains. Patterson responds to this attempt at justification for plural-elder leadership by looking back in time to a noted pastor-elder: "A century and a half ago Spurgeon, strongly influenced by Reformed soteriology, had nevertheless opted for the pattern of single pastor-leader, although other elders served with him. They were not equal in anyone's estimation."[24]

Those called to pastor must lead their church. They are wise to include a variety of people, certainly some holding the office of deacon, to assist in leadership. This can be accomplished in numerous ways for effectiveness. But it must be stressed that if the pastor will not lead, his abdication places the church in a dangerous and precarious position. He is God's chosen leader for the congregation.

3. *Cooperation between the two church offices must be enhanced through effective communication.* Communication is a primary factor in all quality relationships. To enhance the relationship between the pastor and deacons, effort must be expended to

---

[24] Cowan, *Who Runs the Church?*, 240.

ensure communication breakdowns do not occur. Many churches accomplish this through a monthly deacons' meeting where information is shared and discussed. In my current ministry, however, monthly deacons' meetings are not the norm. When it became apparent that we were experiencing a lack of communication between deacons and myself, I instituted a monthly Pastor-Deacon Roundtable. The singular purpose of this gathering is to ensure effective communication. It requires little preparation and yet provides large dividends as I reiterate the teamwork required for success to be realized.

4. *Sincere integrity and accountability must be upheld by all who serve in a church office.* In today's world authority and the ability to lead are easily lost. Issues of failed integrity are far too common in both offices in the church. Dreadful stories make the headlines in local newspapers of those in church service falling to temptation. The office of pastor has more profile than deacon, and it may seem failures in this office occur more frequently than among deacons. This is simply not true but only a by-product of media sensationalism. Being voted on by a congregation does not make the pastor the leader of the church. The right to lead in the Lord's church is earned over time but lost in a heartbeat! Conscious efforts regarding accountability among all in church leadership will aid in reducing the failures for both. Akin correctly provides:

> Calling and following God-called leaders does not mean there is to be no accountability. There is accountability both to God and to the congregation. There also needs to be some form of close or "inner circle" accountability as well. Sexual scandal has ravaged the body of Christ in recent decades, and the fallout has been horrific. Almost without exception those who have fallen admitted that they had neglected their daily walk with Christ through the regular reading of His Word, lost intimacy with their

mate, and failed to establish real and genuine accountability with men who could look them in the face and ask the hard questions and demand answers.[25]

*5. God's leaders must possess a surrendered and humble attitude toward kingdom service.* God blesses humility in service and disdains pride. Leaders who embrace the biblical definition of the roles and responsibilities of the church offices and who surrender their lives to lead accordingly are most effective. This humility and surrender stands against personal power plays and agendas for those in church leadership. The effective church leader lives a surrendered life of humility and leads accordingly.

*6. A fresh encounter with the joy of Christ-focused service in the church.* Everyone in church leadership needs a daily reminder that Jesus is looking for servants who care more about His desires and agenda than their own. Pastors called to lead a local congregation grow weary due to the stress and pressures faced in the daily grind of ministry. Deacons ordained to serve in the church experience their greatest frustrations when operating outside of their office responsibilities. Conflict is greatest when the servants in the two offices take their eyes off of Jesus Christ. Therefore, we all need a fresh encounter of the joy of Christ-focused service at times. Each of us needs to be reminded that ministry is a daily process of stooping low and humbly picking up that instrument of death, the cross, and carrying it for Christ's sake. In Matt 16:24, Jesus admonished all who come after Him to "deny himself, and take up his cross and follow Me" (NASB). Nothing can beat the daily refocusing of our lives of service for Jesus' glory for increasing cooperation between the two church offices as we bend our backs in service to our Lord.

---

[25] Brand and Norman, eds., *Perspectives on Church Government,* 71.

# 8

# The Offices and Women:
# Can Women Be Pastors?
# or Deacons?

*Thomas White with Joy White*

Perhaps the most controversial topic in the *Baptist Faith and Message* 2000 states, "Its (the church's) scriptural officers are pastors and deacons. While both men and women are gifted for service in the church, the office of pastor is *limited to men* as qualified by Scripture."[1] Two particular items from this statement deserve immediate attention. First, the statement limits the office of pastor to men. Second, the confession makes no claim on the office of deacon. From this the implication may be drawn that the majority of Southern Baptists believe Scripture prohibits women from serving as pastors while disagreement remains concerning women deacons. This chapter will first discuss the Baptist belief that women should not serve as pastors and then discuss both sides of the issue as to whether women should serve as deacons. On the first matter there is wide consensus, and on the second this chapter will advocate the majority position recognizing that some strong conservatives continue to hold dissenting views.

---

[1] *Baptist Faith and Message* 2000 Article VI, http://www.sbc.net/bfm/bfm2000 .asp#vi, accessed May 9, 2009. Emphasis added.

Although the confession of faith does not elaborate on its limitation of the office of pastor to men, Malcolm Yarnell writes:

> In the late twentieth century, some Southern Baptists also considered the novel idea of ordaining female pastors. Although the concept was culturally vogue, it contradicts biblical precedent regarding order in creation and the church, and is thus firmly denied in our confession (1 Timothy 2:11–15; 1 Corinthians 14:34–35).[2]

In this particular article, the confession lists three passages which have implications for women pastors: 1 Tim 3:1–15; Eph 5:22–32; and 1 Tim 2:9–14. This chapter will be limited to a discussion of these three passages and their implications as the scope of this book has limited itself to the Southern Baptist Convention's article on the church contained in the 2000 *Baptist Faith and Message*. Additionally, space prohibits a thorough discussion, which would take a book dedicated to the complementarian and egalitarian views on gender roles.[3]

## 1 TIMOTHY 3:1–15

No sensible human questions whether women have the ability to teach. Beyond the experience of having mothers and

---

[2] M. B. Yarnell III, "Article VI: The Church," in *Baptist Faith and Message 2000: Critical Issues in America's Largest Protestant Denomination,* ed. D. K. Blount and J. Wooddell (Lanham, MD: Rowman & Littlefield, 2007), 63.

[3] For the complementarian position which believes that men and women are equal but God has ordained distinct roles from creation, consult the following: S. B. Clark, *Man and Woman in Christ: An Examination of the Roles of Men and Women in Light of Scripture and the Social Sciences* (Ann Arbor: Servant Books, 1980); A. J. Köstenberger and T. R. Schreiner, eds., *Women in the Church* (Grand Rapids: Baker, 2005); J. Piper and W. Grudem, eds., *Recovering Biblical Manhood and Womanhood* (Wheaton: Crossway, 2006); and W. Grudem, *Evangelical Feminism and Biblical Truth* (Colorado Springs: Multnomah, 2004). For the egalitarian position, which believes that men and women are equal with no distinctions in roles, consult: R. W. Pierce and R. M. Groothuis, eds., *Discovering Biblical Equality* (Downers Grove: InterVarsity, 2004), and G. Bilezikian, *Beyond Sex Roles: What the Bible Says About a Woman's Place in Church and Family* (Grand Rapids: Baker, 2006).

schoolteachers from whom we have benefited, Scripture contains clear references to the teaching role of Pricilla (Acts 18:26) and Lois and Eunice (2 Tim 1:5; 3:14).[4] Additionally explicit passages such as Titus 2 instruct older women to teach younger women, and the role of women in public prayer is mentioned in 1 Cor 11:2–16. We must, as the Scripture does, hold a high regard for the ability and ministry of women teachers.

The Bible also provides clear prohibitions against women teaching or having authority over men. Scripture contains no example of a woman teaching an assembled group in public; it prohibits the practice. Some may think Deborah contradicts the previous statement; however, Judg 4:5 states that she sat under a tree while people came to her for judgment. Barak led the armies into battle—not Deborah.[5] This private instruction parallels Priscilla's private instruction in the New Testament. Beyond the fact that the Bible contains no example, there are clear and implicit prohibitions against such action. One implied prohibition is found in the qualifications for a pastor or elder in 1 Timothy 3.

First Timothy 3 provides many qualifications for the role of pastor. For the current discussion, the requirement to be a "husband of one wife," and the requirement for one who "rules his own house well" provide an implied restriction from women serving as pastors. It goes without saying that a woman could not be the "husband" of one wife. While Paul's statement literally reads, "a one-woman kind of man,"[6] it does not provide a reciprocal statement for a one-man kind of woman. The implication is that only men should serve in the office of pastor.[7]

---

[4] In Acts 18:26, the word translated as "explained" is plural indicating that both Aquila and Priscilla explained to Apollos more accurately the way of the Lord.

[5] Gilbert Bilezikian goes so far as to refer to Deborah as a "one-person supreme court." See Bilezikian, *Beyond Sex Roles*, 53. For more information on Deborah, see Grudem, *Evangelical Feminism and Biblical Truth*, 82, 131–36.

[6] J. MacArthur, *First Timothy* (Chicago: Moody, 1995), 104.

[7] W. Grudem states, "In fact, the Greek term here, *aner*, can mean either 'man' or 'husband,' but with either meaning it is the Greek term that specifically designates

In addition, the Bible gives clear indication that males should be leaders in the home. Peter writes in 1 Pet 3:1–7, "Wives, likewise, be submissive to your own husbands" (NKJV). Paul writes in Eph 5:22–24, "Wives, submit to your own husbands, as to the Lord. For the husband is head of the wife, as also Christ is head of the church; and He is the Savior of the body. Therefore, just as the church is subject to Christ, so let the wives be to their own husbands in everything" (NASB). A wife cannot be the ruler of her own home while following the biblical mandate to submit to the loving leadership of her husband. Because other passages indicate female submission to the headship of the husband, a woman cannot biblically rule her house well.[8] This requirement for the office of pastor/elder restricts the office to men.

One might argue that this prohibition was cultural and that in Paul's time a woman pastor would have been a problem whereas modern society has come to accept such practices and this explains the lack of a similar statement for women.[9] Many reject women preachers only because they have never seen one. As the rise of television and feminism erodes this pragmatic restriction, complementarian arguments must be founded firmly on Scripture and not experience. Public acceptance of a changing role does not make the practice endorsable. For example, modern culture accepts and in many cases encourages homosexuality, yet a biblical worldview holds homosexuality as sin. As we will discuss later, Paul appeals in multiple locations to the created order before the fall when establishing guidelines for gender. His appeal to creation places the commands in a perfect prefallen world thus providing timeless instruction. So while this implied prohibition may

---

a male human being. This means elders had to be men." See *Evangelical Feminism and Biblical Truth*, 80.

[8] It is also worthy of notation that men are never commanded to be submissive to their wives.

[9] C. C. Kroeger and M. J. Evans, eds., *The IVP Women's Bible Commentary* (Downers Grove: InterVarsity, 2002), 742 states, "There is enough cultural bias in the list of qualifications that due caution is needed."

not appeal to creation, corresponding New Testament teaching on gender roles rises above culture establishing timeless principles for order in the house of God.

Another objection may arise that such a strict interpretation could rule out anyone not married or who did not have children from serving as a pastor.[10] This is not, however, the intent of these guidelines. If such were the case, then Paul would disqualify both Jesus and himself. The wording means that a church leader should be a one-woman kind of man. A single man planning and preparing well to be the spiritual leader of the helpmate that God may provide fulfills the qualification of a one-woman kind of man. Without a similar statement for women, the implied prohibition still stands. Similarly, a man may develop characteristics of ruling his own house well no matter the size of the house. Family devotions, spiritual leadership, and prayer may all occur in a household with or without children. Other biblical passages indicate that the male bears the responsibility for leading in the home which prohibits a female from "ruling her house well" in the biblical sense of the task.[11]

A final objection may be that a more-talented and better-equipped female is preferable to a less-talented male pastor. First, such a statement indicates the consumer and entertainment-driven nature of our culture that desires a more-talented communicator and more-dynamic personality. Such consumerism undermines the role of the Holy Spirit and fails to consider that it is God's Word which will not return void and not the words of an entertaining communicator. Second, biblically speaking a female cannot be better equipped than a male for the role of pastor. One of the qualifications for being a pastor is being male. You may be comparing two equally disqualified candidates, but unless a person fits all the qualifications, he should not serve as pastor.

---

[10] See Kroeger and Evans, *The IVP Women's Bible Commentary*, 742.
[11] Examples of such passages are Ephesians 5 and 1 Peter 3.

## EPHESIANS 5:22–32

*Wives, submit to your own husbands as to the Lord, for the husband is the head of the wife as also Christ is the head of the church. He is the Savior of the body. Now as the church submits to Christ, so wives are to submit to their husbands in everything. Husbands, love your wives, just as Christ loved the church and gave Himself for her to make her holy, cleansing her in the washing of water by the word. He did this to present the church to Himself in splendor, without spot or wrinkle or any such thing, but holy and blameless. In the same way, husbands should love their wives as their own bodies. He who loves his wife loves himself. For no one ever hates his own flesh, but provides and cares for it, just as Christ does for the church, since we are members of His body. For this reason a man will leave his father and mother and be joined to his wife, and the two will become one flesh. This mystery is profound, but I am talking about Christ and the church. (HCSB)*

The *Baptist Faith and Message* quotes this passage as one of the supporting passages for the article on the church. While this article nowhere prohibits women from teaching men, the article does provide an important biblical foundation for gender role distinctions. While some would argue that Eph 5:21 provides the lens through which the subsequent verses must be seen, this viewpoint does not withstand scrutiny. Ephesians 5:21 states, "Submitting to one another in the fear of God" (NKJV). This verse provides the transition to the entire household code that continues into chapter 6. Verse 21 cannot be interpreted in a way that undoes the instruction for wives to submit to their own husbands by stating that husbands must also submit to wives.[12] If such were the case, then

---

[12] Some have argued the case for mutual submission. See I. H. Marshall, "Mutual Love and Submission in Marriage," in *Discovering Biblical Equality*, 186–204.

Ephesians 6 would indicate that parents should submit to children and owners to slaves.[13] The verb *hupotassō* means a "submission in the sense of voluntary yielding in love."[14] The motivation for submission is fear or reverence for God just as Jesus humbled Himself in voluntary submission to the point of death on a cross (Philippians 2). This passage mentions specific examples where submission is needed. Slaves submit to owners, children submit to parents, wives submit to husbands, and the church submits to Christ.

The command for a wife to submit to her husband rules her out from serving as a pastor. A wife could not submit to her husband at home while leading him at church, and the verse states that the wife must submit to her husband "in everything." In addition, the pattern of male leadership at home carries over into the church when men properly fulfill their responsibility as spiritual leaders. In fact, the requirements on men are much greater in this passage than those on women.

How can any man truly love his wife as Christ loved the church? Some may argue that Christlike love would require a love so great that it results in mutual submission. To the contrary, Christ in laying down His life for the church held an exclusive truth and exclusive salvation. Jesus did not submit to the desires of the church but lead her by demonstrating loving leadership, demanding holiness and not mutual submissiveness. The church must follow her leader—Jesus Christ.

Toward the end of this passage, the recurring practice of connecting gender roles to creation occurs. Paul quotes Gen 2:24 saying, "For this reason a man will leave his father and mother and be joined to his wife, and the two will become one flesh." Within the comparison of the marriage relationship and Christ's connection to the church, Paul refers back to the original purpose of marriage

---

[13] G. W. Knight III, "Husbands and Wives as Analogues of Christ and the Church," in *Biblical Manhood and Womanhood*, 168.

[14] BDAG, 1042, section 1b.β.

in the created order. "Back when God was planning what marriage would be like, He planned it for this great purpose: it would give a beautiful earthly picture of the relationship that would someday come about between Christ and His church."[15] Whenever one distorts the roles in marriage, or the roles in the church, one distorts the picture of the gospel.

### 1 TIMOTHY 2:9–14

*Also, the women are to dress themselves in modest clothing, with decency and good sense; not with elaborate hairstyles, gold, pearls, or expensive apparel, but with good works, as is proper for women who affirm that they worship God. A woman should learn in silence with full submission. I do not allow a woman to teach or to have authority over a man; instead, she is to be silent. For Adam was created first, then Eve. And Adam was not deceived, but the woman was deceived and transgressed. (HCSB)*

First Timothy 2 contains the most explicit prohibition against women serving as pastors of a local church.[16] During the meetings of the committee appointed to present a revision of the 1963 *Baptist Faith and Message*, at least one person argued to keep the biblical wording rather than stating "the office of pastor is limited to men as qualified by Scripture."[17] Because all churches do not

---

[15] Knight, "Husbands and Wives," 175.

[16] For a complete treatment, see Köstenberger and Schreiner, *Women in the Church*; S. B. Clark, *Man and Woman in Christ*, 191–208; or D. Moo, "What Does It Mean Not to Teach or Have Authority over Men?: 1 Timothy 2:11–15," in *Recovering Biblical Manhood and Womanhood*, 184, where he identifies six items for discussion in this passage. This passage represents one of three additional passages listed in the *Baptist Faith and Message* revision from 1963 to 2000 (Heb 11:39–40 and Revelation 2–3 are the other passages). Thus 1 Timothy 2 provides the primary basis for restricting the office of pastor to men. See http://www.sbc.net/bfm/bfmcomparison .asp, accessed June 16, 2009.

[17] http://www.sbc.net/bfm/bfm2000.asp#vi, accessed June 16, 2009. I have

extend this biblical prohibition to women teaching men in Sunday school classes or having authority through various denominational roles, the convention confession only restricts females from the office of pastor.

The local church provides the context of the passage. Just prior, Paul discusses the necessity of fighting the good fight against those teaching heresy in the church—specifically two men named Hymenaeus and Alexander. Following the prohibition, in chapter 3, Paul discusses the qualification for the officers of a church concluding with verse 15 stating, "You may know how you ought to behave in the household of God, which is the church of the living God." Thus, the discussion of women teaching men finds itself bracketed by ecclesiastical instruction.[18] The immediately preceding verse 10 gives instruction for women to pursue good works. They must learn in quietness and submission. Dorothy Patterson states, "The call for 'quietness' (sometimes translated 'silence') is a concrete example and a consistent expression of the overarching principle of submission."[19] The adjoining statement in verse 12 then prohibits women from certain good works—namely teaching or having authority over men. With the setting in a church context, no prohibition exists against learning algebra from a female teacher or against women sharing the gospel in personal evangelism, individual instruction, or women teaching other women and children.

The debated prohibition states, "I do not allow a woman to teach or to have authority over a man." With the context established, this chapter will now overview the important points noting some areas of disagreement.

Paul uses the word *didaskein*, which in the New Testament

---

confirmed this through personal interviews before the meeting of the Southern Baptist Convention in 2000.

[18] Grudem concurs. See *Evangelical Feminism and Biblical Truth*, 65.

[19] D. K. Patterson, "What Should a Woman Do in the Church?" in *Women in the Church*, ed. A. Köstenberger and T. Schreiner, 161.

generally means "the careful transmission of the tradition concerning Jesus Christ and the authoritative proclamation of God's will to believers in light of that tradition."[20] This use provides further evidence alongside the context limiting the restriction to teaching in an ecclesiastical context. Paul also combines teaching with authority (*authentein*), which has been translated as "having or exercising authority."[21] The authority under consideration would not be ultimate authority as God and the Scriptures retain ultimate authority. Neither is the issue usurping the authority of the husband, as this prohibition stands open-ended to authority over any man. The Bible prohibits placing a woman in spiritual leadership over a man. This position may not necessarily have teaching responsibilities, but the position would be in an ecclesiastical context.[22]

Some believe that a woman may teach men under the authority of the senior pastor. In academic circles, both complementarians and egalitarians dislike this practice. Complementarians believe it is functional egalitarianism to have women teaching assembled church groups with the disclaimer that it is under the authority of the pastor. This is really no different from a woman teaching without the approval of the pastor.

Egalitarians believe that women can teach men and do not like them doing so under the authority of the pastor. These situations occur practically in a church setting where the pastor grants authority to a woman to teach or have authority over men under his leadership. Multiple problems exist in these cases. First, it

---

[20] Moo, "What Does It Mean?" 185.

[21] The NKJV uses the word "exercising" while the NIV uses the word "have." See A. Köstenberger, "Syntactical Background Studies to 1 Timothy 2:12 in the New Testament and Extra-Biblical Greek Literature," http://www.cbmw.org/images/articles_pdf/kostenberger_andreas/syntactical1tim2_12.pdf, 262, accessed June 25, 2009.

[22] For information on how some have applied this, consult https://www.cbmw.org/Journal/Vol-12–No-2/JBMW-Forum-Q-and-A-on-Women-Teaching-Mixed-Gender-Sunday-School, accessed September 9, 2009, or the CBMW discussion of 50 Crucial Questions found here https://www.cbmw.org/Online-Books/Fifty-Crucial-Questions/Fifty-Crucial-Questions, accessed September 9, 2009.

places the woman in a role contrary to Scripture. Second, the Bible never grants anyone the authority to set aside commands, and by doing so, the pastor inadvertently sets himself up as the judge over God's revealed Word. Third, Paul does not state that teaching is prohibited "unless she is under the authority of the elders."[23]

No pastor or husband can grant a woman permission to teach or have authority over men since the Scripture has prohibited the action. This would be similar to a pastor's setting aside biblical restrictions against fornication and encouraging church members to try out married life without the commitment. It would be similar to a pastor's granting permission to members not to witness just because they are not very effective. While no pastor would grant permission for sins of omission or commission, somehow the sin of granting women "permission" to teach or have authority over men has become commonplace.

Philip Payne has questioned whether teaching and having authority are one or two commands, contending that they are identical in nature.[24] This interpretation attempts to blur the issue by stating that only "authoritative teaching" is prohibited. Douglas Moo has the evidence on his side when he responds that the connecting word *oude* joins closely related but not identical words. Thus, while relation exists between teaching and having authority, the terms are not identical.[25]

Linda Belleville argues that Paul only planned to correct women intending to dominate men. She writes:

---

[23] For more information on this topic, see Grudem, *Evangelical Feminism and Biblical Truth*, 381–83.

[24] Moo and Payne have discussed the meaning of this word in multiple exchanges. See Payne, "Libertarian Women at Ephesus: A Response to Douglas J. Moo's Article '1 Timothy 2:11–15: Meaning and Significance,'" *Trinity Journal* (1981): 169–170; Moo responded with "The Interpretation of 1 Timothy 2:11–15: A Rejoinder," *Trinity Journal 2* (1981): 198–99; Payne responded, "The Interpretation of 1 Timothy 2:11–15: A Surrejoinder" (unpublished paper that is included in "What Does the Scripture Teach About the Ordination of Women?").

[25] Moo, "What Does It Mean?" 187 n 20.

Paul aims to correct inappropriate behavior on the part of both men and women. . . . "Let a woman learn in a quiet and submissive fashion. I do not, however, permit her to teach with the intent to dominate a man. She must be gentle in her demeanor." Paul would then be prohibiting teaching that tries to get the upper hand—not teaching per se.[26]

While this interpretation fits the agenda of justifying women's teaching, the linguistic evidence does not support the theory.

Köstenberger correctly argues that the context affirms the translation of *authentein* as "have authority" and not "to domineer."[27] After studying the biblical and secular uses, he argues that *oude* never joins opposing terms. The clear translation of "teaching" as positive requires the positive word "authority" rather than "domineer" according to the rules of Greek grammar. Thus, other ecclesiastical tasks that carry authority over men with or without teaching would be prohibited. This might exclude some deacon bodies that serve in an authoritarian manner rather than a servant position. There will be more discussion on deacons to follow, for now the clear teaching of this verse prohibits women from teaching or having authority over men in an ecclesiastical context.

The question arises as to whether this prohibition was cultural or timeless.[28] Perhaps anticipating the question, Paul transcends

---

[26] L. Belleville, "Teaching and Usurping Authority 1 Timothy 2:11–15," in *Discovering Biblical Equality,* 223. G. Fee writes, "The word translated authority, which occurs only here in the NT, has the connotation 'to domineer.' In context it probably reflects again on the role the women were playing in advancing the errors—or speculations—of the false teachers and therefore is to be understood very closely with the prohibition against teaching." See G. Fee, *1 and 2 Timothy, Titus,* New International Biblical Commentary (Peabody, Mass: Hendrickson, 1988), 73.

[27] A. Köstenberger, "A Complex Sentence Structure in 1 Timothy 2:12," in *Women in the Church: A Fresh Analysis of 1 Timothy 2:9–15,* ed. A. Köstenberger, T. Schreiner, and H. S. Baldwin (Grand Rapids: Baker 1995), 81–103. See also Grudem, who agrees with Köstenberger's research, *Evangelical Feminism and Biblical Truth,* 314.

[28] Belleville, "Teaching and Usurping Authority," 219.

culture with his teaching by appealing to the created order going back before the fall to establish gender distinctions. Moo writes, "For by rooting these prohibitions in the circumstances of creation rather than in the circumstances of the fall, Paul shows that he does not consider these restrictions to be the product of the curse and presumably, therefore, to be phased out by redemption."[29] In other words, gender roles were a part of the prefallen, perfect world and a part of God's plan from the beginning.

Paul states, "For Adam was created first, then Eve. And Adam was not deceived, but the woman was deceived and transgressed." In this statement two slightly different but not mutually exclusive reasons explain why Paul appealed to creation. The first reason is the order of creation. Adam was created first, and Eve was created to be his helper. Douglas Moo and others claim that the problem was with role reversal. Eve took an improper role of leadership rather than helping. The serpent deceived her. Then Adam, not deceived, chose to disobey God and to follow the woman committing the sin of idolatry among other sins.[30]

Some contend that arguing for different roles based on the order of creation would result in a system where the animals ruled over man. They fail to acknowledge that man was given dominion over the garden and all that was in it.[31] Furthermore, Adam's priority among humans comes as the first created human being. Douglas Moo says it this way:

> Paul emphasizes that man was created "first, then" Eve; the temporal sequence is strongly marked (*protos*, "first," and *eita*, "then"). What is the point of this statement? Both the logic of this passage and the parallel in 1 Cor 11:3–10

---

[29] Moo, "What Does It Mean?" 190 n 33.

[30] For a more detailed discussion, see T. R. Schreiner, "An Interpretation of 1 Timothy 2:9–15: A Dialogue with Scholarship," in *Women in the Church*, 140–46; D. Doriani, "A History of the Interpretation of 1 Timothy 2," in *Women in the Church*, 213–67; and Moo, " What Does It Mean?"

[31] Grudem discusses this. See *Evangelical Feminism and Biblical Truth*, 68.

make this clear: for Paul, the man's priority in the order of creation is indicative of the headship that man is to have over woman.[32]

A second explanation for appealing to creation is that Adam was not deceived but the woman was deceived. Grudem writes, "Paul is saying something about the nature of men and women as God created them."[33] Schreiner supports this position stating:

> Satan approached the woman first not only because of the order of creation but also because of the different inclinations present in Adam and Eve. Generally speaking women are more relational and nurturing and men are more given to rational analysis and objectivity.[34]

While 1 Timothy 2 clearly prohibits women from teaching or having authority over a man, there are many important biblical functions that women should do. One that often raises questions is the writing of books and commentaries. To that, Wayne Grudem has a clarifying answer:

> Another modern parallel to the private conversation between Priscilla and Aquilla and Apollos would be *the writing of books on the Bible and theology by women.* When I read a Bible commentary written by a woman, for example, it is as if the author were talking privately to me, explaining her interpretation of the Bible, much as Priscilla talked to Apollos in Acts 18:26.[35]

Grudem provides a helpful discussion of various tasks in the

---

[32] Moo, "What Does It Mean?" 190.

[33] Grudem, *Evangelical Feminism and Biblical Truth*, 70; Grudem claims this is the most common position citing Dorian, "A History of Interpretation of 1 Timothy 2," 213–68.

[34] Schreiner, "Interpretation of 1 Timothy 2:9–15," in *Women in the Church,* 145–46.

[35] Grudem, *Evangelical Feminism and Biblical Truth,* 75.

local church and where they fall in terms of teaching and having authority.[36] Moo offers a good closing summary:

> In light of these considerations, we argue that the teaching prohibited to women here includes what we would call preaching . . . and the teaching of Bible and doctrine in the church, in colleges, and in seminaries. Other activities—leading Bible studies, for instance—may be included, depending on how they are done. Still others—evangelistic witnessing, counseling, teaching subjects other than Bible or doctrine—are not, in our opinion, teaching in the sense Paul intends here.[37]

## WHAT ABOUT WOMEN DEACONS?

While the majority of Baptist churches have refrained from having women deacons or deaconesses, a minority opinion throughout American Baptist history has advocated this view.[38] Some of these churches allowed deaconesses in support of the modern feminist movement while others defended this as a scriptural position.[39] The discussion has once again risen to prominence with conservative churches such as Capitol Hill Baptist Church supporting the practice with biblical argumentation. Honestly, good arguments exist on both sides of this debate, but more evidence exists against women deacons or deaconesses. This section will discuss the arguments on both sides demonstrating why churches should avoid the practice of deaconesses. In order to accomplish this purpose,

---

[36] For a discussion of what women should do in the church, consult Grudem, *Evangelical Feminism and Biblical Truth*, 84–101.

[37] Moo, "What Does It Mean?" 186.

[38] For more on the historical discussion among Baptists, one may critically consult C. W. Deweese, *Women Deacons and Deaconesses: 400 Years of Baptist Service* (Macon: Mercer, 2005).

[39] For example, R. B. C. Howell who served as the second president of the Southern Baptist Convention and pastor of the First Baptist Church of Nashville supported deaconesses. R. B. C. Howell, *The Deaconship: Its Nature, Qualifications, Relations, and Duties* (Philadelphia: Judson, 1946).

several questions must be answered. Were the first deacons instituted in Acts 6? Does 1 Tim 3:11 refer to deaconesses, deacons' assistants, or wives of deacons? Was Phoebe a deaconess?

## WERE THE FIRST DEACONS INSTITUTED IN ACTS 6?

Philippians 1:1 (c. AD 60–62) and 1 Tim 3:8–13 (c. AD 62–64) are the only two passages of Scripture in which deacons are indisputably mentioned.[40] In these passages Paul does not explain the origin or duties of deacons, apparently assuming his readers had previous knowledge about their existence and function. From where did this previous knowledge come? Some believe this knowledge came from Acts 6:1–6 which "has traditionally been regarded as the record of the instituting of the first deacons."[41]

In Acts 6:1–6, "seven men of good reputation, full of the Spirit and wisdom" were chosen to "serve tables" (NASB). Many commentators throughout church history, beginning with Irenaeus (c. AD 185), have assumed that these men were the first deacons.[42] Objectors to this view rightly note that the Greek noun *diakonos,*

---

[40] The Greek noun (*diakonos*) is used many times in Scripture. It is used in the sense of a "waiter at a meal" (John 2:5,9); "the servant of a master" (Matt 22:13); "servant of God" (1 Tim 4:6); etc. *Diakonos* means "'helper,' 'minister,' or 'servant'" and depicts the attitude of Christ himself who 'came not to be served but to serve' (Mark 10:45). Philippians 1:1 and 1 Tim 3:8–13 are the only times *diakonos* indisputably means a "fixed designation for the bearer of a specific office." See G. Kittel, ed., *Theological Dictionary of the New Testament: Volume II* (Grand Rapids: Eerdmans, 1964), 88–89, and D. W. Shaner, "Women in the Church: A Biblical Interpretation of an Ethical Problem," *Foundations* 23 (1980): 215.

[41] E. A. McKee, *John Calvin on the Diaconate and Liturgical Almsgiving* (Geneva: Librairie Droz S.A., 1984), 140.

[42] Irenaeus, "Against Heresies" book 4, chapter 15, in *Nicene and Post-Nicene Fathers*, ed. P. Schaff (Peabody: Hendrickson, 1999), 480 says, "Luke also has recorded that Stephen, who was the first elected into the diaconate by the apostles." Others who have assumed Luke was referring to deacons in Acts 6 include John Calvin, "Commentary upon the Acts of the Apostles," *Calvin's Commentaries*, vol. 18 (Grand Rapids: Baker, 1999), 238, and J. L. Dagg, *Manual of Church Order* (Charleston: Southern Baptist Publication Society, 1858; reprint, Harrisonburg: Gano, 1990), 266.

from which the English word *deacon* is derived, does not appear in this passage. In fact, the English word *deacon* never occurs in Acts.[43] Nevertheless, the related noun *diakonia* and verb *diakonein* are both used.[44]

In the NASB, *diakonia* is translated "serving," and *diakonein* is translated "to serve." The need for the seven men arose because the Hellenistic "widows were being overlooked in the daily serving [*diakonia*] of food" (Acts 6:1b). Because it was "not desirable for us [the apostles] to neglect the word of God in order to serve [*diakonein* from *diakoneō*] tables" (Acts 6:2b NASB), the seven men were selected by the congregation to assist with this task. They were then "brought before the apostles; and after praying, they laid their hands on them" (Acts 6:6b NASB).

Although Acts does not explicitly call these men deacons, they should be regarded as such for several reasons, or at a minimum as the precursor to deacons. First, qualifications were required for them to be selected. They had to be "men of good reputation, full of the Spirit and wisdom" (Acts 6:3 NASB). John Hammett notes that these qualifications are consistent with the more complete list of qualifications for deacons found in 1 Tim 3:8–13.[45] Second, the task for which they were selected was one of service, which is consistent with what the word *deacon* literally means: "'helper,' 'minister,' or 'servant.'"[46] Third, the seven men performed some of the same functions as the later deacons.[47] Fourth, they were set apart by the laying on of hands. Alexander Strauch comments, "The laying on of the apostles' hands indicates authorization to

---

[43] J. B. Polhill, *Acts*, The New American Commentary, vol. 26, ed. D. S. Dockery (Nashville: B&H, 1999), 182.

[44] F. F. Bruce, *The Book of the Acts*, New International Commentary on the New Testament, ed. G. Fee (Grand Rapids: Eerdmans, 1988), 122.

[45] J. Hammett, *Biblical Foundations for Baptist Churches: A Contemporary Ecclesiology* (Grand Rapids: Kregel, 2005), 192.

[46] Shaner, "Women in the Church," 215.

[47] J. MacArthur Jr., *The MacArthur New Testament Commentary: Acts 1–12* (Chicago: Moody, 1994), 182.

serve in an official capacity."[48] Such action by the apostles would seem to indicate the establishment of something important and not just selecting a few men for normal service. Fifth, many "church fathers of the first and second centuries . . . refer to the seven men of Acts 6 as deacons."[49]

In addition to the church fathers, numerous contemporary commentators and theologians argue for this view.[50] P. E. Burroughs in his work *Honoring the Deaconship* reasons, "As the Apostles were the forerunners of the pastors who later served the churches in a distinctly spiritual capacity, so these men were beyond doubt the forerunners of the deacons who later came to serve the churches in material affairs."[51] Strauch asserts that there must be a connection between the seven and deacons when he writes:

> Since an office in the church called *diakonos* is concerned with the physical needs of people (1 Timothy 3:8–13) and since an official body of men was appointed to help meet (*diakoneō*) the physical needs of the poor (Acts 6:1–6), we cannot but assume there is a connection between the two groups. The inclination to associate the church officers called "servants" (*diakonoi*) in 1 Timothy 3 with those

---

[48] A. Strauch, *The New Testament Deacon: Minister of Mercy* (Colorado Springs: Lewis & Roth, 1992), 51–52.

[49] As already alluded to, Irenaeus held to this view. In addition to his quote, one may see Hippolytus, "Refutation of All Heresies," book 7 chapter 24, in *Nicene and Post-Nicene Fathers*, ed. P. Schaff (Peabody: Hendrickson, 1999), 115, which says concerning Nicolaus, "He, as one of the seven (that were chosen) for the diaconate, was appointed by the Apostles." Note 5 on this sentence states, "He understands that the seven (Acts vi. 5) were deacons." See also, Victorinus, "On the Creation of the World," in *Nicene and Post-Nicene Fathers*, ed. P. Schaff, 342, which references the "seven deacons" when referring to Acts 6.

[50] This is a common view held by many. See Strauch, *New Testament Deacon*, 44–54; R. Saucy, *The Church in God's Program* (Chicago: Moody, 1972), 154–55; J. F. Walvoord and R. B. Zuck, eds., *The Bible Knowledge Commentary: New Testament Edition* (Wheaton: Victor, 1988), 737; Hammett, *Biblical Foundations*, 192; P. E. Buroughs, *Honoring the Deaconship* (Nashville: Sunday School Board, 1929), 17.

[51] Burroughs, *Honoring the Deaconship*, 17.

whom the apostles appointed to "serve tables" (*diakoneō*) in Acts 6 is quite natural. At the very least, the similarities should not be ignored.[52]

Hammett provides an additional insight when writing, "If Acts 6 is not linked to the origin of deacons, we have an office with no precedent in Jewish society, with no origin described in Scripture, and yet an office that was widely and readily accepted by New Testament churches."[53] The only plausible explanation is that the seven men mentioned in Acts 6 were at the very least the forerunners of the deacons mentioned by Paul in Phil 1:1 and 1 Tim 3:8–13. Their purposes were service and unifying the congregation so that the apostles could dedicate themselves to prayer and the ministry of the word.

## THE SIGNIFICANCE OF ACTS 6

While not explicitly containing guidelines for the office of deacon, Acts 6 does contain wisdom that should be considered by current generations. Of particular significance to the current study is the fact that seven "men" were selected. In the Greek language two words can be translated "man," *anēr* and *anthrōpos*. When *anēr* is used, it "designates a 'male person,' as opposed to a female."[54] In contrast, the word *anthrōpos* is a gender-neutral term. It "primarily designates a 'human being,' regardless of sex."[55] In Acts 6:3, using the more gender-specific term, *andras*, the apostles instructed the congregation to chose seven men [*anēr*]. It is not likely this is a coincidence.

John MacArthur asserts that the choice of the seven men is

---

[52] Strauch, *New Testament Deacon*, 48–49.

[53] Hammett, *Biblical Foundations*, 192.

[54] E. H. Carpenter and P. W. Comfort, *Holman Treasury of Key Bible Words* (Nashville: B&H, 2000), 331.

[55] Carpenter and Comfort, *Holman Treasury of Key Bible Words*, 331. For more support, see also Kittel, *TDNT*, vol.1, 361–67. Although Kittel's does not so succinctly state this, his work confirms that this general distinction can be made.

meaningful because "God's design for the church is that men assume leadership roles."[56] If the seven men selected in Acts 6 were indeed the forerunners for the deacons later mentioned by Paul in Phil 1:1 and 1 Tim 3:8–13, it is noteworthy that the text required that they all be males.

## WHAT IS THE MEANING OF *GYNAIKAS* IN 1 TIMOTHY 3:11?

The quintessential passage for any discussion of deaconesses is 1 Tim 3:11. In 1 Tim 3:8–13, Paul provides a list of qualifications for deacons. In the midst of this passage, in verse 11, Paul interjects qualifications for the *gynaikas*. Because the Greek word *gynē* can mean either "woman" or "wife," it is not clear to whom Paul was referring.[57] Commentators provide three primary possibilities for the identification of these women. Each of these three possibilities will be discussed as separate sections.

### The *Gynaikas* as Women Deacons, i.e. Deaconesses

Some commentators contend that *gynaikas* in 1 Tim 3:11 refers to women deacons. *The Interpreter's Bible* provides a succinct but thorough overview of the support for *gynaikas* referring to deaconesses. It notes:

(1) the Pastorals are primarily concerned with church officials;
(2) the adverb likewise, as in verse 8, introduces a new category parallel to "deacons," etc.;
(3) the parallel if not identical list of virtues suggests parallel officials;
(4) it is strange that requirements should be made only of deacons,' and not of bishops' wives; and
(5) the writer would have made his meaning clear by using the personal pronoun "their" with the noun "women."[58]

---

[56] MacArthur, *Acts*, 182.

[57] W. D. Mounce, *Pastoral Epistles*, Word Biblical Commentary, vol. 46 (Nashville: Thomas Nelson, 2000), 202. See also Kittel, *TDNT*, vol.1, 776–89.

[58] F. D. Gealy, "The First and Second Epistles to Timothy and the Epistle to

First, all recognize and agree that this discussion concerns itself with the church officials. Immediately preceding the verse in question is a discussion of overseers and deacons. Thus, the discussion of an office of deaconesses would be consistent with the overall genre of 1 Timothy and would fit into the immediate context. Important to this view is that the adverb "likewise" in verse 11 "introduces a new category parallel to 'deacons.'"[59] The Greek word (here "likewise") "indicates a transition from one distinct class to another."[60] This is the same word used in verse 8 when Paul transitions from talking about elders to deacons. Thus, it is logical that this "suggests that a distinct, though similar group is now under consideration."[61]

This is further supported by the fact that the "must be" from verses 8 and 11 is not explicitly in the text but is carried over from its usage in verse 2, suggesting that verse 11 "is parallel to the two preceding sections."[62] Put simply, the "one and the same verb coordinates the three: the overseer, deacons, women."[63] Those who advocate this view assert that this "syntactic sign thus points to a distinction of these 'women' from the preceding *diakonoi*."[64] Therefore, a third distinct office may be the topic of verse 11.

Additionally, this view contends that the requirements listed for the women in 1 Tim 3:11 are similar to those required for deacons in verses 8–10. Verse 11 states that the qualifications are *mē diabolous, nēphalious, pistas en pasin.* Although the qualifi-

---

Titus: Introduction and Exegesis," in *The Interpreter's Bible*, ed. G. A. Butrick (Nashville: Abingdon, 1955), 11:417.

[59] Ibid.

[60] R. M. Lewis, "The 'Women' of 1 Timothy 3:11," *Bibliotheca Sacra* 136 (Apr-June, 1979): 167.

[61] G. W. Knight III, *The Pastoral Epistles: A Commentary on the Greek Text,* New International Greek Testament Commentary (Grand Rapids: Eerdmans, 1992), 493.

[62] Ibid.

[63] W. Hendriksen and S. J. Kistemaker, *Exposition of Thessalonians, the Pastorals, and Hebrews:* in *New Testament Commentary* (Grand Rapids: Baker, 1957), 132.

[64] J. H. Stiefel, "Women Deacons in 1 Timothy: A Linguistic and Literary Look at 'Women Likewise' (I Tim 3:11)," *New Testament Studies* 41 (July 1995): 448.

cations are not identical, they do suggest someone of exemplary character and faithful to the cause of Christ. Thus some conclude that "the parallel if not identical list of virtues suggest[s] parallel officials."[65]

Correspondingly the question arises why requirements would not be made of overseers' wives. Marshall contends that the "lack of a reference to the wives of overseers makes it unlikely that the reference here is to the wives of deacons."[66] He further questions, "Why should the wives of deacons, as opposed to overseers, need special qualifications?"[67]

Lastly, proponents of this view rightly note that the Greek text does not include a personal pronoun or a definite article linking these *gynaikas* with the deacons.[68] Schreiner notes, "The reference would clearly be to wives if Paul had written 'their wives' (requiring simply the addition of the Greek word *autōn*) or 'the wives of deacons' (requiring simply the addition of the Greek word *diakonōn*)."[69] Since the Greek text includes neither of these terms, Schreiner dissents and suggests that "women deacons rather than wives are probably in view."[70]

## The *Gynaikas* as Deacons' Assistants

The proponents for this unique position use many of the above arguments for deaconesses because they too do not believe 1 Tim 3:11 refers to deacons' wives. However, instead of claiming that the *gynaikas* in 1 Tim 3:11 are deacons, several commentators and theologians assert instead that they were women who assisted

---

[65] *The Interpreter's Bible*, 417.

[66] Marshall, *Pastoral Epistles*, 493.

[67] Ibid.

[68] Several translations of the Bible insert the personal pronoun "their" into the text for clarity. This word is not found in the Greek text. The KJV, the NKJV, and the NIV do this as do several other versions.

[69] T. Schreiner, *Two Views on Women in Ministry*, ed. J. R. Beck and C. L. Blomberg (Grand Rapids: Zondervan, 2001), 194.

[70] Ibid.

deacons.[71] The primary reasoning for this view in contradistinction to the prior view is "the fact that no special and separate paragraph is used in describing their necessary qualifications."[72] Instead, "verse 11 falls in the midst of a discussion on *male* deacons."[73] William Hendriksen notes that the qualifications for these women are "wedged in between the stipulated requirements for deacons" indicating "that these women are not to be regarded as constituting a third office in the church, the office of 'deaconesses,' on par with and endowed with authority equal to that of deacons."[74] Robert Lewis concurs:

> It would seem strange for Paul to introduce a third office of the church so briefly and then return to the former topic of male deacons without some further explanation. With the detailed qualifications for both elder and deacon so plainly spelled out, why a parenthesizing of the deacons' female counterpart? If these women held a full third office of the church, why do they not merit a paragraph on their own?[75]

Because Paul does not put these women in a category of their own, some believe they were helpers to deacons.

Lewis contends that these women who assisted the deacons were unmarried women. He argues that Paul did not include any qualifications for them regarding their families "because they had no need of any" due to their singleness.[76] He reasons that married women would be too focused on their families to serve in this ca-

---

[71] Proponents of this view include Hendriksen and Kistemaker, *Exposition of Thessalonians, the Pastorals, and Hebrews*; Lewis, "The 'Women' of 1 Timothy 3:11"; and Howell, *The Deaconship*. Although Howell claims to advocate "deaconesses," he describes them as "female assistants to deacons", thus, it is believed that he fits best in this category (cf. 30, 115).

[72] W. Hendriksen, *1 and 2 Timothy and Titus,* New Testament Commentary (Grand Rapids: Baker, 1957), 132.

[73] Lewis, "The 'Women' of 1 Timothy 3:11," 172.

[74] Hendrikson, *1 and 2 Timothy and Titus*, 133.

[75] Lewis, "The 'Women' of 1 Timothy 3:11," 173.

[76] Ibid., 174.

pacity. He views this as consistent with the thrust of the Pastoral Epistles in which

> women are generally urged to return to that function for which God has especially designed them; that is, their homes, their children, and their husbands are to be their primary concern (1 Timothy 2:9–15; 5:8,14,16; 2 Timothy 3:14–15; Titus 2:3–5). Thus a wife serves the church primarily through her ministry in the home.[77]

Ultimately, a married woman's "duties at home would deny her the availability and/or flexibility needed" to serve as a deacon's assistant.[78] The role of women has also effected Hendriksen's interpretation of 1 Tim 3:11. He believes that regarding the *gynaikas* of 1 Tim 3:11 as deacons would be "contrary to the spirit of Paul's remarks concerning women and their place in the church."[79]

### The *Gynaikas* as Deacons' Wives

A third possibility is that the *gynaikas* in 1 Tim 3:11 were deacons' wives. Regarded as the "traditional understanding" of this passage, this is a widely held view reflected in many Bible translations.[80] *The Interpreter's Bible* provides a succinct overview of the support for deacons' wives. It states:

1. If deaconesses had been meant, a more specific word would have been used.
2. The description of qualifications is too brief to refer to a category of officials.
3. Women officials are treated at length in 5:9–16.
4. The sequence of thought is less awkward if wives rather than deaconesses are meant. Then the subject matter of

---

[77] Ibid.

[78] Ibid., 175.

[79] Hendriksen, *1 and 2 Timothy and Titus*, 133.

[80] Stiefel calls this view as the "traditional understanding" of the passage. Cf. NIV, NKJV, KJV, ESV, HCSB, TLB, NLT, and TEV.

verses 8–13 is deacons—deacons' wives—deacons' married and family life.

5.  Deacons' wives would often accompany their husbands in pastoral visitation and would have the same temptations to gossip and drunkenness. They therefore should be characterized by the same virtues as their husbands.[81]

These arguments will be expounded upon in more detail, thus explaining the arguments for *gynaikas* in 1 Tim 3:11 referring to deacons' wives.

Proponents of this view question, "If the writer meant deaconess, why use *gynaikas*?"[82] This view asserts that the wording seems to indicate that Paul's intended meaning was wives. This can be assumed for two specific reasons. First, Paul used the same word, *gynaikos*, in a different case "in the very next verse where it must refer to the deacon's wife."[83] It would be odd as well as confusing to use the same word back to back and have it mean two completely different things. Second, Paul could have easily used a more specific term if the intended meaning was deaconesses. Although there was not a specific word for deaconesses in Greek during the New Testament times, "the Greek noun *diakonos*, although masculine in form is among a select number of second declension nouns that can be either masculine or feminine. Thus the masculine form can apply to women."[84] For the sake of clarity, Paul could have used the masculine form with a feminine article. William Mounce concurs. He writes:

> Paul shows a readiness, both in the PE [Pastoral Epistles] and elsewhere, to create words to meet his needs. It would have been very easy for him to have written τὰς διακ-

[81] *The Interpreter's Bible*, 417.
[82] Hammett, *Biblical Foundations for Baptist Churches*, 199.
[83] Mounce, *Pastoral Epistles*, 203.
[84] Strauch, *New Testament Deacon*, 116.

όνους or perhaps διακονίσσας and prevent what would
be otherwise confusing if in fact he had changed topics.[85]

This position is even supported by some who favor the view of
women deacons. Patrick Fairbairn writes, "It still is somewhat
strange, however, that the general term *women* (γυναῖκας) is employed, and not the specific *deaconesses* (τὰς διακόνους), which
would have excluded all uncertainty as to the meaning."[86] In other
places such as Titus 2, Paul demonstrated the willingness to create
new words when needed to express biblical concepts.

Those arguing for deacons' wives point out that the list of
qualifications for the *gynaikas* "is much shorter than that for deacons or elders;" in fact, it is "too short for a new office."[87] Indeed,
the controversial section is so short that translators do not give it a
new paragraph. Hendriksen notes

> no special and separate paragraph is used in describing
> their necessary qualifications, but that these are simply
> wedged in between the stipulated requirements for dea-
> cons, with equal clarity indicates that these women are not
> to be regarded as constituting a third office in the church,
> the office of "deaconess" on par with and endowed with
> authority equal to that of deacons.[88]

One would think that an office in the church, especially since this
would be the only place it is discussed in the New Testament,
would have a longer discussion and not be listed in the middle
of the discussion of the office of male deacons. Basically, "the
sequence of thought is less awkward if wives rather than deaconesses are meant."[89]

Even dissenting views acknowledge the strength of this

---

[85] Mounce, *Pastoral Epistles*, 203.

[86] P. Fairbairn, *Pastoral Epistles* (Minneapolis: Klock & Klock, 1980), 150.

[87] Hammett, *Biblical Foundations for Baptist Churches*, 200.

[88] Hendriksen, *1 and 2 Timothy and Titus*, 133.

[89] *The Interpreter's Bible*, 418.

argument. Schreiner states, "It would be unusual to switch the subject to female deacons in the middle of the discussion (verse 11) without giving explicit indication of the fact by some phrase such as 'the women *who serve as deacons* likewise must be serious.'"[90] Thus, the logical flow of thought in 1 Tim 3:8–13 "is deacons—deacon's wives—deacon's married and family life."[91] In addition, the *New American Commentary* states, "In favor of viewing these as 'wives' of the deacons is the fact that deacons are addressed on each side of the verse."[92] Marshall, while opposing this view, recognized the fact that "the qualifications concerning 'women' are placed in the midst of the deacon code, instead of on their own, and the cursory nature of the qualifications and the lack of detail do not suggest that something so important as the church office is in mind."[93] One would think that the office of deaconess would require a separate discussion and would not be wedged in the middle of the discussion of the office of deacon, as previously argued by those who favored the deacon's assistant position.

A professor at Wake Forest College commented:

> Then we are asked to believe that he interrupts his statement in the midst to say all he is ever to say about deaconesses, in one verse, and then returns in two other verses to complete what he had begun to say about deacons. Not a word he says before verse eleven and not a word he says after it can be applied to any but deacons. I submit that it is in accord with common sense and probability that Paul intended in verse eleven also to state a qualification for

---

[90] T. Schreiner, "The Ministries of Women in the Context of Male Leadership," in *Biblical Manhood and Womanhood*, ed. J. Piper and W. Grudem (Wheaton: Crossway, 1991), 505.

[91] *The Interpreter's Bible*, 418.

[92] T. Lea and H. Griffin, *1, 2 Timothy, Titus*, New American Commentary, ed. D. Dockery (Nashville: B&H, 1999), 119.

[93] Marshall, *Pastoral Epistles*, 493.

the office of deacon and had not remotely in his head the idea of deaconess.[94]

Another argument proposed in support of *gynaikas* meaning deacons' wives is that "the topic of women workers is taken up in detail" later in 1 Tim 5:9–16.[95] Some believe that the older widows referred to in chapter 5 were women workers in the church. J. N. D. Kelly agrees, asserting that it is "absolutely clear that there was a definite order of widows."[96] He believes these women "had practical duties to perform in the community."[97] Thus, some such as Easton conclude that it would be "inconceivable" for there to be "two distinct classes of women, 'deaconesses' and 'enrolled widows,' whose duties would be precisely the same."[98] Nevertheless, the exact function of the elderly widows "is a much disputed question."[99]

Last, it makes more sense for this to be referring to the wives of deacons rather than a new office because the context of the family is important. Schreiner in a dissenting view writes, "A requirement for the wives of deacons would be appropriate in this context, since Paul sees the status and conduct of a man's family as an essential qualification for church office."[100] This also explains a major objection from those supporting deaconesses. Functionally, the wives of deacons are more likely to serve alongside their husbands than the wives of elders are. For this reason the wives must be women of exemplary character in order not to create division or chaos. Alexander Strauch states it well when he says:

---

[94] G. W. Paschal, "Deaconesses" *Biblical Recorder* (January 23, 1929): 4.

[95] B. S. Easton, *The Pastoral Epistles: Introduction, Translation, Commentary and Word Studies* (New York: Scribner's, 1947), 134.

[96] J. N. D. Kelly, *A Commentary on the Pastoral Epistles*, Black's New Testament Commentaries (London: Adam & Black, 1963), 115.

[97] Ibid., 116.

[98] Easton, *The Pastoral Epistles*, 134.

[99] D. Guthrie, *The Pastoral Epistles*, Tyndale New Testament Commentaries (Grand Rapids: Eerdmans, 1957), 102.

[100] Schreiner, "The Ministries of Women in the Context of Male Leadership," in *Biblical Manhood and Womanhood,* 505.

"But why," people often ask, "are the wives of deacons mentioned and not the wives of overseers?" The answer lies in the nature of the diaconate, which is not a teaching, governing office like the eldership. First Timothy 2:12 states, "But I do not allow a woman to teach or exercise authority over a man. . . ." Pastor-elders (shepherds) teach and govern the whole church. Their wives are not to assist in the governing of the church.

The diaconate, on the other hand, provides loving service to the needy. Wives can assist their deacon husbands in this service without violating their God-ordained role in the local church. Indeed, at times their assistance may be demanded, as in cases involving the care of single mothers, children, and sick or elderly women. The wives are not deacon officials, however. They don't hold the office of deacon or any special title.[101]

In addition to the argument that wives would be more involved in the ministry, one other option exists. Perhaps, because "likewise" is used with both deacons and wives, and because the verb "must be" has been supplied in verse 2, this comment could refer both to wives of deacons and the wives of elders.

In summary, the arguments from this passage favor the position that deacons' wives are in view:

1. *Gynaikas* is used one verse later and obviously means wife. Paul would not use the same word this close together with two different meanings without an explanation.
2. Paul could easily have used the feminine article to clarify or create a word as he did in other locations; thus, the argument that no word exists for deaconess is not persuasive.
3. The description is too brief (one verse) and is bracketed by a discussion of male deacons; thus, the use of *likewise*

---

[101] Strauch, *New Testament Deacon*, 127.

only indicates the addressing of wives and not the mention of a new office.

4.  The different function of overseers as teaching and having authority explains the lack of prohibition to their wives. Deacons' wives would likely serve alongside them.

5.  Women are treated at length in 1 Tim 5:9–16. There would not be a separate discussion for the same function.

One cannot contend that 1 Timothy establishes the office of deaconess with certainty. In fact, the evidence indicates that 1 Tim 3:11 addresses the wives of deacons.

## WAS PHOEBE A DEACONESS?

This is the third crucial question in determining if the Bible advocates deaconesses. Once again commentators are divided over the issue. Some argue that Phoebe was a deaconess of the church of Cenchrea, and others argue that she was simply a servant of the church.[102] At the core issue is whether *diakonos* in Rom 16:1 should be translated "deaconess" or "servant." Both sides have valid arguments.

### Phoebe as a Deaconess

The first view presents the position that Phoebe was a deaconess. Two main arguments support the interpretation of this passage as referring to the office of deaconess. First, perhaps the best argument for this is included in Hammett's work although he takes a mediating position. Hammett states, "In support of the deaconess interpretation it must be noted that none of these other texts refer to a *diakonos* of a specific church, as does Romans 16:1. It suggests some type of official service."[103] Since this is the only

---

[102] But see BDAG, 230, which calls Phoebe a "courier" (διάκονος), and T. L. Wilder, "Phoebe: the Letter-Carrier of Romans?" (paper presented at the Evangelical Theological Society's annual meeting, November 17, 2005), who argues that Phoebe was the "letter-carrier" of Romans.

[103] Hammett, *Biblical Foundations for Baptist Churches,* 201.

occasion where *diakonos* is linked with a specific church, perhaps the office of deacon is in view.

Second, the argument presented by Schreiner and others says that the use of the masculine noun suggests the office is used. By using the masculine noun in reference to Phoebe, Paul linked this service with the masculine noun used in 1 Timothy.[104] Osborne agrees with Schreiner and even goes further by stating, "One would have expected the feminine *diakonia*. In fact some have concluded that she was the pastor of the congregation."[105] However, even supporters of the office of deaconess disagree with the conclusion that Phoebe was in a position of authoritative leadership.[106]

These two arguments do not conclusively prove that the use here refers exclusively to the office of deacon. Osborne's argument can just as easily be used against his position in referring to the 1 Timothy passage which establishes the office. Why did Paul not use the feminine word if he wanted the office of deaconess? Osborne's argument is not convincing. The relationship with the church will be addressed later. Let us now examine the alternative view that Paul simply meant Phoebe was a servant.

## Phoebe as a Servant

There are two basic reasons Phoebe should be viewed as a servant. First, the normal translation of *diakonos* is "servant." Those in favor of translating *diakonos* as "servant" note that "of the twenty-nine times *diakonos* is used in the New Testament, servant is overwhelmingly the normal translation."[107] In fact, the term is used of Jesus in Matt 20:28 which says, "Even as the son of man came not

---

[104] T. Schreiner, *Romans*, Baker Exegetical Commentary on the New Testament (Grand Rapids: Baker, 1998), 787.
[105] G. R. Osborne, *Romans*, the IVP New Testament Commentary Series (Downers Grove: IVP, 2004), 403. Those concluding she was pastor include Fiorenza and Jewett. IVP as a publishing house, Fiorenza, and Jewett all support the egalitarian position and may have other motives behind their various interpretations.
[106] Schreiner, *Romans*, 788.
[107] Hammett, *Biblical Foundations for Baptist Churches,* 200.

to be served but to serve." This verse uses both the passive form and active verb form of the word *diakonos* in reference to Jesus; however, the translation of *diakonos* in this instance is "servant."[108] The fact that the word does not always refer to the office means that the Rom 16:1 use could simply mean "servant." The linking of this passage with the church at Cenchrea can be explained by the fact that Phoebe served only at that one church or that Paul could have been identifying this Phoebe from other people by the same name noting her place of service. The purpose of linking *diakonos* to this particular congregation could simply have been for clarification especially considering the timing of the book.

Second, the office of deacon may not have existed when Paul wrote Romans. The book of Romans was probably written between AD 55 and 59. Paul's first letter to Timothy was not written until between AD 62 and 64. Thus to establish an office in the local church from one word in one verse written before any explanation of the qualifications for that office exists (other than what is mentioned in Acts 6) would be suspect.[109] Even Hammett, who presents both views, ultimately concludes that the "linkage of Phoebe with a specific church suggests some type of recognition, but to call her a deaconess seems to anticipate later developments and is without clear biblical precedent."[110]

In the end, the passage in Romans cannot be conclusively used to establish the office of deaconess. The arguments for understanding Phoebe as a servant are just as strong, if not stronger, than understanding her to occupy the office of deaconess. This passage may be interpreted either way. This result that cuts

---

[108] T. W. McClain, "CON," *Word & Way* (May 17, 1984): 7.

[109] And if one contends that Acts 6 is the foundation for deacons, they must answer why no women were chosen. Either way a problem exists for contending Phoebe was more than a servant of the church. With so many examples of *diakonos* in its various forms not being translated as deacon in the New Testament, a heavy burden of proof rests on those who contend that she was.

[110] Hammett, *Biblical Foundations for Baptist Churches,* 201.

both ways means the overall evidence must be weighed and some conclusions drawn.

## CONCLUSION

Today in many churches the office of deacon has sadly strayed from its biblical roots. Instead of being a position of service to unify the church, it has become an office of leadership and authority that frequently divides the church. Many modern deacons possess similar authority to the biblical office of overseer. In its current state in a majority of Baptist churches, women would be biblically ineligible for the office of deacon due to scriptural injunctions found in 1 Tim 2:12, and so forth. Nevertheless, this is not the biblical pattern for the office. Thus for women to serve as deacons, the biblical understanding of servant deacons would first have to be restored. But the question remains, "Does the Bible advocate deaconesses?"

Reasonable arguments exist on both sides; however, the biblical evidence leans against an office of deaconess. The reasoning for this is founded upon the interpretation of Acts 6 as the precursor to the later diaconate. Since Luke clearly reports that the church was to select seven "men" for the task at hand, it is argued that the same should be true today.

Additionally, the arguments put forth by those advocating deaconesses in 1 Tim 3:11 are largely explained by the opposing view. As stated by John Hammett, "The only one of the five arguments for deaconess that cannot be cogently explained by the opposing view is the last, the absence of the pronoun *their* before *wives*, and that is an argument from silence."[111] On the other hand, a number of the arguments for *gynaikas* meaning deacons' wives go unanswered. While Rom 16:1 leads some to contend for women deacons, it remains inconclusive at best. Due to the early date of Romans, it is unlikely that Paul meant to refer to Phoebe as an office holder in the church. Nevertheless, she was undoubtedly a respected servant,

---

[111] Ibid. 200.

which highlights the valuable ministry women have in the church, even if they are not formal office holders. For the purposes of this chapter, which seeks to elaborate on the Baptist view of the church, it is noteworthy that the *Baptist Faith and Message* does not include Romans 16 in the references listed at the bottom of the article giving indication that the Southern Baptist confession does not interpret Romans 16 as having implication on the officers of the church.

The issue of deaconesses is a difficult and sensitive issue that should not be taken lightly. Church leaders must weigh the biblical evidence carefully. While disagreement over the office of deaconess will continue, hopefully all churches will heed the clear biblical mandate for proper male leadership. Unless men faithfully serve and lead in the home and in the church, the future of our society looks bleak.

# 9

# The Universal and Local Church

*Thomas White*

In February 2004, a new Web site called "Facebook" launched as the idea of an industrious Harvard student.[1] The site, initially for Harvard students only, became a worldwide networking phenomenon and sent researchers scrambling to determine what the real impact of social networking would be.[2] While some thought the new tool would help relationships, others were much more skeptical.

Neuroscientist Susan Greenfield stated,

> I often wonder whether real conversations in real time may eventually give way to these sanitized and easier screen dialogues, in much the same way as killing, skinning and butchering an animal to eat has been replaced by the convenience of packages of meat on the supermarket shelf.[3]

---

[1] S. Yadav, "Facebook: The Complete Biography," http://mashable.com/2006/08/25/facebook-profile/, accessed May 8, 2009.

[2] T. A. Workman, "The Real Impact of Virtual Worlds: How digital culture shapes students' minds," http://chronicle.com/weekly/v55/i04/04b01201.htm, accessed May 8, 2009.

[3] D. Derbyshire, "Social websites harm children's brains: Chilling warning to parents from top neuroscientist," http://www.dailymail.co.uk/news/article-1153583/Social-websites-harm-childrens-brains-Chilling-warning-parents-neuroscientist.html, accessed May 8, 2009.

Another claims, "Online interactions do not necessarily remove people from their offline world but may indeed be used to support relationships and keep people in contact, even when life changes move them away from each other."[4] Keeping real-world and virtual relationships in proper balance seems to be the key. Greenfield concludes, "I'm not against technology and computers. But before they start social networking, they need to learn to make real relationships with people."[5]

The use of social networking sites like Facebook in the proper balance increases friendships and enhances the networking process. However, obsession with the online world that overemphasizes virtual networking to the neglect of real-world relationship harms participants. Some create fictional lives in the virtual world that barely resemble the real thing. Such overemphasis prevents development of conversation skills and the ability to interact with others. Out of balance, a tool created to increase friends and networking may reduce relationships.

The same thing occurs in the proper balance of the universal and local church. When the invisible, universal Church takes precedence over the local, visible congregation, then we have a situation not unlike a virtual world becoming more important than the real world. The ideal meant to help the actual begins to injure because of improper emphasis. Overemphasis on the universal Church to the minimizing of the local church can be demonstrated in quotes like the one given by George Barna in his book *Revolution*. He says, "Whether you become a Revolutionary immersed in, minimally involved in, or completely disassociated from a local church is irrelevant to me (and, within boundaries to God)."[6]

---

[4] N. B. Ellison, C. Steinfield, and C. Lampe, "The Benefits of Facebook 'Friends': Social Capital and College Students' Use of Online Social Network Sites," http://jcmc.indiana.edu/vol12/issue4/ellison.html, accessed May 8, 2009.

[5] Derbyshire, "Social websites harm children's brains."

[6] G. Barna, *Revolution* (Carol Stream, IL: Tyndale House, 2005), 29.

But more on these practical matters later; we must first partake of the meat before enjoying our dessert.

## INTRODUCTION

*Ekklēsia* is the Greek word normally translated as "church" in the New Testament. H. E. Dana begins his church manual by stating, "There is no term in the New Testament which has suffered more misapprehension and distortion of meaning in its transition into modern speech than the term *ekklesia*."[7] Our bumbling and confusion over the term "church" begins at an early age. Perhaps all of you have heard and seen the illustration that begins with fingers interlocked and hands folded over.

> *"Here is the church." The two index fingers then point to the sky.*

> *"Here is the steeple." Suddenly the demonstrator opens and turns his hands inside open.*

> *"Open it up and there are the people."*

From this childhood exercise, children begin to understand that the "church" is a building where people worship. Yet nowhere in the New Testament does the original word *ekklēsia* carry with it the connotation of building.

The fog grows thicker as history has added any number of unbiblical adjectives to the word *church*. Your choice of adjectives includes *local, visible, militant, one, holy, Catholic, universal, invisible, triumphant, institutional, apostolic, emergent, emerging, Internet, cowboy,* and perhaps even *dysfunctional*. We have regional churches like the Presbyterian Church of the United States. We have the Roman Catholic Church, and then we have those pesky Baptist churches. We even have independent, fundamental, KJV-only churches. The newest slogan to catch on is "one church

---

[7] H. E. Dana and L. M. Sipes, *A Manual of Ecclesiology* (Kansas City: Central Seminary Press, 1944), 13.

in many locations." Frankly, with the fog as thick as pea soup, I am surprised anyone can find a church much less understand what it is.

In this presentation I will seek to wade through the fog and clarify the proper biblical understanding of the church. In doing so, I will address three current theological trends which undermine the importance of the local church. I will prove that we should maintain priority on the local congregation while acknowledging a final and future assembly (the universal Church). I do not plan to deny the concept of a universal Church as the concept properly interprets some passages of Scripture; however, the proper balance of emphasizing the local while acknowledging the universal must be maintained. This theological position will then be applied to practical items like: (1) the ecumenical movement, (2) Barna's *Revolution,* and (3) Internet churches. Let's begin where we should always begin our theology, with a biblical foundation.

## BIBLICAL FOUNDATION

It will be helpful to begin by looking at the original Greek word that is translated by the English word *church*. *Ekklēsia* is the Greek word frequently translated as "church." J. Hammett states that *ekklēsia* is formed "from two Greek words, *ek*, 'out,' and *kaleō*, 'to call.' Thus the *ekklēsia* is composed of 'the called-out ones.'"[8] Some have debated whether the original audience would have understood the "called out" idea. K. L. Schmidt believes it to be essential and writes, "*Ekklēsia* is in fact the group of men called out of the world by God."[9] In order to further examine what *ekklēsia* meant during the time of its original deployment, we will look at its use in the Septuagint and its secular Greek usage drawing

---

[8] J. Hammett, *Biblical Foundations for Baptist Churches* (Grand Rapids: Kregel, 2005), 26.

[9] K. L. Schmidt, "ἐκκλησία," in *Theological Dictionary of the New Testament*, ed. G. Kittel, trans. and ed. G. W. Bromiley (Grand Rapids: Eerdmans, 1965), 3:531.

conclusion upon what the term *ekklēsia* would have indicated to first-century Christians. After establishing the original meaning of *ekklēsia*, we will look at the usage in the New Testament proving that the primary meaning of the word is a local congregation.

## Old Testament Usage

In the Old Testament two Hebrew words, *'ēdāh* and *qāhāl*, are used to discuss God's people. *'Ēdāh* characterizes the covenant of community as a whole, while *qāhāl* is the ceremonial expression for the assembly that results from the covenant—the Sinai community or spiritual Israel if you will.[10] In the Septuagint (LXX), the Greek translation of the Hebrew Old Testament, *ekklēsia* is never used for *'ēdāh*, the term that denotes a class of people. But *ekklēsia* is used 77 times for *qāhāl*, which indicates an actual assembly resulting from the covenant. Additionally, in every instance I examined, *ekklēsia* only translates *qāhāl* when a called assembly of the Lord's people is intended. Mark Dever states, "This word for assembly, *qahal*, is closely bound up in the Old Testament with the Lord's distinct people—Israel. The rich association between the assembly of God and the distinct people of God then carries over to the New Testament."[11] To summarize, the usage in the Septuagint indicates that *ekklēsia* means an assembly or gathering of God's people.

## Secular Usage

The apocrypha employs the term *ekklēsia* about 20 times, and it is translated in the LXX as "congregation" or "gathering" every time. H. E. Dana commented concerning *ekklēsia*, "The word came, especially in the inter-biblical period, to denote a local gathering for purposes of worship."[12] B.H. Carroll provides sever-

---

[10] *New International Dictionary of New Testament Theology,* 1:295.

[11] M. Dever, "The Church," in *A Theology for the Church* (Nashville: B&H Academic, 2007), 769.

[12] Dana and Sipes, *A Manual of Ecclesiology,* 30.

al quotations from ancient Greek writers where the term *ekklēsia* is used to mean "assembly." For example:

1. Thucydides 2,22: "Pericles, seeing them angry at the present state of things . . . did not call them to an assembly (ecclesia) or any other meeting."
2. Thucydides 6,8: "And the Athenians having convened an assembly (ecclesia) . . . voted, etc."
3. Aristophanes *Act.* 169: "But I forbid you calling an assembly (ecclesia) for the Thracians about pay."[13]

In addition to evidence from the LXX and secular Greek usage, many lexicons demonstrate that the meaning of *ekklēsia* should be an assembly or gathering. Consider the following:

1. Thayer states that *ekklēsia* means "a gathering of citizens called out from their homes into some public place; and assembly."
2. Liddell and Scott state that *ekklēsia* means "an assembly of citizens summoned by the crier, the legislative body."[14]
3. Even Bauer maintains as the primary meaning of *ekklēsia* as an "assembly, as a regularly summoned political body."[15]

The evidence demonstrates that in the first century *ekklēsia* meant "a called-out congregation, assembly, or gathering." With this understanding, we must attempt to set aside the cultural baggage we carry and examine the proper usage of *ekklēsia* in the New Testament.

---

[13] B. H. Carroll, *Ecclesia: The Church* (Paris, AR: The Baptist Standard Bearer, 2006), 35–36. Carroll quotes more than I give, but the point is still made concerning the meaning of *ekklēsia*.

[14] The first two references are taken from W. Rone, *Southern Baptists and the Concept of a Catholic (Universal) Church (Visible and Invisible)* (Paducah, KY: Paducah Printing Co, 1959), 19.

[15] W. Bauer, W. F. Arndt, F. W. Gingrich, and F. W. Danker, *Greek-English Lexicon of the New Testament and Other Early Christian Literature*, 2nd ed. (Chicago: University of Chicago Press, 1979), 240.

New Testament Uses

I have personally identified 114 times where the word *ekklēsia* is found in the New Testament.[16] Out of the 114 occurrences, there are three secular uses characterizing riots (Acts 19:32,40–41). These usages are translated as an assembly or gathering of a secular nature. Two occurrences of the *ekklēsia* describe or quote the Old Testament (Acts 7:38 and Heb 2:12), and in these occasions the word is translated as "congregation" or "assembly." The remaining 109 occurrences of *ekklēsia* refer to a Christian assembly of some sort. These 109 uses can be broken down into three general categories of usage that we will briefly discuss:

1.  General use: This refers generally to the church as Jesus established it during His earthly ministry.
2.  Local and concrete use: In this sense the term refers to one *ekklēsia* (1 Cor 1:2) or to many *ekklēsiai* (1 Cor 16:19) by using the singular and plural.
3.  Future use: The final and future "assembly" of Christ's own in heaven commonly referred to as the universal Church.[17]

*General Usage.* The first category is the generic use of the word *church* as an "idea" or "institution." This category of usage has frequently been overlooked, and so we will examine some examples of words used generically to help clarify the meaning of "church." First, consider the recent systematic theology titled *A Theology for the Church*.[18] "Which church?" you might ask. Good question. The universal Church contains the redeemed of all ages,

---

[16] Carroll, *Ecclesia*, 14 states that there are 117; however, he seems to have been operating off of an English translation. Dever, *Theology for the Church*, 771 agrees with 114. The final number may change depending on whether Acts 2:47 is included in the manuscript used. Generally it is excluded because it is not in the best manuscripts, and it has been in this presentation.

[17] Rone, *Southern Baptists and the Concept of a Catholic (Universal) Church (Visible and Invisible)*, 3.

[18] D. L. Akin, ed., *A Theology for the Church* (Nashville: B&H Academic, 2007).

but the book's title surely cannot have the latter meaning in mind. Obviously, the intended meaning is that the book is written for churches in general.

Another example is the use of the word *press* when referring to the secular media. I could correctly state that the "press" possesses a liberal bias. In fact, I have stated as much on multiple occasions. Now I know there is neither a "universal press" nor an "invisible press." I also understand that all of those working in the "the press" are not liberal. I am confident there are two or three conservatives and that all of them work for Fox News. At any rate, this generic use is common.

Furthermore, consider the word *family*. I may say to you that the liberal press is waging an ungodly attack on the "family." Do I mean that there is a universal and perhaps invisible family somewhere, perhaps in "never, never land," that is under siege? No. Of course I do not. I use the word *family* generically to represent the idea of families. Nevertheless the masses clearly understand the statement that the liberal press is attacking the family.

This principle can also be seen in Scripture. Take for example Gen 1:26, "Then God said, 'Let Us make man'" (NASB). Did the Lord intend only to have one man on the face of the earth? No, in fact He gave the command to be fruitful and multiply. This command is similar to the Great Commission. God understood that by establishing one man with the purpose of multiplication He would establish the race known as mankind including many individual men. Similarly when God established the "church" in Matthew 16, He understood that the church would multiply creating many churches, which may still be referred to generically as "the Church."

L. R. Scarborough said it well when he wrote:

Christ founded one (church) as a model within the Kingdom and left orders for it to be duplicated and multiplied everywhere in the world. . . . It is our task to keep these churches in their pristine purity on their Christly foundations, treasure their ordinances, impassion and apply their doctrines, multiply this model, and through them preach the truth, teach the doctrines, and carry the crucified but risen and triumphant Christ to every lost man as quickly as we can.[19]

Let's quickly look at a few examples. First Timothy 3:15 states, "But in case I am delayed, *I write* so that you may know how one ought to conduct himself in the household of God, which is the church of the living God, the pillar and support of the truth" (NASB). Here the word clearly indicates the generic idea of the church. Colossians 1:24 states, "Now I rejoice in my sufferings for your sake, and in my flesh I do my share on behalf of His body [i.e. the church] in filling up that which is lacking in Christ's afflictions" (NASB). Paul suffered for the literal Church on this earth and not for a universal, invisible assembly, and yet his suffering did not occur for one single church but for the generic Church.

*The Concrete Local Congregation Usage.* Differences exist over how many times the word *ekklēsia* refers to a visible local congregation. Dana states, "Eighty-five times the local idea is positively certain."[20] B. H. Carroll states it differently believing that all but four occurrences refer either to "the *particular assembly* of Jesus Christ on earth or to his *general assembly* in glory."[21] Edward Hiscox states, "Of the *one hundred and ten* instances in which *ekklēsia* is rendered *Church* in the New Testament, more than *ninety* are applied to a visible, local congregation or company of disciples, meeting in a given place for a given purpose."[22]

---

[19] L. R. Scarborough, *Christ's Militant Kingdom* (Nashville: Sunday School Board, 1924), 53–54.

[20] Dana and Sipes, *A Manual of Ecclesiology,* 33.

[21] Carroll, *Ecclesia: The Church,* 16.

[22] E. T. Hiscox, *New Directory for Baptist Churches* (Philadelphia: Judson, 1894), 24.

Wendell Rone states, "The terms 'church' and 'churches' are used in at least 92 instances [the author lists 95], out of the total 109, to refer to the literal and concrete expressions of the divine institution—'the church.'"[23] J. M. Pendleton lists four possible exceptions before stating that his concern lies with the large majority of uses, which designates the local visible church.[24] To summarize, Baptist specialists in ecclesiology believe that 85 to 95 of the 109 uses refer to the local visible congregation.

Rone concludes:

The idea of assembling or congregating, or coming together is vital to its use and has been inherent in its use. A thorough study of the use of *ekklēsia* in Biblical and Classical Greek will reveal the fact that the word is *never* used in an unassembled or uncongregated sense.[25]

After discussing the majority of uses, Dana agrees when he states, "The prevailing and fundamental idea of *ekklēsia* is that of a local body organized on democratic principles for purposes of worship and service."[26]

Time and space do not allow for every use of the local and concrete sense to be discussed; however, I will provide a few. Acts 14:23 states, "When they had appointed elders for them in *every church*" (NASB). Acts 15:41 uses the plural stating, "And he went through Syria and Cilicia, *strengthening the churches*" (NKJV). Paul's letter to Corinth was addressed to "the church of God which is at Corinth" (NKJV). He closes out that first letter by stating in 1 Cor 16:19, "The churches of Asia send you greetings. Aquila and Prisca, together with the church in their house, send you hearty greetings in the Lord" (ESV). Galatians is written "to the

---

[23] Rone, *Southern Baptists and the Concept of a Catholic (Universal) Church (Visible and Invisible)*, 5.

[24] J. M. Pendleton, *Baptist Church Manual* (Nashville: Broadman, 1966), 6.

[25] Rone, *Southern Baptists*, 1. Emphasis added.

[26] Dana and Sipes, *A Manual of Ecclesiology*, 67.

churches of Galatia." Thessalonians is written to "the church of the Thessalonians." In the book of Revelation, letters are written to "seven churches" with each location being specifically identified: the church of Ephesus, the church in Smyrna, the church in Pergamos, the church in Thyatira, the church in Sardis, the church in Philadelphia, and the church of the Laodiceans. To summarize, the vast majority, almost 90 percent of the New Testament uses refer to a local assembly in the singular or the plural.

*Final and Future Assembly Usage.* This category is often referred to as the universal Church; however, that term has been so misused that it provides more confusion than clarity. For this presentation I have used "final and future assembly" of Christ in glory to denote what most consider the universal Church. Again, I am not denying the existence of the universal Church but merely desiring to clarify what it is and how this affects those few passages that demand this interpretation. We must recognize three facts about the final and future assembly. First, many of its members are now in heaven. Second, many of its members are here on earth. Third, many of its members are yet to be born and thus exist neither on earth nor in heaven.[27]

With these three considerations, the only logical conclusion is that the final and future assembly cannot gather in the present time. Without a "gathering," how can there be an *ekklēsia*? Many of its members do not yet exist, and with others in heaven, the first meeting will be after the return of our glorious and triumphant Savior Jesus Christ. This glorious assembly of believers will then continue to meet for all eternity. We have great expectations of complete unity in that final assembly. For now the final and future assembly (universal Church) exists as a theological concept, an expectation of greatness to come. As with eschatology and sanctification, we live in an already/not yet tension. We may look forward to the great assembly with confidence that it will one

---

[27] Carroll, *Ecclesia*, 17.

day gather. We may speak of it. But currently the future and final assembly cannot gather.

Let us look at a few verses that may indicate this theological concept. Ephesians 5:27 states "that He might present to Himself the church in all her glory, having no spot or wrinkle or any such thing; but that she should be holy and blameless" (NASB). This verse apparently has a futuristic concept in the meaning. Many include Heb 12:23 in this category: "to the general assembly and church of the firstborn who are enrolled in heaven, and to God, the Judge of all, and to the spirits of righteous men made perfect" (NASB). Although the word *ekklēsia* is not used, Rev 7:9 expresses the idea, "After these things I looked, and behold, a great multitude, which no one could count, from every nation and *all* tribes and peoples and tongues, standing before the throne and before the Lamb, clothed in white robes, and palm branches *were* in their hands." These and perhaps a few other passages demand the concept of a future and final assembly. Thus, fidelity to Scripture demands that we hold as a theological concept the future and final assembly (the universal Church).

*Conclusion of the Biblical Evidence.* The biblical evidence demonstrates that the concept of a final and future assembly exists, but Scripture primarily focuses on the current, visible, and local congregation. Many theologians have understood this proper balance. For example Herschel Hobbs acknowledges the universal with a focus on the local. J. M. Pendleton acknowledged the redeemed in the aggregate and yet wrote, "In a large majority of instances it is used in the Scriptures to denote the local assembly, convened for religious purposes."[28]

Edward Hiscox first published a directory for Baptist churches in 1859. His volume was so popular that it was translated into seven languages and updated in 1893.[29] Its longevity can be

---

[28] Pendleton, *Baptist Church Manual*, 6.
[29] Hiscox, *New Directory for Baptist Churches*, 7–10.

demonstrated by the fact that it remains in print and available on Amazon.com. Hiscox says:

> There is then, the visible, local Church, and the invisible, universal church. In the latter case the word represents a conception of the mind, having no real existence in time or place, and not a historical fact, being only an ideal multitude without organization, without action, and without corporate being.[30]

Even John Dagg emphasized the local assembly acknowledging, "The church universal is in progress of construction, and will be completed at the end of the world, after which it will endure forever.[31]

We must similarly emphasize the local, visible church in our theology while continuing to acknowledge the minority use of a future and final assembly (universal Church). Having now examined the biblical foundation, let's briefly look at the historical development of the meaning of *ekklēsia*.

## HISTORICAL DEVELOPMENT

### One, Holy, Catholic, Apostolic Church: *Ekklēsia* and the Fathers

The writings of the early church fathers demonstrate a shift from a local church to a universal, visible concept. Noted historian J. N. D. Kelly states, "What these early fathers were envisaging was almost always the empirical, visible society; they had little or no inkling of the distinction which was later to become important between a visible and an invisible Church."[32] To demonstrate the shift, one could begin with Clement of Rome, who wrote around

---

[30] Ibid., 24.

[31] J. Dagg, *A Treatise on Church Order* (Charleston, SC: Southern Baptist Publication Society, 1858; rpt. ed., Harrisonburg, VA: Gano, 1982), 137.

[32] J. N. D. Kelly, *Early Christian Doctrine* (New York: Harper & Row, 1960), 191.

AD 95–97 and used the word *ekklēsia* four times, and in each use the word demands a local sense.[33]

Ignatius, who was martyred around AD 107, used *ekklēsia* 39 times in the epistles of Ignatius. Dana says concerning those uses, "At least thirty times the word is used in an unquestionably local significance."[34] Of the nine remaining, five are generic, three are universal, and one is unclear. By the late second century we see the trend reverse to focus on the universal Church and not the local. Irenaeus in his work *Against Heresies,* written c. AD 180, used *ekklēsia* 130 times with 103 of those uses focused on a universal meaning.[35]

By the third century and the time of the writings of Cyprian, a change occurred with references to a universal yet visible church. Cyprian used the term "The Catholic Church" repeatedly, and his famous statement indicates his emphasis on the visible Catholic Church: "He cannot have God for his Father who has not the Church for his mother," indicating that there is no salvation outside the Church.[36] Cyprian emphasized a much broader concept than I allow, but he did not present an invisible universal congregation. With Augustine, we see continued development of the universal emphasis. On this matter Dana states, "Augustine emphatically declared for the 'the totality of the one church,'" and that "the word church in its local use but rarely occurs in his writings."[37]

To summarize, during the patristic era

there appears a gradual and persistent departure from New Testament standards as set forth in the teachings and practices of the apostles, and that this progressive perversion has come as a result of the neglect of the local conception

---

[33] Dana and Sipes, *A Manual of Ecclesiology,* 99. See *I Clement.*

[34] Dana and Sipes, *A Manual of Ecclesiology,* 101.

[35] Ibid., 107–8.

[36] Cyprian, *De unit. Eccl.* 6.

[37] Dana and Sipes, *A Manual of Ecclesiology,* 116–17.

of the New Testament and formulation of the theory of a universal Church.[38]

## The Universal Invisible Concept of the Reformers

Although the topic could be a complete paper to itself and oversimplification can be dangerous, it is in this case necessary to say that the fragmentation of the Roman Catholic Church dealt the reformers with some difficult questions to answer. The universal, visible Church had been split. How after the split could the Church be one? Although one struggles to find a clearly articulated and coherent ecclesiological position, the answer was to divide the Church into the visible and the invisible Church. The visible Church may not have unity on earth, but the invisible Church could retain unity. Luther frequently refers to the "the universal church." And "it is reported that on one occasion he was asked what the church was, and he replied, 'The Church is invisible'; but the functions which he assigns to it could not be performed by an invisible agency, unless that agency were a spiritual personality."[39]

Meanwhile Calvin refers to the church in ambiguous ways. He states, "We profess to 'believe the church' refers not only to the visible church (our present topic) but also to all God's elect."[40] While he claims to focus on the "visible church," he refers to the "visible church as mother of believers" in language reminiscent of Cyprian.[41] One historian notes, "It is, indeed, strange that in his (Calvin's) analysis of the use of *ekklēsia* in the New Testament he does not even recognize its local application, denoting only two meanings, the invisible church of all ages and the visible universal Church, present in the world."[42]

---

[38] Ibid., 118.

[39] Ibid., 139.

[40] J. Calvin, *Institutes of the Christian Religion*, Library of Christian Classics (Louisville: WJK, 1960), 1012–13, book 4, chapter 1, section 2.

[41] Ibid., book 4, chapter 1, section 4.

[42] Dana and Sipes, *A Manual of Ecclesiology,* 142.

When Was "Church" First Used?

During the development of *ekklēsia*, different words translated the term. Our common current word *church* originated from the Greek word *kyriakos,* which means "belonging to the Lord."[43] Malcolm Yarnell explains the progression from there:

> *Kuriakon* indicated Christian houses of worship in the Constantinian era. German soldiers in the Roman army thus called a church building, *kirika.* Returning to their homes, they took with them the term which became the Anglo-Saxon *circe*, German *kirche*, Scottish *kirk*, and English "church."[44]

By this point hopefully you understand that *ekklēsia* means "a called assembly, gathering, or congregation" and not necessarily "church." So the logical question arises, If it means congregation, why and when did we begin translating this term as church? The earlier English translations actually used the word *congregation* to translate *ekklēsia.* Doing our best to remove ourselves from our cultural bias, we must think about all those verses that create such problems being properly translated as "congregation" rather than "church." Dana explains, "The word 'church' having been first substituted by the Genevan revisers in 1560."[45] He further states, "In the officially approved translation of the Anglican church the word 'congregation' stood in Matt 16:18 until changed by the Authorized Version in 1611."[46]

So why was it that in 1611 translators began to use the term *church.* They had no option. King James gave several rules of translation. The king's third rule stated that "the old ecclesiastical words (were) to be kept, as the word church not to be translated

---

[43] Bauer et al., *Greek-English Lexicon*, 576.

[44] M. Yarnell, "The Church" in *The Baptist Faith and Message 2000: Critical Issues in America's Largest Protestant Denomination* (Lanham, MD: Rowman & Littlefield, 2007), 56.

[45] Dana and Sipes, *A Manual of Ecclesiology,* 22.

[46] Ibid.

congregation."[47] Two items draw attention in the king's third rule. He desired that the translators not translate such words as baptizoμ as "immerse," keeping the "old ecclesiastical words." He also did not think that was explanation enough for one specific term so he determined to mention the word *church* by name. This left no doubt or discussion over the translation of *ekklēsia* in the King James Version of the Bible, and for thousands of years, an unregenerate king has determined the English word which would provide meaning for the biblical concept.

Perhaps the reason for the king's insistence upon translating *ekklēsia* as "church" came from his dislike for the Puritans, who chose the term *congregation*. S. E. Anderson states, "King James and his Church of England leaders were vexed and annoyed with the Puritans who wanted to purify (hence the name) their Established Church."[48] Since we are a little late to the party and may not be able to withdraw the usage of the word *church,* the least we can do is understand the proper emphasis on the congregation in the original word *ekklēsia*.

## The *Baptist Faith and Message*

### The 1925 Baptist Faith and Message

This confession is based on the New Hampshire Confession of Faith written in 1833. The New Hampshire Confession does not even mention or acknowledge the universal Church. In like manner, the 1925 *Baptist Faith and Message* does not mention a universal invisible Church. It states:

---

[47] James M. Pendleton, *Christian Doctrines: A Compendium of Theology* (1878; rpr. Valley Forge, PA: Judson, 2010), 343. For a complete list of King James's rules see W. F. Moulton, *The History of the English Bible* (London: Charles H. Kelly, 1911), 196. This rule is also discussed by F. F. Bruce, *The English Bible: A History of Translations* (New York: Oxford University, 1961), 98. See also S. E. Anderson, *Real Churches or a Fog: A Defense of Real, Local Churches: A Denial of a Foggy, Universal Church* (Texarkana, TX: Bogard, 1975), 13–14.

[48] Anderson, *Real Churches or a Fog*, 13.

A church of Christ is a congregation of baptized believers, associated by covenant in the faith and fellowship of the gospel; observing the ordinances of Christ, governed by his laws, and exercising the gifts, rights, and privileges invested in them by his word, and seeking to extend the gospel to the ends of the earth. Its Scriptural officers are bishops, or elders, and deacons.

It was not until 1963 that the official Southern Baptist Confession of Faith mentioned any concept beyond the local meaning of *ekklēsia*.

### The 1963 Baptist Faith and Message

In 1963, the article on the church underwent a few changes; however, the most important for our current discussion is the additional phrase that reads, "The New Testament speaks also of the church as the body of Christ which includes all of the redeemed of all the ages." This phrase did not come without controversy. At the convention, held in Kansas City, discussion arose over the phrase "which includes all of the redeemed of all ages." Many objected to this reference to the universal Church. At this moment,

> Hobbs, with Albert McClellan's coaching, called the group's attention to a J. M. Pendleton quotation acknowledging New Testament use of church to mean the redeemed in aggregate. Since Pendleton had been a leader of the Landmark movement, that settled matters.[49]

And with this discussion, the Landmark movement actually contributed to the acknowledgment of a universal concept in the New Testament.

Herschel Hobbs claimed that the addition to the 1963 *Baptist Faith and Message* was "the first new development in ecclesiology

---

[49] J. Fletcher, *The Southern Baptist Convention: A Sesquicentennial History* (Nashville: B&H, 1994), 209. This phrase occurs in Pendleton's *Church Manual*, 5.

among Southern Baptists since 1845."[50] Hobbs further clarified
the addition by stating the meaning of *ekklēsia*:

> The word "church" in the New Testament never refers to
> organized Christianity or to a group of churches. It de-
> notes either a local body of baptized believers or includes
> all the redeemed through all the ages. The greater empha-
> sis among Baptists, as in the New Testament, is on the
> local church.[51]

### *The 2000 Baptist Faith and Message*

This revision of the confession changes the wording but not the
focus of the article on the church. The new wording acknowledged
the redeemed in the aggregate by stating, "The New Testament
speaks also of the church as the Body of Christ which includes
all of the redeemed of all the ages, believers from every tribe,
and tongue, and people, and nation."[52] The revision added biblical
language from the book of Revelation to express more clearly the
futuristic and final assembly of the redeemed of all ages. In addition the 2000 *Baptist Faith and Message* rightly maintains the
emphasis on the primacy of the local church. We should do likewise. Thus, currently we focus on the local congregation and the
ministry given to us in the present age and not focus our theology
or practice on an age to come.

## PRACTICAL APPLICATION

### The Ecumenical Movement

The first practical problem is known as the ecumenical movement. Emphasizing the local church to a denial of the universal
will repeat the errors of Landmarkism. But an overemphasis on

---

[50] H. H. Hobbs, *The Baptist Faith and Message* (Nashville: Convention Press,
1971), 146, chapter 7, footnote 2.

[51] Ibid., 75.

[52] Available online at http://www.sbc.net/bfm/bfm2000.asp.

the universal Church and a minimization on the local will result in unhealthy ecumenical tendencies.

This ecumenical tide comes ashore in different ways with various visible impacts. Sometimes it rolls in as interdenominational partnerships for the gospel. Perhaps you have heard it called, "widening the tent of cooperation." More problematic is the wave known as "evangelical ecclesiology." Finding an evangelical ecclesiology continues to be elusive because ecclesiology separates rather than unites evangelicals. The highest concern should be expressed over a full-blown universal Church theology that seeks to join Catholics and Evangelicals together in a universal visible Church, usually still reporting to the pope. Such efforts compromise too many important theological doctrines.

At the same time the Southern Baptist Convention developed the 1925 confession, which had no reference to the universal Church, the British Baptists were developing a statement which began,

> We believe in the Catholic Church as the holy society of believers in our Lord Jesus Christ, which He founded, of which He is the only Head, and in which He dwells by His Spirit, so that though made up of many communions, organized in various modes, and scattered throughout the world, it is yet one in Him.[53]

This British influence has come across the pond.

Ecumenical support in the theology of the universal Church can be seen in quotes like this one:

> I consider myself a member of all religions. I have known for a long time that I am of the Universal Church, which is not a particular structure anywhere. It is everywhere. And

---

[53] Ernest A. Payne, *The Fellowship of Believers* (London: Carey Kingsgate, 1952), 143. Cited in N. H. Maring and W. S. Hudson, *A Baptist Manual of Polity and Practice* (Valley Forge, PA: Judson, 1966), 44.

I've learned that, in my reading, I can walk with spiritual people of all times, all places, and all religions.[54]

Proponents believe that we should demonstrate the love of Christ to broaden our tents of cooperation. They desire complete unity. A unity that will be present in the final and future assembly, but here on earth such unity requires theological compromise. I agree with cooperation so long as it does not include compromise. After all, the prayer of Jesus recorded in John 17 asks that all would be one, and when possible, Christians should cooperate.

Unfortunately, errant theology, humanity's depravity, and the evil one make complete unity impossible until that future and final assembly. Unity in love must contain unity in truth. Once cooperation demands compromise, then it is the love for Christ that compels me to stand for truth of His Word.

Christ's laws do not always unite. Jesus told His disciples in Matt 10:21–22, "Brother will deliver brother over to death, and the father his child, and children will rise against parents and have them put to death, and you will be hated by all for my name's sake. But the one who endures to the end will be saved" (ESV). We do not expect unity on this earth; we expect tribulation. Even when dealing with those who call themselves "brothers," we must understand that unity without truth is not true unity. First Corinthians 5 demands separation from a "brother." Through discussions of proper baptism, the meaning of the Lord's Supper, congregational church government, and local church autonomy, divisions may occur. Second Thessalonians 3:6 states, "Now we command you, brothers, in the name of our Lord Jesus Christ, that you keep away from any brother who is walking in idleness and not in accord with the tradition that you received from us."

While the focus on the local church and sound biblical doctrine

---

[54] Wilson Van Dusen, "The Universal Church and the Sacred Source: Part I. On the Universal Church," in *Religion East and West*, no. 5 (October 2005): 11, http://www.drbu.org/rew/pdf/Issue5.pdf, accessed May 1, 2009, 11.

may create division, we also acknowledge the final and future assembly. Practically this means that we should recognize and cooperate with those of like faith and practice. We should pray for the success of other local churches understanding that we are working together for the kingdom of Christ. Selfishness or self-promotion has no place in the work of Christ.

We should help our fellow churches rebuild from destruction. We should uphold the discipline of other churches and not too quickly receive strangers into our fellowship. We should cooperate with those of like faith and practice but never cooperate to the point that it undermines the integrity of the local congregation or compromises the laws of Christ. A theology focused on the local but acknowledging the universal maintains the proper balance of integrity in the local church with a cautioned longing for the unity that will only be present in the final and future assembly.

## Revolution

I have titled this next undercurrent "Revolution," which comes from the title of a book by George Barna.[55] His title accurately describes his views as a revolution against the local church. This revolution is being fueled by consumerism and customization.

Consumerism appears in that we have allowed society to influence religion, and we have become religious consumers who see local churches as nothing more than purveyors of religious goods. Just as we demand choice in consumerism, we now demand choice in religion. In a book entitled *Shopping for God*, James Twitchell compares our need for religious choice to that of secular choice, "AT&T offering 'the right choice'; Wendy's, 'there is no better choice'; Pepsi, 'the choice of a new generation'; Coke, 'the real choice'; and Taster's Choice Coffee is 'the choice for taste.'"[56] In the church this comes across in demanding the right program, the right service time, the right music for each congregant's personal

---

[55] George Barna, *Revolution* (Carol Stream, IL: Tyndale House, 2006).
[56] James Twitchell, *Shopping for God* (New York: Simon & Schuster, 2007), 70.

preference. You must have the latest and greatest or risk becoming a religious K-Mart or Circuit City—a bankrupt reminder of an age gone by.

Customization has also affected religion. This principle can best be seen in the iPod. Remember back to those ancient days when the older among us were kids. We had to buy an entire cassette tape, and then a little later we had to buy an entire CD. Now consumers simply go to the Internet and purchase the one song they want without any obligation to purchase other songs. They can even create their own playlist. You can have a page on the Internet called "MySpace," which you can customize to fit your own personality. In fact, it seems this generation is all about "you."

In religion this means, you do not have to go to church. You do not even have to believe as I do. You can have your beliefs. I can have mine. And we can both be right even though we completely disagree. You can watch a television sermon, go to a Christian concert, listen to the radio, read a good book, and put together your own cafeteria-style buffet of religious nourishment expecting no one to criticize you since you are so religious.

I am not sure which Barna statement bothers me most. Perhaps when he says, "If the local church is the hope of the world, then the world has no hope."[57] He goes on to say, "You see, it's not about *church*. It's about *the Church*."[58] "Or, put more succinctly, the Revolution is about recognizing that we are not called to *go* to church. We are called to *be* the Church."[59] Perhaps he has forgotten Heb 10:23–25, which states do "not forsake our own assembling together, as is the habit of some, but encouraging *one another*; and all the more, as you see the day drawing near."

Finally he says, "We should keep in mind that what we call 'church' is just one interpretation of how to develop and live a faith-centered life. We made it up. It may be healthy or helpful,

---

[57] Barna, *Revolution*, 36.
[58] Ibid., 38.
[59] Ibid., 39.

but it is not sacrosanct."[60] I respectfully believe that Barna has failed to notice that Jesus Christ established only one human institution and that institution was the *ekklēsia*. Furthermore, when Jesus confronted Saul on the road to Damascus, He did not ask Saul why he persecuted the church. He stated, "Saul, Saul, why do you persecute me?" (NIV). Perhaps this is why on Paul's first missionary journey he retraced his steps appointing elders among every congregation. The church is the body of Christ and the bride of Christ, and if we are ashamed to identify with the local church and all its flaws, then we will be ashamed when we stand before the Lord Jesus Christ with all of our flaws.

I am not alone in my criticism. Kevin Miller states, *"Revolution is passionate for the church, so long as it's the capital-C church, the universal group of believers in Jesus, the church I can't see and don't have to relate to."*[61] Miller continues, "His book merely reveals every thin spot in evangelical ecclesiology. We flamingly disregard 2,000 years of guidance under the Holy Spirit. We elevate private judgment above the collective wisdom of apostles, martyrs, reformers, and saints."[62]

Perhaps an illustration from a different age will help. Samuel A. Maverick was born in 1803 and died in 1870. This Texas pioneer did not brand his cattle. Instead he left his cattle free to roam across the range without identification. Other ranchers sometimes adopted these cattle calling them "mavericks." The original word *maverick* meant "an unbranded calf, cow or steer."[63] It came to mean "a rootless wanderer or rebel." Just as these calves wandered aimlessly with no identification revealing to whom they belonged, a new "revolution" of "maverick Christians" desire to wander the

---

[60] Ibid., 37–38.
[61] http://www.christianitytoday.com/ct/2006/january/13.69.html, accessed September 24, 2008.
[62] http://www.christianitytoday.com/ct/2006/january/13.69.html?start=2, accessed September 24, 2008.
[63] Anderson, *Real Churches or a Fog*, 99.

range of American Christianity without bearing the identification of a member of the only human institution that Jesus Christ established. The only problem is that the New Testament knows nothing of a churchless Christian.

This minimization of the local church comes closer to home when parachurch institutions take precedence over the local church. For example, when college students allow positive events like Campus Crusade or Fellowship of Christian Athletes to become the supplier of their religious goods, neglecting the local congregation. While these organizations help to disciple and mature believers, and I commend these groups, for their evangelistic work, they create problems through minimizing the local church. Many participants experience difficulty moving away from a parachurch group focused on meeting their needs in everything from timing to style of worship. Reintegration into a local assembly with babies who cry, kids as distractions, and the elderly with needs does not feel right to these students. A better scenario connects college ministries to local churches where participants can gather during the week on the college campus while maintaining a connection to the local church. In this way parachurch organizations may complement the church rather than be a detriment to it.

## Internet Church: Taking Jesus "Virtually"

A final undercurrent seeking to promote a foggy, universal relationship over the true meaning of *ekklēsia* comes in the form of the modern church growth movement and more specifically technologically enhanced extensions of the local church. From the full-blown Internet campus to the latest fad known as the multisite church, these organizations seeking to be "one church in many locations" undermine the meaning of the word *ekklēsia*.[64]

---

[64] This is the slogan for lifechurch.tv which can be seen on the Web site www.life church.tv. For a more complete discussion of the multisite campus movement, see chapters 8–10 of T. White and J. M. Yeats, *Franchising McChurch: Feeding Our Obsession with Easy Christianity* (Colorado Springs: David C. Cook, 2009).

One of the most extreme examples is LifeChurch.tv, which has multiple locations in Oklahoma and others in Mesa, Arizona; Wellington, Florida; Albany, New York; Hendersonville, Tennessee; and Fort Worth, Texas. In addition to these geographical locations, the church has a "global Internet campus" and a virtual campus in the world of Second Life. Craig Groeschel, senior pastor of LifeChurch.tv, stated in an interview with NBC, "When Jesus told us to go into all the world, we took Him very literally." Perhaps it would be more accurate to say that LifeChurch.tv has taken Jesus virtually.[65]

The most extreme example is the virtual location on the Web site www.secondlife.com that mimics the physical location.[66] People create computer animated "avatars" which can be human or not but allow the computer user to interact with other people online while attending "church." Perhaps the use of avatars and winged creatures makes you feel a little uncomfortable. However, you should realize that I have personally taken my avatar into this virtual community asking such questions as, "Do you go to real church anywhere?" The responses range from infuriation to confusion. For the majority of "avatars," this is "real church." They virtually "gather," they can chat back and forth by typing or speaking into a computer microphone, they build relationships through social networking sites like Facebook or MySpace, and they pay their tithe through PayPal. Does this really constitute what the New Testament term *ekklēsia* communicates?

A little closer to home is the new phenomena of the multisite church. One book claims, "Well over 1,500 churches are already multisite. One out of four megachurches is holding services at multiple locations. One out of three churches says it is thinking about developing a new service in a new location. Seven out of the

---

[65] See www.secondlife.com. For example, videos, see http://www.youtube.com/watch?v=1MB4Gwg0k_U or http://www.youtube.com/watch?v=i9ZjjIjPXNs, accessed October 18, 2008.
[66] See www.secondlife.com, accessed October 18, 2008.

country's 10 fastest-growing churches offer worship in multiple locations, as do nine of the 10 largest churches."[67] Groeschel, pastor of Life Church in Oklahoma City, states that "the move from horseback preacher to satellite broadcast is simply a shift from circuit rider to closed-circuit rider."[68]

In the multisite movement where campuses can be right across town or all the way across the country, the *ekklēsia* will not gather. In addition, we encourage consumerism by communicating that only the most entertaining speakers should be heard. It does not matter that congregational polity no longer exists since the founding church hires the staff, sets the budget, and determines members. It does not seem to matter that local-church autonomy disappears as the founding church makes all the decisions for every off-site location. What matters are the three Bs: the budget, the buildings, and the bodies. As long as all three Bs continue to grow, the church is considered successful. Yet I must question whether multiple locations that never gather have compromised the meaning of *ekklēsia*.

At some locations this separation occurs on the same piece of land. The family may ride to church together, separate for the service of their choice, and then never see one another until they meet at the car. Take, for example, North Coast Church, where you can choose from "five different venues for worship. The church calls its main sanctuary setting 'North Coast Live.' Video Cafe, was the first alternative venue established in 1998."[69] In this setting you can sit in patio chairs while served Danishes and Starbucks coffee.

Another service is called "Traditions." "It's described as an 'intimate and nostalgic worship experience led from a baby grand piano—a mix of classic hymns, old favorites and contemporary

---

[67] G. Surratt, G. Ligon, and W. Bird, *The Multi-Site Church Revolution* (Grand Rapids: Zondervan, 2006), 9.

[68] Ibid., 91.

[69] "Video Venues to the Rescue," http://www.churchexecutive.com/article.asp ?IndexID=237, accessed October 5, 2009.

worship choruses.'"[70] Perhaps the most creative version, called "The Edge," "resembles a nightclub, with a high-energy band and big subwoofers."[71] In addition to compromising the *ekklēsia,* this also creates a consumer-based religious mentality where our biggest concern becomes not spiritual growth but the satisfaction of our spiritual consumers.

OK, let's bring it even closer to home. Have you thought about your recent decision to have two separate worship services? Does that decision not undermine the meaning of *ekklēsia*? Perhaps it grows worse if one service offers contemporary music while another offers traditional. We may have created two "gatherings" and unintentionally encouraged consumerism by communicating that the church service should cater to desires and preferences of the congregant. Perhaps multiple services or an overflow room are OK for a temporary time while a building is under construction, but the point of my question is to help you raise awareness that our practical decisions have theological implications.

Even closer to home would be the local church that sends the kids off to Noah's Playtime Park with the newest slides and a fire truck baptistery to boot. The teenagers go to a uniquely named facility, perhaps "Area 51" where Xbox and other games entice them to come back. Meanwhile the parents go to the "grown-up" worship service to drink Starbucks and eat Danishes. Is this what the New Testament means with the word *ekklēsia*?

Such separation in the primary worship time has implication on the men attempting to lead their families spiritually. There is meaning when my daughter sees her daddy sing praises to God knowing that he sings horribly and at no other location. There is meaning to my family watching me open my Bible and listen to a text-driven message submitting myself to God's Word. The segregation of the family at every worship opportunity can

---

[70] Ibid.
[71] Ibid.

result in a consumer-driven worship that undermines the leadership of the father and does not teach concern for those unlike you.[72] What will happen to the ministry to the widows and orphans when consumer-driven worship has filtered through all of our congregations?

The objection often arises that such focus on the church being gathered is not realistic. Similar critiques have been leveled against the "believers' church." As the argument goes, one unbeliever accepted as a member damages the believers; thus, drop the unrealistic goal. The response is the same. A truly regenerate church may never exist, but that is the goal set forth in Scripture. All members may never assemble at one time, but the goal should exist, and plans that make the goal impossible are problematic. Similarly, Christians will never be holy as God is holy, but that too is the ideal of Scripture. No one contends every member must be present to constitute the church, but the intent to assemble bears important implications on the congregation.

## THE PROBLEMS OF FOCUSING ON
## THE UNIVERSAL CHURCH

In an attempt to summarize the problems of focusing too heavily on a theory of a universal Church, I offer you this list of four:

1. Focusing too heavily on the universal Church theory cannot be reconciled to the meaning and use of the New Testament term *ekklēsia*.

2. Focusing too heavily on the universal Church theory minimizes the local assembly in many ways including func-

---

[72] I do not mean to imply that age-graded classes are always evil. I can see wisdom in age-graded education. It allows children to learn on a level that teaches them the basics. Such age-graded education should function in addition to the primary time of corporate gathering. It does not need to be an either/or situation. It should be a both/and situation. The entire family gathers for worship while age-appropriate teaching occurs at other times during the week.

tioning officers and the discipline of the local church that does not occur at a universal level.

3. Focusing too heavily on the universal Church theory encourages theological minimalism and ecumenical movement while minimizing the regulative principle of the New Testament.

4. Another problem of the universal Church theory is that it makes caring for the brethren or administrating the church impossible.

The New Testament presents several duties that require both knowing who the believers are and ministering to one another. This cannot be accomplished outside of a local assembly. For example, in 1 Corinthians 5, the congregation was critiqued for not putting the sinner out from among them. Out from among what? Obviously some form of membership was held. Such discipline would not be possible in an ambiguous universal Church. In 1 Tim 5:9, we see a list of widows who are to be served, and Heb 13:17 indicates that leaders will give account for those literally under their watch.

Perhaps the most convincing argument beyond the meaning of the word *ekklēsia* is the New Testament commands to behave in certain ways to other Christians. Below are compiled 12 "one another" passages. These passages provide a good overview of what the fellowship of a church should look like, and it does not indicate a universal assembly. The duties of those one another passages can be broken down as follows:

1. Love one another (John 13:34–35; 15:12–17; Rom 12:9–10; 13:8–10; Gal 5:15; 6:10; Eph 1:15; 1 Pet 1:22; 2:17; 3:8; 4:8; 1 John 3:16; 4:7–12).

2. Seek peace and unity (Rom 12:16; 14:19; 1 Cor 13:7; 2 Cor 12:20; Eph 4:3–6; Phil 2:3; 1 Thess 5:13; 2 Thess 3:11; Jas 3:18; 4:11).

3. Avoid strife (1 Cor 10:32; 11:16; 2 Cor 13:11; Phil 2:1–3).

4. Rejoice and suffer with one another (Rom 12:15; 1 Cor 12:25; Gal 6:2; 1 Thess 5:14; Heb 4:15; 12:3).

5. Care for one another physically and spiritually (Matt 25:40; John 12:8; Acts 15:36; Rom 12:13; 15:26; 1 Cor 16:1–2; Gal 2:10; 6:10; Heb 13:16; Jas 1:27; 1 John 3:17).

6. Watch over one another and hold one another accountable (Rom 15:14; Gal 6:1–2; Phil 2:3–4; 2 Thess 3:15; Heb 12:15).

7. Edify one another (1 Cor 14:12–26; Eph 2:21–22; 4:12–29; 1 Thess 5:11; 1 Pet 4:10; 2 Pet 3:18).

8. Bear with one another (Matt 18:21–22; Mark 11:25; Rom 15:1; Gal 6:2; Col 3:12).

9. Do not sue one another (1 Cor 6:1–7).

10. Pray for one another (Eph 6:18; Jas 5:16).

11. Separate from people destructive to the church (Rom 16:17; 1 Tim 6:3–5; Titus 3:10; 2 John 10:11).

12. Contend for the gospel (Phil 1:27; Jude 3).[73]

## CONCLUSION

In this presentation we have seen the meaning of the term *ekklēsia* is a "called-out assembly or gathering." Scripture primarily uses the term to denote a local congregation although a final and future assembly (universal Church) can be seen as a theological concept interpreting a few uses. We have also seen that throughout the history of the Southern Baptist Convention, and in several main Baptist writers a proper emphasis on the local church has been maintained. Commenting on the 2000 *Baptist Faith and Message*, Malcolm Yarnell rightly notes, "The *Baptist Faith and Message* 2000 focuses upon the local church, in line with the New Testament emphasis."[74] He further states, "The church which contains all the redeemed will exist only in glory."[75] While the *Baptist Faith and Message* acknowledges the

---

[73] Source unknown.
[74] Yarnell, "The Church," 63.
[75] Ibid., 65.

theological concept known as the redeemed of all ages, the majority of confessions dealing with the church focus on a local and visible church of this age. We must make sure that we continue to place the emphasis in the proper location.

If we place the emphasis where it belongs, on the local church and neither on a universal concept nor our own personal fame, then our desire will be to plant more of these local churches and to encourage others to attend local churches and build that final and future assembly, one local congregation at a time.

I was not saved in an invisible church. I was saved in a visible, local congregation. I was not baptized in an invisible, universal Church. I was baptized in a visible, local congregation. I have never partaken of the Lord's Supper in an invisible, universal Church. I have remembered and celebrated the Supper of our Lord in a visible, local congregation. I was not married in an invisible, universal Church. I was married as a covenant before the Lord in a visible, local congregation. Why is it that with all that occurs in the visible, local congregation, we continue to look for an invisible, universal one?

I desire neither to compromise by broadening the tents of cooperation nor to participate in a revolution against the local church. Instead, I desire to support and participate in the only human institution the Lord Jesus Christ established on this earth. I desire to build up the visible body of Christ. I desire to hold high the church for which Christ gave His life. Through the local church we must take the gospel of Jesus Christ to all 6.5 billion people on this planet ensuring that as many as possible enter both the local and universal Church. Let us all, go therefore and make disciples, baptizing them in the name of the Father, Son, and Holy Spirit, teaching them (in the local church) to observe all things He has commanded so that one day that glorious and spotless bride will gather in a final and future assembly at the great and glorious return of our Lord Jesus Christ.

# Author Index

# Scripture Index